monet's
garden in giverny:
inventing the landscape

monet's
garden in giverny: inventing the landscape

Edited by Marina Ferretti Bocquillon
Essays by Marina Ferretti Bocquillon,
Françoise Heilbrun, Vanessa Lecomte and Gabrielle van Zuylen

musée des impressionnismes giverny

5 CONTINENTS

Published in conjunction with of the exhibition *Monet's Garden in Giverny: Inventing the Landscape* organized by the Musée des Impressionnismes Giverny from 1 May to 15 August 2009

This exhibition received exceptional loans from the Musée d'Orsay

Musée d'Orsay

Musée des Impressionnismes Giverny
99, rue Claude Monet
27620 Giverny, France
www.mdig.fr

5 Continents Editions
via Cosimo del Fante, 13
20122 Milan, Italy
www.fivecontinentseditions.com

ISBN: 978-88-7439-526-2
Distributed in the United States and Canada by Harry N. Abrams, Inc., New York
Distributed outside the United States and Canada, excluding France and Italy, by Abrams UK, London

Cover
Claude Monet, *Water Lilies*, 1904
Musée Malraux, Ville du Havre (see cat. no. 15)

Back cover
Anonymous for *L'Illustration, Claude Monet before his House in Giverny*, spring 1921 (see cat. no. 45)

EXHIBITION

Curators
Marina Ferretti Bocquillon, Scientific Director, Curator with Vanessa Lecomte, Associate Curator, in association with Diego Candil, General Director

Conservation
Véronique Roca

Registrar
Olivier Touren

Installation
Didier Dauvel, Didier Guiot

Education
Hélène Furminieux

Public Relations
Géraldine Raulot, Giverny
Catherine Dufayet Communication, Paris

Tourism
Laurette Roche

CATALOGUE

Musée des Impressionnismes Giverny
Editor
Vanessa Lecomte
with the assistance of Audrey Klébaner

5 Continents Editions
Editorial coordination
Marie-Laure Jouve
Laura Maggioni

Art direction
Annarita De Sanctis

Translations
Simon Pleasance and Fronza Woods

Editing
Andrew Ellis

Production
Enzo Porcino

LENDERS

Denmark
Ny Carlsberg Glyptotek, Copenhagen

Spain
Museo Thyssen-Bornemisza, Madrid

United States
Terra Foundation for American Art, Chicago

France
Archives Départementales de l'Eure, Évreux
Archives Durand-Ruel, Paris
Latour-Marliac Sarl, Le Temple-sur-Lot
Lycée Claude Monet, Paris
Musée d'Art et d'Histoire Marcel Dessal, Dreux
Musée Clemenceau, Paris
Musée Malraux, Ville du Havre
Musée Marmottan Monet, Paris
Musée Municipal A.-G. Poulain, Paris
Musée d'Orsay, Paris
Philippe Piguet Collection
Private collection. Courtesy Galerie Bernheim-Jeune
Truffaut, Évry
Véronique et Philippe Perdrix Collection

Italy
Galleria Nazionale d'Arte Moderna, Rome

Switzerland
Fondation Beyeler, Basel
Fondation E. G. Bührle, Zurich
Galerie Beyeler, Basel
Musées d'Art et d'Histoire, Geneva

United Kingdom
Private collection

And all the lenders who wish to remain anonymous.

ACKNOWLEDGEMENTS

We wish to express our particular gratitude to:

Giverny, the Musée des Impressionnismes

Anne Boisse, Marie Bosson, Didier Dauvel, Catherine Fox, Hélène Furminieux, Didier Guiot, Audrey Klébaner, Laurent Lefrançois, Céline Muller, Xavier Poc, Géraldine Raulot, Véronique Roca, Laurette Roche, Olivier Touren.

Évreux, Conseil Général de l'Eure

Jean Louis Destans, Dominique Soulier, Sophie Sérafin, Francis Courel, Christian Chermeux, Philippe Huthwohl, Yves Bousquet, Sonia Verbist, Fatima Meslem, Aïcha Lebh, Jean-Loup d'Hooren, Benoit Forcuit, Laurent Sodini, Évelyne Gliozzo, Claire Scotton, Stéphanie Cléradin, Éric Memeto, Thierry Leroy.

Our thanks also go to all those who gave us assistance and advice throughout the long task of preparing the exhibition, as well as to those who helped us to actually set it up:

Jacqueline Aubart, Marine Bancilhon, Laurence Barret, Stéphane Bayard, Véronique Beauregard, Michael Beck, Benoîte Beaudenon, Hadrien Bocquillon, Léonore Bocquillon, Philippe Bocquillon, Pierre Bouho, Katherine Bourguignon, Martine Bozon, Myriam Bru, David Butcher, Philippe Büttner, Françoise Cachin, Helen Carey, Marie-Christine Chauffeteau, Mathias Chivot, Marc-Antoine Claivaz, Maria Vittoria Marini Clarelli, Guy Cogeval, Pina Comar, Déborah Copel, Catherine Couturier, France Daguet, Lara Daly, Guy-Patrice Dauberville, Jean-François Denize, Patrick Derom, Catherine Dufayet, Ann Dumas, Jean-Claude Dupuy, Caroline Durand-Ruel Godfroy, Flavie Durand-Ruel, Joseph Durand-Ruel, Paul-Louis Durand-Ruel, Dominique Durussel, James Dyke, Laurent Echaubard, Ute Eggeling, Isabelle Evrard, Karim Farza, Jérôme Faucheux, Flemming Friborg, Hugues Gall, Marie Garet, Vanina Gasly, Bruno Gaudichon, Thierry Gausseron, Caroline Genet, Gilles Gentil, Léonard Gianadda, Elizabeth Glassman, Lukas Gloor, Stéphane Guégan, Emily Hall, Amélie Hardivillier, Annette Haudiquet, Françoise Heilbrun, Guillaume Henry, Alan Hobart, Jane Humley, Sophie Imbert, Ljiljana Jovic, Valérie Joxe, Samuel Keller, Violaine de La Brosse-Ferrand, Paul Lang, Isabelle Laurence, Nathalie Lecerf, Géraldine Lefebvre, Alice Le Guen, Lise Lentignac, Matthieu Leverrier, Sophie Lévy, Claudette Lindsey, Dominique Lobstein, Angelo Lui, Lee Marks, Sara Martinez-Sarandeses, Caroline Mathieu, Marianne Mathieu, André Mayer, Dan Mayer, Deborah Mayer, Sandra Mazière, Cäsar Menz, Maïlys Messager, Odile Michel, Axelle Moreau, Tanja Narr, Monique Nonne, Pierre Nora, Helena Pastianis, Sylvie Patin, Muriel Pavesi, Line Clausen Pedersen, Adeline Pelletier, Véronique et Philippe Perdrix, Philippe Piguet, Hélène Pinet, Joachim Pissarro, Sandrine Pissarro, Marc Plocki, Nicolas Portnoï, Véronique Postic, Maria Letizia Profiri, Jussi Pylkkanen, Donald H. Ratner, Catherine Ricciardelli, Christopher Riopelle, Purificación Ripio, Anne Roquebert, Francesca Rose, Brigitte Rubon, Jonas Chr. Ryborg, Patrice Schmidt, Anne Serre, Thomas Seydoux, Robert Sheldon, Guillermo Solana, Katy Spurrell, Jacques Taddei, Vérane Tasseau, Antoine Terrasse, Philippe Thiébaut, Veerle Thielemans, Tina Thunø, Baronne Thyssen-Bornemisza, Barbara Tomassi, Silvana Turzio, Isabelle Vazelle, Hélène Verdier, Ariane Westin-McCaw, Gabrielle van Zuylen.

The publisher would like to express a special thanks to Francesca Rose for her precious collaboration.

Paintings by Claude Monet on view in Giverny... the statement seems simple, almost banal, not to say obvious. But to achieve this has involved the pooled energy of a determined group of people, including Guy Cogeval (president of the Musée d'Orsay), Elisabeth Glassman (president of the Terra Foundation for American Art), Laurent Fabius (former prime minister and president of the Communauté d'Agglomération de Rouen), Alain Le Vern (president of the Région Haute-Normandie), Didier Marie (president of Conseil Général de la Seine-Maritime), Gérard Volpatti (president of the Communauté d'Agglomération des Portes de l'Eure), Philippe Nguyen Thanh (mayor of Vernon), and not least myself. The Département de l'Eure has conscientiously carried out the re-organization of the Musée de Giverny, coordinating all those involved so as to ensure that the results be complementary and harmonious.

Ambitious designs invariably have a compelling backstory involving real women and men working in unison, and the new Musée des Impressionnismes is no exception. May this preface offer a chance to pay tribute to their unflagging commitment.

In addition to the links with Claude Monet's house and renowned garden, the exhibition "Monet's Garden in Giverny: Inventing the Landscape" prompts a general reconsideration of the relationship between the Giverny artist and his garden. Like a modern-day Pygmalion, Monet was forever preparing plant compositions, the better to capture them on canvas. A hundred years or so later, these works painted in Giverny are have once more on made accessible for an inaugural show that is particularly poignant, as they establish a living dialogue with the original landscape-*cum*-garden.

I wish therefore to express my deepest gratitude to Hugues Gall, director of the Fondation Claude Monet, and to the various lenders, public and private alike, who have so generously agreed to contribute to this exhibition. I must also congratulate the efforts of the museum's team, headed by Marina Ferretti Bocquillon and Diego Candil, which have ensured that this exhibition is now on view at Giverny, within the appointed time.

Jean Louis Destans
PRESIDENT OF THE EPCC

What better place than Giverny, this village lying in the heart of the Seine valley, to open a new Musée des Impressionismes. Giverny is ideally placed in this region rich in preserved sites, which, from Paris to the coast of Normandy, saw the major stages of the Impressionist adventure unfold. Claude Monet was the first to set up a permanent home here in 1883. The artist was forty-two when he discovered this delightful Norman village of a mere 300 inhabitants. He lived here in Giverny for more than half his life and the village subsequently became one of the most famous sites in art history. Very quickly a large colony of American painters settled here between 1885 and 1915, and enlivened the village and its environs. But they were far from being the only people to follow Monet's example of seeking idyllic surroundings in which to work: in 1884 Camille Pissarro left Osny, near Pontoise, where he had lived, and went to live permanently at Éragny-sur-Epte, near Gisors, with just fifteen miles between him and his old friend Monet. Although the light and the Seine valley landscapes were the principal attraction for many artists, it was the proximity of Pissarro and Monet which induced Paul Signac to spend the summer of 1886 in Les Andelys, where he painted his first series of neo-Impressionist landscapes. Nor was it anything haphazard that prompted Pierre Bonnard to purchase a house—*Ma Roulotte*—in 1912 at Vernonnet, barely three miles from Monet's home.

Much later on, in 1969, Joan Mitchell in turn moved to the region, to Vétheuil, where she was joined by her companion, the Canadian painter Jean-Paul Riopelle.

Giverny had long been a place of pilgrimage for painters. In 1980 the Fondation Claude Monet opened the gardens and the artist's house to the public, and they came in droves, often from afar. Henceforth, thanks to the Musée des Impressionnismes, visitors will also have a chance, in Giverny, to admire the works painted in this historic place close to the sites which inspired them. And it is a pleasure as much as it is a moral duty for the Musée d'Orsay to assist and cooperate with this new institution. My warm thanks go to the president of the Conseil Général de l'Eure, Jean Louis Destans, for having successfully planned the best possible future for this inspired place, and for having found the wherewithal to give it a new life. My thanks also go to Elizabeth Glassman, president of the Terra Foundation for America Art, for having so subtly encouraged the discreet changes that have occurred at the old Musée d'Art Américain.

I have no doubt that, in the capable hands of Marina Ferretti Bocquillon and Diego Candil, the Musée des Impressionnismes in Giverny will enjoy a dazzling future.

Guy Cogeval
PRESIDENT OF THE MUSÉE D'ORSAY

In 2007, the Terra Foundation for American Art took the official decision to focus its activities on assistance for the study of American art, and embarked on an ambitious project for the Giverny site. There was a crucial meeting with Elizabeth Glassman, president of the Foundation, and Jean Louis Destans, president of the Conseil Général de l'Eure, to give form to the new Musée des Impressionnismes in Giverny, with the help of the Région Haute-Normandie, the Département de la Seine Maritime, the Communauté d'Agglomération des Portes de l'Eure and that of Rouen, and the town of Vernon. The Musée d'Orsay, for its part, undertook to become our advisory committee partner, and the project got under way with much gusto. All that remained to be done was itemize the Museum's new mission, and set up the inaugural exhibition, in record time... This was only made possible through the ongoing support of the Conseil Général (here, in particular, we would like to thank Dominique Soulier and Sophie Sérafin) and the unfailing generosity of the Musée d'Orsay, which has not only afforded us some outstanding loans, but also backed our requests to other lenders. Our heartfelt gratitude goes to their respective presidents, Jean Louis Destans and Guy Cogeval.

The theme of the first show at the Musée des Impressionnismes, "Monet's Garden in Giverny: Inventing the Landscape" most logically pays tribute to the father of Impressionism, reminding us that it was above all in the twentieth century that Giverny became a hub of French art. For through the creation and then the depiction of his garden, Monet plunged at the turn of the century into a second art revolution. Impressionist objectivity gradually gave way to a powerful lyricism which was a harbingered of, among other things, all the daring and audacity of 1950s American abstraction.

Our exhibition is also designed to be a tribute to the wonderful place of memory represented by the artist's house and gardens, bequeathed to the Fondation Claude Monet which, under the aegis of the Académie des Beaux-Arts, would undertake splendid restoration work on them, and then open the gardens to the public in 1980. Our thanks go to its director, Hugues Gall, for all the help he has given us.

Diego Candil
GENERAL DIRECTOR

Marina Ferretti Bocquillon
SCIENTIFIC DIRECTOR-CURATOR

Table of Contents

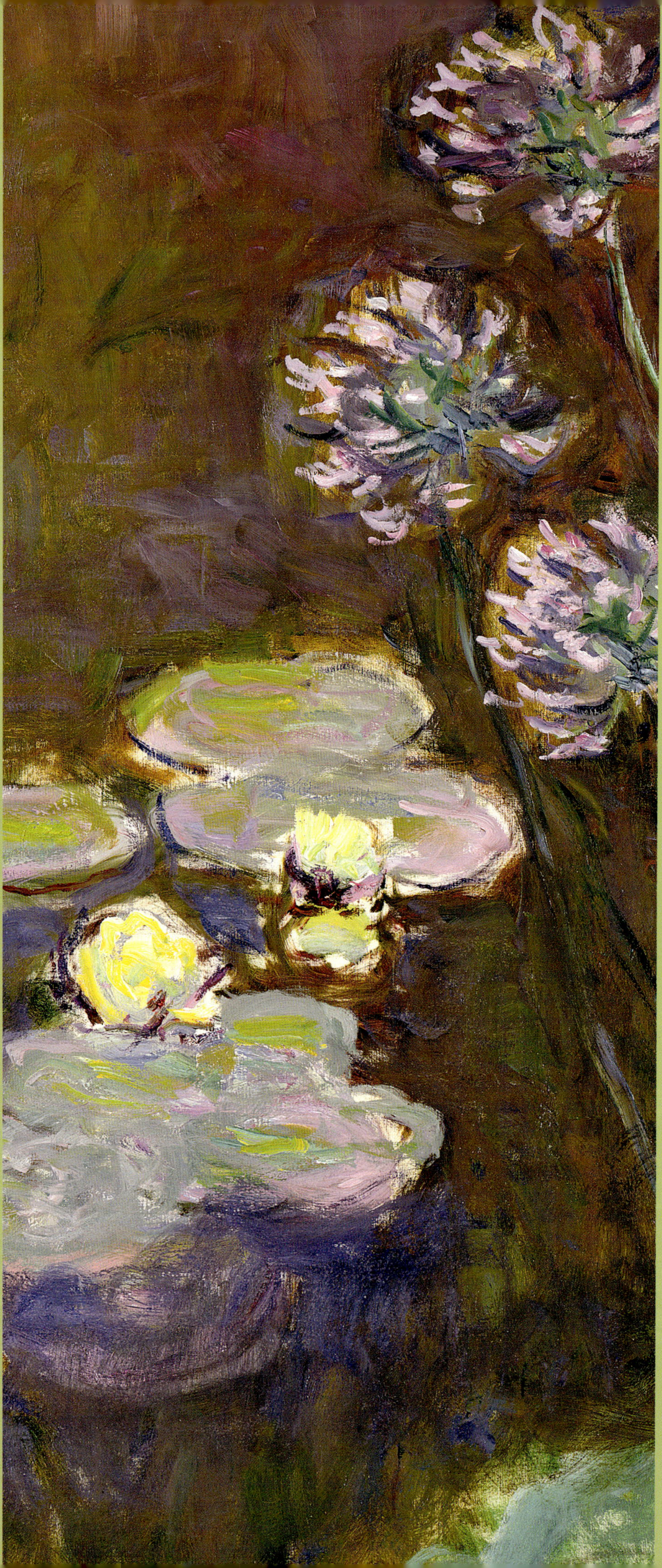

Marina Ferretti Bocquillon

Monet's Garden in Giverny

Monsieur Monet, whose vision, such a lure,
Is unaffected by either
Winter or summer, as he paints Giverny,
Situate near Vernon, in the Eure.[1]
Stéphane Mallarmé

When Monet set up home in Le Pressoir in Giverny in 1883, he embarked on a new life. The painter was forty-three, and the heroic years of Impressionism were already a thing of the past. In 1880 or thereabouts, those involved in the initial group had scattered, with everyone individually seeking new artistic avenues. Monet was already one of the more famous among them. He was the only Impressionist painter invited to be a pallbearer at Édouard Manet's burial that same year, 1883. Thenceforth he became the leading figure in the French artistic avant-garde.
The artist's private life also took on fresh impetus. After the death in 1879 of his first wife, Camille, he lived with Alice Hoschedé, who looked after his two sons, Jean and Michel Monet, as well as her own six children from her marriage with the collector and patron Ernest Hoschedé: four daughters—Suzanne, Blanche, Germaine and Marthe—and two sons, Jacques and Jean-Pierre. It was a tribe, no less, of ten which therefore moved into Le Pressoir in 1883. Ernest Hoschedé died in March 1891, and on 16 July 1892 Alice most officially became Mme Monet. From the start, the painter wielded all the paternal authority of a veritable father figure over all the children, ever keen to maintain the unity of the clan. The Hoschedé girls posed for him—Suzanne in particular, being the most charming of the four. The children would help carry his canvases painted from life, and Blanche herself became a painter, the only one who could claim to have been taught by Monet. For their part, the boys helped with garden tasks and shared Monet's enthusiasm for that activity. One of the Hoschedé sons even published an article on botany.[2]

As Jean-Pierre Hoschedé pointed out in his memoirs, Monet's passion for gardening and his contact with Gustave Caillebotte, all began at Argenteuil. At both Argenteuil and Vétheuil, Monet had grown modest gardens, but "in Giverny he had a large

page 10:
Water Lilies and Agapanthus (detail),
see cat. no. 19

orchard with, in front of the house, just a few flowerbeds, and two long beds on either side of the central path, with its entrance on the Chemin du Roy."[3] The geometric structure of the original Clos Normand still existed, but this was nevertheless the beginning of a far-reaching change. Monet had visited many gardens, and he remembered them all. His particular preference for flowers showed an English influence, but with massing effects that called to mind Dutch tulip-fields (cat. no 5). As for Japan, it was all the rage at the time, but familiar to Monet through photographs as well as the prints he collected (fig. 5 p. 43).[4] So Japanese aesthetics were naturally echoed in certain details of the water garden, like the footbridge known as the "Japanese bridge." But the bursting profusion of plants, which nowadays still amazes visitors to the Fondation Claude Monet , has nothing Japanese about it, and conjures up certain Mediterranean gardens much more. The result of these varied influences was a unique creation, spanning almost twenty years. Monet invented a landscape which was like no other, and which, for want of any better term, would be defined as the very template of the "Impressionist garden."

For the man who had long been the "impecunious Monet," the garden—its creation and its upkeep—was an unheard-of luxury, but everything was thoroughly controlled and mastered. The head gardener, Félix Breuil, and his team of five would receive precise orders, passed on to Alice when the artist was not in Giverny, and Monet even went so far as to help finance the asphalting of the road through Giverny to stop the dust from soiling his sumptuous water lilies.[5] The artist left nothing to chance, primarily because he knew that his garden would be his outdoor studio. As soon as he planted the first flowers in 1883, his intention was actually to paint them: "I've had gardening to do, which has taken up a bit of my time, picking some flowers to paint them when the weather is bad."[6] And when he applied for the permit required to make the pond, it was again to have "things to paint."[7] By working out the landscape he wanted to depict, Monet innovated in two ways. For if the landscape painter's approach was thus oddly reversed, what was there to be said about the method of the Impressionist who had fought the idea of the structured landscape as it was taught at École des beaux-arts?
The garden in Giverny was not just a favorite motif; it became, for Monet, the instrument of a radical artistic development. By creating the landscape he wanted to paint, Monet furnished himself with the wherewithal to achieve his artistic ambition. What he wanted to do, thenceforth, was capture "the envelope of things,"[8] that is, the space that separates us, air and light, the fluidity of the atmosphere, things impalpable and their ready, deliberate progression, was at a radical remove from that legendary Impressionist spontaneity. In Giverny, the artist unearthed new areas of exploration, and the painter of modern life gradually turned into an apologist for luxuriant nature. In those years Monet also espoused new artistic practices, shifting from the traditional field of painting to the series in 1890, and thereafter to his obsession with a single theme, in the exclusive depiction of the garden. The Giverny garden became his quintessential motif at the turn of the century. From 1900 to his death in 1926, Monet painted, and bequeathed us, nearly 400 pictures, not counting the panels at the Orangerie in Paris (fig. 7). More than half these works were devoted to his garden. After the Venetian series, undertaken in 1908, he never painted anything other than the garden he had created, and he made this theme almost exclusively his own.[9] His stepdaughter, Blanche Hoschedé, was the only person authorized to paint it, and it seems that she did so rarely before Monet's death (cat. no. 30). Outside of these

works, the only picture painted within Le Pressoir property in Monet's lifetime was one by an American artist, John Leslie Breck (cat. no. 29), produced shortly after Monet's arrival in Giverny. But in no time Monet wearied of his kindly and invasive admirers. With regard to Monet's demand for exclusivity, Paul Cézanne observed, and not unwittily: "Then he's like a lord who pays for the haystacks he likes. The corner of a field suits him, so he buys it. With a tall flunkey and guard-dogs, so that people don't bother him."[10] Monet had to fight to be alone when he worked. This was the ransom of his fame, which was growing in leaps and bounds at that time.

Starting in 1881 Paul Durand-Ruel's purchases became more regular, and Monet had more and more one-man exhibitions. In March 1883, the month before he moved to Giverny, Monet showed fifty-six recent works at the gallery where the first *Haystacks* also went on view, in 1891. They were followed in 1892 by the *Poplars*, a dozen versions of the *Water Lily Pond* in 1900 and, in 1909, the first show devoted exclusively to the water garden, *Water Lilies. Series of Water Landscapes.* Other galleries joined the fray, and in 1885 Monet took part in the International Exhibition organised by Georges Petit. From then on, this latter was numbered among Monet's dealers, and it was in his luxurious premises on the Rue de Sèze that the first "Monet-Rodin" exhibition was held, in 1889. In 1888, Théo Van Gogh, for his part, showed the seascapes painted in Antibes at the galerie Boussod-Valadon. Lastly, the brothers Josse and Gaston Bernheim-Jeune, who had enjoyed a special bond with Monet since the end of the nineteenth century, were added to the circle of his dealers. The artist's correspondence shows that, from December 1900 on, Monet developed business relationships with them, and, over the years, the tone of the letters became thoroughly friendly.[11] In 1902 the exhibition "Recent Works of Camille Pissarro and new Series by Claude Monet *Vétheuil*" marked the start of a lengthy collaboration, and from then on Monet's works were regularly exhibited at the galerie Bernheim-Jeune, be it in group or solo shows. In 1912 Monet exhibited twenty-nine views of Venice. Bernheim-Jeune Editions also put out major volumes devoted to Monet.[12]

Around the Garden

As he fathomed how to lay out his garden, between 1883 and 1899, Monet did not actually depict it; instead he chose most of his subjects from outside his property. The first flowers painted at Giverny were for a commissioned work, the decoration of his dealer Paul Durand-Ruel's living-room doors: "It's giving me hell. Since my return, I've produced six which I've had to destroy, just one to my liking has survived"[13] and, on 30 October, "I'm working on your panels, which are causing me quite a headache."[14] A month later he sent Durand-Ruel the first panels: "How many have I made that I've had to erase! More than twenty, maybe thirty. I'm busy with the small ones right now and hope they'll be easier, although the ones I've made have to be started again"[15] (cat. nos. 1 and 2). Henceforth his letters were peppered with recurrent doubts, an exactingness that was seldom satisfied, and the undeniable trouble he was having in finishing his canvases. On several occasions, Monet even destroyed his works. In 1890 he wrote to his friend Berthe Morisot: "This blasted painting is tormenting me and I can't do anything about it. I am just scratching and wearing out canvases."[16] The American painter Lilla Cabot Perry, a friend and neighbour of the artist in Giverny, confirmed that, in a fit of anger, he had once kicked and torn a canvas, before resuming work on it. In 1908 or thereabouts the artist also told her that Monet had burnt about thirty canvases with which he was displeased.[17]

1 | *The Luncheon*, ca. 1873
Oil on canvas, 160 × 201 cm (63 × 79 1/8 in.)
Musée d'Orsay, Paris (RF 2774)

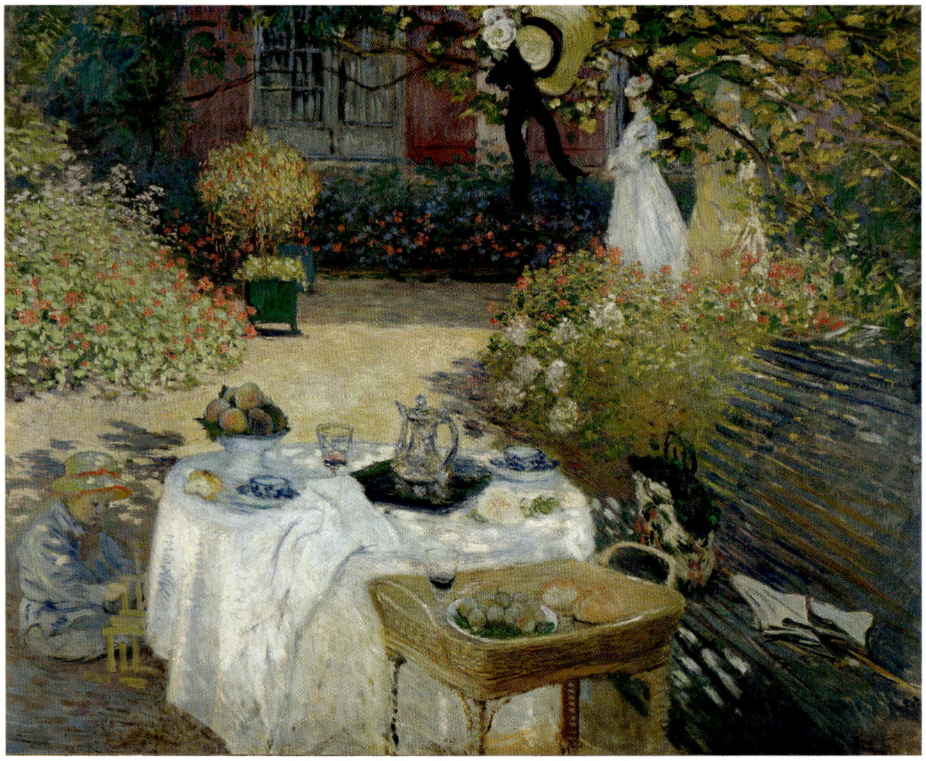

After moving to Giverny, in 1886 and 1887 Monet also painted a few pictures of figures in the immediate surroundings of Le Pressoir, in particular two versions, *Woman with a Parsasol* and *In the 'Norvégienne'* (cat. no. 6). At that time Monet wrote to Théodore Duret: "I'm working as never before on new attempts, outdoor figures the way I understand them, treated like landscapes. This is an age-old dream that is still bothering me and one that I'd like to realise once; but it's so difficult!"[18] *In the 'Norvégienne'* illustrates how these figures were "treated like landscapes." There is no sky in the picture, nothing moves, not a breath of wind ruffles the water's surface, and a mysterious sensation of immersion in nature washes over the observer. But Monet was very quick to abandon the genre of the figure once and for all. Was this because it was "so difficult"? Or to avoid bothering his favourite models, the Hoschedé girls, as he suggested during an interview given to the Duke of Trévise?[19] Or, again, was it to avoid having professional models in the house, which might have caused Alice to be jealous—as suggested by one of the Durand-Ruel sons?[20] All are possible, but if Monet had really wanted to carry on painting figures, none would have sufficed, and the real reason lay elsewhere. What interested him above all else—which was something he could not forego—was nature, and nature gave rise to a real sense of worship in him. "I make no other wish than to be more closely involved with nature, and I covet no other fate than to have—in accordance with Goethe's precept—worked and lived in harmony with her laws. She is the greatness, power and immortality beside which creatures seem to be no more than miserable atoms."[21] In the early 1890s this avowed pantheism prompted Monet to undertake the first "series," a method which he ushered in Giverny by painting the *Haystacks* around 1891, then the *Poplars* in 1891–92 (cat. no. 7). The paintings of *Rouen Cathedrals*, started in 1892 and 1893, were not finished or exhibited until 1895. Then, in 1896 and 1897, came the *Mornings on the Seine* (cat. no. 8), painted at dawn, from a boat.[22] The latter were a direct harbinger of Monet's later work on the *Water Lilies*, for here Monet was even keener to capture the tiniest variations of light, and time passing, the "envelope of things", as he put it, in reference to Corot.[23]

He certainly took evident pleasure in exploring subjects in the immediate surroundings of Le Pressoir, but he also readily strayed further afield for long periods, for bouts of painting during which he worked with great zeal. He was in fact a tireless traveller and, among the Impressionists, the one who journeyed most. Normandy was a special area of exploration, in the period when he painted—in addition to the immediate environs of Giverny—Étretat, Rouen cathedral, Pourville, Varengeville, and Vétheuil. But Monet also stayed on the shores of the Mediterranean in 1884 and 1888, in Brittany and Holland in 1886, and in the Creuse valley in 1889, not forgetting a trip to Norway in 1895, and his regular visits to London. In 1908 he went with Alice to Venice, and the "water lily city" was his last destination as an itinerant painter.[24] Monet did not travel like a tourist and rarely visited museums and monuments, because his primary goal was to find the motif.[25] It subsequently behoved him to work as hard as possible on as many canvases as he could manage, often thirty or so, all clamouring to be finished upon his return. These expeditions called for lots of organisation because, on top of the journey itself, there was the daily matter of transporting all the pictures he was simultaneously working on. All these factors gave rise to fatigue and expense, not to mention the artist's disappointment when the weather was inclement. And once the initial tasks had been acquitted, Monet was still at the mercy of whimsical climatic conditions, about which he was forever grumbling in his letters.

The Gardener's Patience

So over the first fifteen years Monet spent in Giverny—with very few exceptions—Monet did not paint his garden. But he meanwhile invested a great deal of energy in it, and the original orchard gradually disappeared. The fruit-trees were replaced by flowers planted in beds and crowded squares, providing a succession of colorful masses in the warmer months. The flowers which carpeted the ground to the point of hiding it completely also invaded the higher ground. Roses climbed along the arbour lining the central path, clematis coiled along stakes, and wisteria disguised the light superstructures over the footbridge. Octave Mirbeau was the first to describe the new look of the former orchard—the so-called "Clos Normand"—in 1891, and he did so as an informed nature-lover, because he, too, was a keen gardener. He was well acquainted with the garden he often visited, so he could easily evoke the progression of the seasons and the wonderful succession of colourful harmonies, offering precise data about the various species, rare and commonplace alike, with their serial flowering, and occasionally giving free rein to a fertile imagination. In Monet's garden, the author of *Le Jardin des supplices* described, in particular, the irises which "brandished their strange, curved petals, frilled with white, mauve, lilac, yellow and blue, streaked with brown variegations and purplish spots, conjuring up in their innermost complexities mysterious analogies, and perverse and tempting dreams." He also described the poppies which "splay, on their hairy stalks, huge gobletfuls of vermilion blood."[26] In more sombre tones, Arsène Alexandre, for his part, emphasised the geometric simplicity of the enclosure's structure, buried beneath the wealth of plant life. "What might give you some idea of it is the floral shows at the Tuileries, with their many layers; but those dazzling layers only last for four or five days, whereas in the Giverny garden there is no respite from the flowers. Wherever you turn, they are at your feet, over your head, growing to chest height, lakes, garlands, hedges of flowers, whose harmonies are at once improvised and calculated, and renewed as season follows season [...]. The garden is divided up into 'squares', in all simplicity, like with the market-gardeners of Grenelle and Gennevilliers. [...] It is this profusion, this horde-like aspect which creates all the garden's character." And the author winds up by mentioning "another garden which would be very curious to describe, too, Clemenceau's garden at Passy."[27] This extraordinary superabundance of plants has Mediterranean overtones, and Monet's stay in Bordighera, Italy, not far from the French frontier, probably had more than a little to do with that.

In 1883—the year he moved to Giverny—Monet had actually explored the Var coast with Auguste Renoir, pressing on as far as Bordighera, famous for its lemon-trees and gardens. The following year, Monet went back there on his own, earnestly beseeching Paul Durand-Ruel not to tell their friend Renoir about his project. The spellbound artist spent several weeks there, exploring subjects that were "extremely difficult to grasp and commit to canvas; everything is so dense; it is delicious to behold."[28] And a few days later, after discovering the famous Moreno gardens, "a garden for which there is no comparison, it is pure enchantment, all the world's plants grow there on open ground, and seem not to be tended: there is a jumble of every variety of palm, every species of orange and mandarin."[29] This extravagance clearly thrilled Monet, and two paintings included here express the sense of fullness that those places inspired in him (cat. no. 3 and 4). In the Norman garden, however, where the vegetation was also dense, it did not have to be as refined and exotic as in the Moreno gardens. We should bear in mind that Monet was also very fond of Dutch tulip-fields and flower-shows (cat. no. 5). The artist was looking for masses of form with powerful hues invading the landscape the way they would come to dominate the surfaces of his canvases, with each flower being part of the overall effect, just as each daub of paint would help to make the whole canvas vibrate.

When Monet purchased Le Pressoir property in 1890, after renting it for several years, the garden had already become the object of all his attention, but its transformation took on a new scale, and he had some greenhouses built in 1892. Monet left home less often, and when he did, he strayed less far afield. He painted the haystacks in the neighbouring field, then the poplars lining the Epte River, a mile and a half upstream from his garden. The Clos Normand already burst radiantly forth in descriptions penned by critics, but it had still not found its way into his pictures.

In February 1893 the painter bought a plot of land beside the Epte, below his own property and on the other side of the railway line. He was now keen to dig out a pond, making a diversion from an arm of the Epte known as the "communal arm," and he duly wrote about this project to the Prefect of the Eure on 17 March 1893.[30] At first, Monet came up against some resistance, but he persevered and finally obtained the required authorisation. He then traced the initial outlines of the water garden, to which he devoted more effort, time and money even than he had to the Clos Normand. Thus, "the willows unfurled their green locks, bamboo culms thrust up from the ground, clumps of rhododendrons lined the paths, and Monet sowed the ponds with water lilies, whose trailing roots floated mid-water, spreading their wide leaves, with flowers, white and pink, mauve and greenish, sprouting."[31] In all likelihood, it was at the 1889 International Exhibition that Monet had the idea for this water lily pond: the Latour-Marliac Nursery had been awarded prizes for its colourful water lilies, and it was from them that Monet ordered his plants in 1894 and 1904 (figs. 5, 6 and 10). Almost ten years later, in 1901, with an additional plot purchased and the no less official permit to divert the course of the arm of the Epte obtained, he tripled the size of the pond. In it the painter created a man-made isle linked to the banks by four small bridges. In 1904, Monet further altered the outlines of the pond, which called for a second order of water lilies from Latour-Marliac. That same year, Maurice Kahn commented that they were "kinds of water lilies with wider leaves, and richer and more subtle shades of colour: there are pink, yellow and white flowers. A small wooden bridge, painted green, spans the pond. Moored to the bridge, a dinghy. All around the pond, water irises. In the background, azaleas, tamarisks, and a weeping willow."[32] Monet had been living in Giverny for more than twenty years and the garden was finally taking on its permanent look. The patience and determination displayed by the artist to achieve this outcome did not escape the Duke of Trévise who observed: "Everywhere there is the loveliest order [...]. Everything is sober, even the luxuriance, everything is prepared, even what seems wild: for these fragile 'water lilies', beside which our own pond lilies are vulgar, we are indebted to the canny tenacity of the master."[33] People who described the garden often used words like "fairytale," "marvel," and "paradise." But Jean-Pierre Hoschedé wrote that, in his view, such novelist's terms were not suitable for Monet's gardens, which were something else. "They were designed and made, not by a gardener, but by an Impressionist, who made them as he would have painted a picture from nature."[34] An artist's garden, then, as Gabrielle van Zuylen shows in these pages.[35] Yet, if the garden can be said to be still "Impressionist," the pictures it inspired in its maker took on a very different dimension.

2 | *The Garden at Montgeron*, 1876–77
Oil on canvas, 173 × 193 cm (68 1/8 × 76 in.)
Hermitage Museum, Saint Petersburg

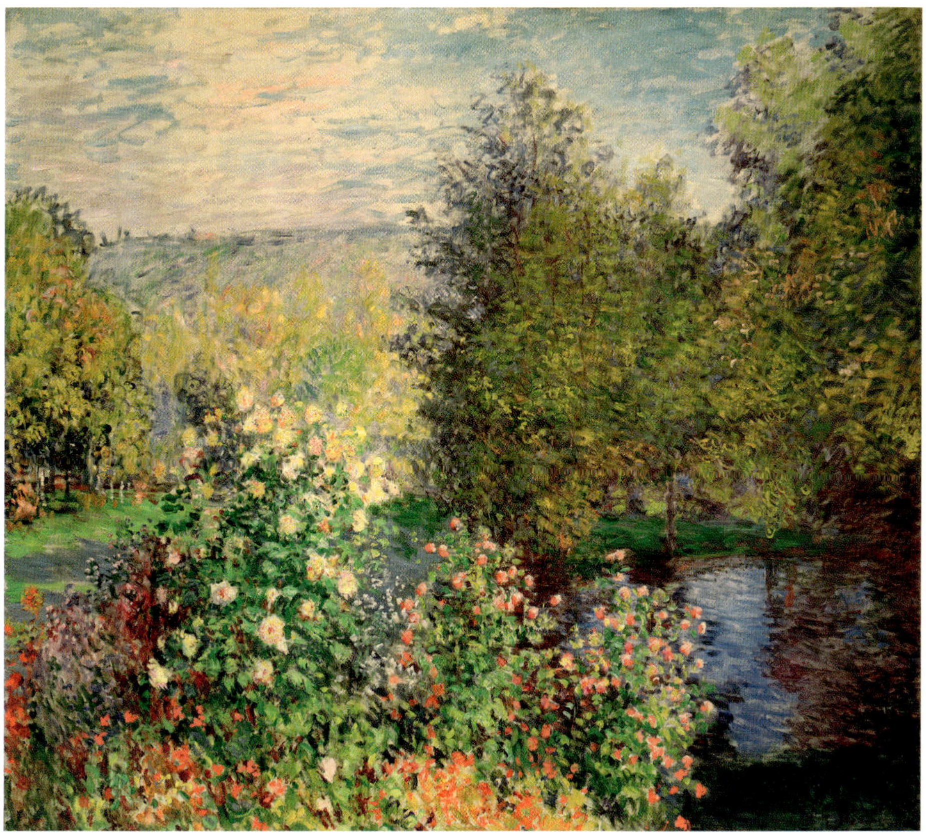

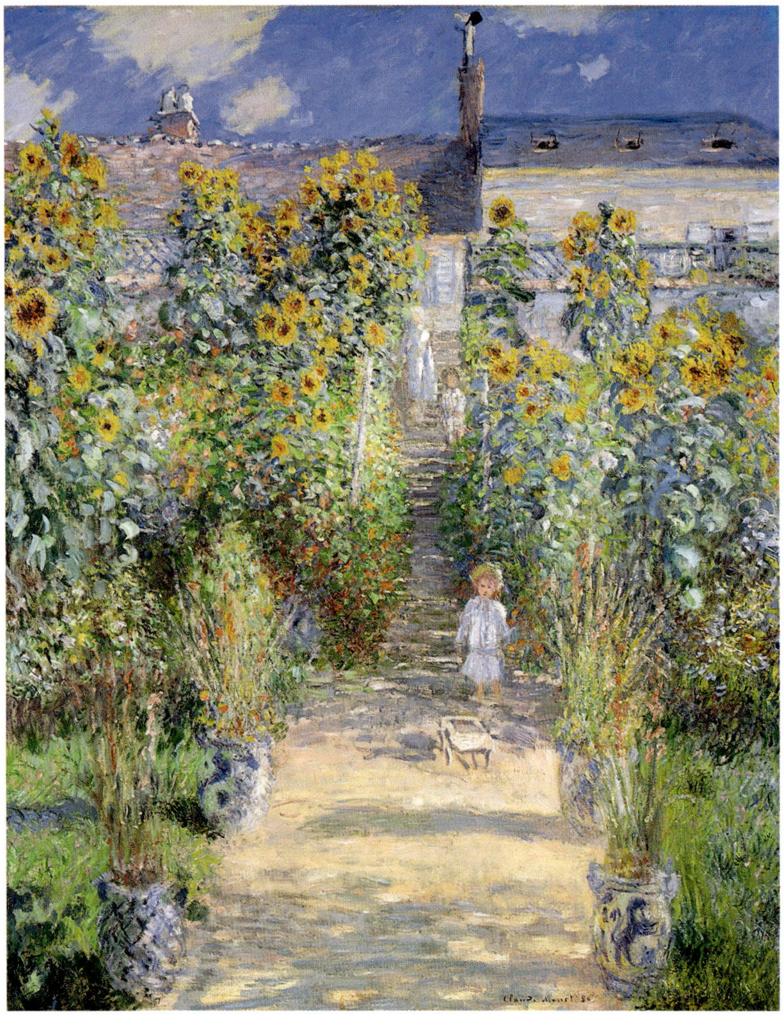

3 | *The Artist's Garden at Vétheuil*, 1881
Oil on canvas, 151.5 × 121 cm
(59 5/8 × 47 5/8 in.)
National Gallery of Art, Washington, D. C.
Ailsa Mellon Bruce collection (1970.17.45)

"I'd like to prevent people seeing how it's done"

The first pictures inspired by the garden were studies of flowers—the three versions of the *Peonies* painted in 1887 (cat. no. 9). These sumptuous studies, fruit of the artist's fascination with the colourful wealth of a rare variety which he was especially proud of owning, were anything but garden views. The painting *Peonies* in the Musées d'Art et d'Histoire in Geneva, shown here, attests to as much: the format is impressive, and boldly treated in a close-up composition, without sky and almost devoid of perspective. None of these studies was exhibited or sold prior to 1922, any more than were two pictures depicting delicate white clematis plants painted in the same period. Perhaps the artist had not found them "pictorial" enough, that is, sufficiently finished to be exhibited. In any event, he kept them for a long time in his studio, without destroying them, as he sometimes did when he was dissatisfied, and the modernity of those canvases was every bit a match for certain works by Emil Nolde painted twenty years later. In 1897 Monet also painted eight studies of water lilies (cat. no. 11), but here again these were studies of flowers, just as he had painted the peonies in 1897, and the chrysanthemums in 1898 (fig. 4). And, again like the peonies, these water lilies remained for many years in his studio, before being exhibited.

According to the catalogue raisonné drawn up by Daniel Wildenstein, the garden first appeared in the artist's œuvre in 1895. The author thus situates two views of the Japanese bridge, subsequently wrongly dated by the artist, which point very directly to the pond views painted in 1899 and 1900. The first, less problematic, view of the Clos Normand also dates from 1895, and is titled *Monet's Garden at Giverny* (cat. no. 10). It is still typically Impressionist and shows a scene of modern life where figure and landscape are harmoniously balanced. There is no sky in the composition, but the diagonal line of the walk creates the perspective, separates the planes, and organises the abundant vegetation. Five years later Monet painted *The Artist's Garden at Giverny* (cat. no. 13), and a new pictorial language came into being. The perspective of the diagonal walk, swiftly checked by the house, was certainly there, but the figure had vanished and the whole space was filled by dense vegetation.

The turn of the century would mark a new departure in Monet's œuvre, for he was now fervently painting the garden he had been working on for so long—a landscape cannily and carefully organised by the artist himself. This relentless work caused him to miss the wedding of his beloved Julie Manet ("I curse the painter who deprives me of the joy of seeing you a bride"[36]), as well as the opening of the Rodin exhibition.[37]

Thirty years ago Robert Herbert published a meticulous study of Monet's technique, in which he took apart the cliché of "Impressionist spontaneity." Based on a close analysis of the layer(s) of paint, he showed that Monet's art was definitely not an instant response to the spectacle offered by nature.[38] Quite to the contrary, over and above any seeming ease, it was the outcome of a sophisticated technique, empirically developed over several years of artistic praxis. Working outdoors and in the studio offset each other and were part of a more complex method than has been hitherto described. To start with, Monet painted his from life, applying quite a thick layer of paint, whose impastos and unevennesses enlivened the whole surface. The artist then focused on the complex task involving colour. He would add several thin layers of paint which, like a glaze, gradually modulated and enriched the canvas. Herbert thus managed to identify up to eighteen different shades of colour over a surface measuring [10 × 15 cm] 4 × 6 inches. This was slow work, because it usually called for a drying period between the different layers of paint. This was how Monet obtained extremely subtle and varied chromatic effects. His magic with colour had nothing immediate about it, and the look of improvisation he tried to keep resulted from the unevennesses of the underlying layer, creating an illusion of spontaneity.

Monet had always had studios and, over the years, he spent more and more time there. When he arrived in Giverny, he converted a barn with a beaten-earth floor into a studio-*cum*-living room, which he subsequently connected to the main house. He had a large window installed in 1885, and made further alterations in 1910.[39] In 1899 he had a second studio built, west of the house near the greenhouses. A third and much larger studio was constructed in 1916 to enable him to make the *Grand Decorations* today held in the Orangerie des Tuileries. The critic Gustave Geffroy, who was one of Monet's close friends, described them thus: "The two studios outside, one to the left near a huge aviary where there are parrots flying and tortoises wandering around amid lettuce leaves; the other to the right. The left studio contains, or used to contain, old works, such as *Luncheon on the Grass*, the *Women in the Garden*, and a selection of Monet's works from every period; the right studio, built more recently (to be precise, during the war) is filled with a series of large canvases of the *Water Lilies*, an overall decoration which goes right round the immense room where the light comes from above, filtered by an awning. There is also a studio—the original one—in the house, which is at the same time a living-room, where the walls are covered with finished paintings and unframed sketches, their edges touching. This is where Monet takes the day's work, which he then looks at for hours, the way I have seen him looking at his Belle-Île canvases, then cleaning them, finishing them and getting them to go together."[40]

We have seen how this "cleaning" played an important part in the creative process, but Monet s contemporaries said little about it. The very idea of studio work ran counter to the notion of the Impressionist painter, seen as a landscape painter working outdoors, fiercely opposed to academic practices. It is a fact that Monet very rarely adopted the traditional method which consisted in producing studies and drawings, then making one or more general sketches before embarking on the final picture. But while he would begin his canvas outdoors, it was in the studio that he would complete and finish it. Very early on, the idea of painting outdoors clashed with the idea of painting taught at the École des Beaux-Arts, much in the same way that truth clashes with falsehood, and this contributed to the success of Impressionism. The collector Georges de Bellio said it loud and clear in a letter sent to Monet in 1883:

"With your prodigious activity and your no less prodigious fluency, painting, for you, is—how shall I put it?—writing from life."[41] The analogy is delightful but misconceived, because it clashes radically with everything we know about Monet's œuvre, the problems he experienced in finishing his works, and his reluctance to abandon pictures with which he still was not entirely satisfied. Reality was well removed indeed from the hackneyed image which the artist and his dealer Paul Durand-Ruel had probably themselves fostered. "Monet never works beyond the desired effect (even if it would only last for ten minutes) and always from life; he works with thick paint, unmixed, with four or five strong colours; he juxtaposes raw hues. The painter does not have what we would call a studio set up in the country in a splendid landscape, not far from Vernon, in Giverny. [...] Never does he add touches in the studio; there is a very small number of pictures by him based on studies."[42] In more subtle terms, Maurice Guillemot said just the same in 1898: "We take refuge in the cool of the studio—living room, more like, because the outdoor painter only works outside." But in the very next paragraph the author noted: "Had we not known—through the secrets of chit-chat—about the length and patience of the labour, his anxiety over the outcome, the conscientious research, the feverish obsession with this two-year work, his statement 'I'd like to prevent people seeing how it's done' would come as a surprise."[43] Monet himself liked others to believe in the illusory ease of his refined harmonies, but he spoke more and more openly about his difficulties to those interviewing him. Most critics who approached him knew as much: "There are some canvases which one would swear were painted with great gusto of an afternoon, on which this illustrious master has worked for several years."[44]

Weary of all this chatter, Monet claimed his freedom in a letter to Durand-Ruel: "And whether my Cathedrals, my Londons and other canvases are painted from nature or not, this is nobody else's business, and of no importance."[45] But his closest friends saw fit to keep the legend alive, and it was Monet painting in his garden whom Sacha Guitry chose to film in 1915.[46]

It was always vital for Monet to immerse himself in nature, and the proximity of his garden offered an almost inexhaustible source of inspiration. But over and above his live observation of the subject, the artist indulged in a process of slow meditation during which, released from the subject, he would masterfully transpose reality. The garden close by thus encouraged the shift from Impressionist objectivity to the powerful lyricism of the late works.

The Patriarch of Giverny

At the turn of the century, the figure of Monet—already acknowledged as the father and leading exponent of Impressionism—gained added importance and he acquired the stature of a giant. He was perceived as one of the geniuses of French painting, his creativity comparable only to that of the sculptor Rodin. The enthusiastic Mirbeau was scarcely ahead of the pack when he wrote in 1891 that "even the most plodding criticism, even the most jealous painters, do not dare dispute the immense power and endless charm of his works. His exhibitions are special and altogether spiritual because they act, as it were, as painting lessons for painters who had first of all been the most blind and hostile to this initiatory and thrilling art, which went right over their intellectual heads."[47] Ever since 1880 Monet had seen fit to assert his presence outside the Impressionist group. He no longer exhibited alongside his erstwhile friends who, for the most part, had gone their separate ways, down avenues where they henceforth expressed themselves as individual artists. Renoir had harked back to the past, Pissarro was involved in Neoimpressionist research, Alfred Sisley was still somewhat repetitively painting in Monet's wake, Edgar Degas had never painted in an Impressionist way, and Cézanne only very slightly. Aware of these divergences, Monet would later acknowledge: "I simply have the merit of having painted live, faced with nature, trying to render my impressions in front of the most fleeting of effects, and I am upset to have been the cause of the name given to a group where the majority had nothing Impressionist about them."[48] He continued seeing friends from those earlier heroic days, Renoir and Pissarro above all, because the now half-blind Degas kept to himself, given that Édouard Manet, Gustave Caillebotte, Berthe Morisot, and Sisley had all died, and Cézanne had moved to the south. Now, however, his friendships extended to other circles. Georges Clemenceau, the inveterate politician, became a close friend, as did Octave Mirbeau, Geffroy, and Sacha Guitry. Monet surrounded himself above all with writers, and in particular those who shared his passion for gardening. It was in their company that he posed for photographers who travelled to Giverny to interview him and visit his garden. The critic Arsène Alexandre, who had known Monet for many years, was the first to note: "His garden. He's indebted to it, he's proud of it."[49] He may have kept out the inquisitive, who would have prevented him from working in peace and quiet, but Monet did get his garden to go down in history, not only through his works, but also by guaranteeing its fame through the press. For the "patriarch" was altogether a man of his day and age, and the modernity of his vision was also expressed by the mastery with which he encouraged the construction of his own image, as Françoise Heilbrun's essay in this book amply proves.[50] In December 1899 Alice and Claude Monet had posed for the photographer Paul Nadar, son of the great Félix Tournachon Nadar, in his studio on the Boulevard des Capucines (cat. no. 59). But subsequently it was in his own home, and preferably in his garden, that Monet, the demiurge, compiled the image he left for posterity. Articles about the artist came thick and fast, usually accompanied by photographs and the image of the patriarch of Giverny was established, underpinned by the painter's friends. It is to Mirbeau that we owe the earliest description of the garden in 1891.[51] The first photographs of the garden were then published in 1905 by Louis Vauxcelles.[52] At the top of the article was a photograph taken by Jacques-Ernest Bulloz showing Monet in his garden, while the following pages were illustrated with shots of the water lily pond, the Japanese bridge and the path in front of the house. That same year, in October, Joseph Durand-Ruel went to Giverny with the outstanding photographer Adolf de Meyer; next it was his friend Sacha Guitry's turn, followed by the minister Étienne Clémentel. Pierre Choumoff accompanied the Duke of Trévise[53] and photographed Monet upon his eightieth birthday on 14 November 1920. Georges Truffaut appeared as a gardening expert to photograph and write about the garden in 1924, and Thérèse Bonney produced some beautiful portraits

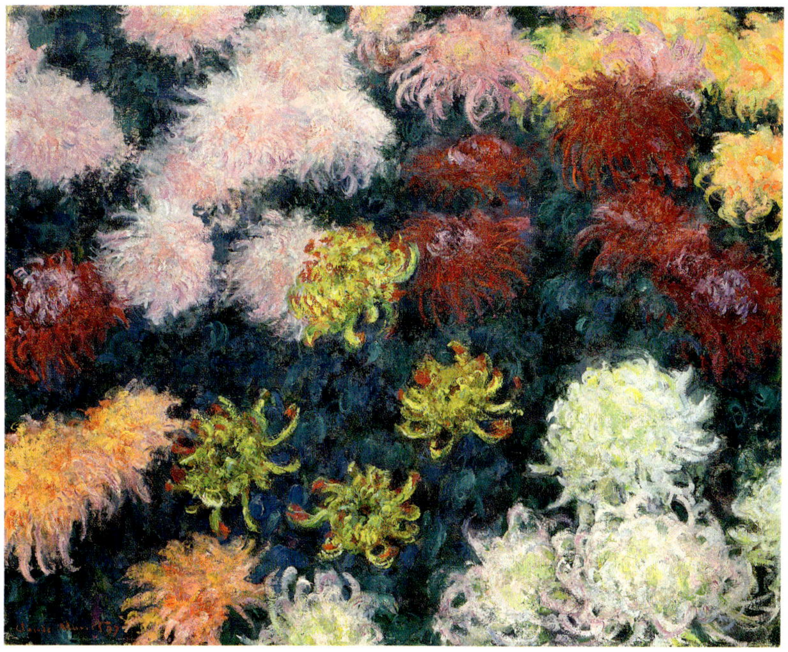

4 | *Bed of Chrysanthemums*, 1897
Oil on canvas, 82 × 100.5 cm ($32\frac{5}{16} \times 39\frac{9}{16}$ in.)
Kunstmuseum, Basle
Permanent loan from the Fondation Emile Dreyfus (G1970.11)

of the painter the following year. After her came Nickolas Muray, who, in the summer of 1926, took the last known pictures of Monet.[54]

Because he was so long-lived, Monet was witness to his own fame. Young painters would cross the Atlantic to ask for his advice—in vain. Collectors and dealers fought over his works, and he henceforth enjoyed a financial ease which helped him to realise his projects. But this longevity came with a price. Monet saw his elegant stepdaughter and favourite model Suzanne die in 1899. Alice Monet likewise passed away in 1911, leaving the artist very much alone from then on. It took him almost two years to recoup energy enough to return to his easel.[55] Then it was his eldest son Jean's turn to die, prematurely, in 1914. The war compounded these tribulations, and let us remember that, in 1913, Monet, afflicted by a cataract, was forever worried about losing his eyesight. The artist's world darkened, literally and figuratively. The presence of his stepdaughter, the painter Blanche Hoschedé-Monet, Jean Monet's widow, eased his loneliness a little. But during the war, it was above all in the *Grand Decorations* project that he found refuge: "I am busily at work and, whatever the weather, I paint. [...] I have embarked upon a major work which greatly interests me,"[56] he wrote to Félix Fénéon, who was at that time running the department of modern painting at the Galerie Bernheim-Jeune. Otherwise, the artist found if not solace, for he was eternally dissatisfied, then at least a reason for living in relentless work. He had become ever more demanding in relation to his works, and told the Duke of Trévise: "When I have no longer needed to sell, I have managed to work; now, I think I am as hard on myself as it's possible to be."[57]

"These water landscapes have become an obsession"

In 1898 Monet embarked on the first series of the pond with the Japanese bridge. Most of the twelve canvases he produced were exhibited in November 1900 at the Galerie Durand-Ruel, where they featured alongside *Mornings on the Seine* (cat. no. 8), and works painted at Varengeville, Dieppe, Pourville, in Norway, and in the Creuse—twenty-five paintings in all, attesting to the way his art was evolving.

From then on, the water garden became the artist's favorite theme. With the various series, he had sought to develop a method to capture the split second and the organization this called for was far removed from any idea of improvisation. The presence of the garden helped him to dodge some of these restrictions and encouraged his artistic evolution. The artist spent much time observing the landscape he had put together, then sketched his canvas on the spot, from life, before starting the task of transposing it. The Giverny pond may have been fascinating, but its dimensions were smallish. The Quebec painter Jean-Paul Riopelle was not the only person to be surprised by that, and even today many people share his feeling: "It's unimaginable—such huge, excessive paintings were made in front of such a small, next-to-nothing pond."[58] When transposed to Monet's panels, this enclosed and measured space actually took on a quite different dimension.

After completing the sequence providing an overall view of the water garden, in 1903 the artist undertook his first series devoted to water lilies. It was not until 1909 that he exhibited the series at the Galerie Durand-Ruel under the title *Water Lilies. Series of Waterscapes*. For the first time, the exhibition showed only works inspired by the pond, presented as the sole motif. Roger Marx who, with Fénéon, was one of the most lucid critics of the day, instantly grasped the change that had come about in the artist's œuvre. "Mr Claude Monet is breaking the final bonds which connected him to the Barbizon school; he is busily renewing his art in accordance with his view of things and his own means." He noted this about Monet's development of his point of view since the 1900 show: "The shore is receding, and will soon be erased; one can hardly see it, at the top of the first pictures. [...] No more land, no more sky, no more limits now; uncompromisingly the dormant, fertile wave covers the field of the canvas; the light pours out, playing joyfully on its surface, littered with verdigris-like foliage; the lilies rise up from it and, superb, thrust skyward their corollas, white, pink, yellow and blue, thirsty for air and sunlight. Here the painter has deliberately moved away from the restrictions of the western tradition; he is not seeking lines which form pyramids and focus the eye on a single point; the character of what is fixed, unchanging, seems to him contradictory with the very principle of fluidity; he wants diffused attention, spread everywhere."[59]

As early as 1908 Monet wrote to his friend, the critic Gustave Geffroy: "These waterscapes and reflections have become an obsession. They are beyond my old man's powers, yet I want to succeed (in describing?) what I feel."[60] From then on he stopped travelling and spent his time essentially studying his garden, in particular the water lily pond, whose surface and reflections became an almost exclusive motif. Monet focused tirelessly on the water in the pond and unflaggingly studied the slightest variations of light and colour. However, the pictures inspired by the water garden were never repetitive. The selection of works we are showing in this catalogue (cat. no. 14 to 18) fully demonstrates as much. Monet tried out new formats, round, square, and elongated; he also adopted unusually huge dimensions. At times he used an endlessly flowing and blending technique or, conversely, he expressed an amazing array of stroke- and brush-work, enabling him to follow the meandering touch of the brush on the canvas. Ever demanding, he refused the convenience of any formula that had proved successful, for him. Monet had already overturned the course of nineteenth-century painting; he also became one of the greatest of twentieth-century French painters.

At the turn of the century, the artist plunged into a new aesthetic adventure, and the American art historian Charles F. Stuckey very rightly compares the post-1900 *Water Lilies* to the masterpieces of Pablo Picasso and Henri Matisse, noting that they are every bit as brilliant as the latter in terms of daring, and gauged by the consequences they were to have on the art of younger generations.[61]

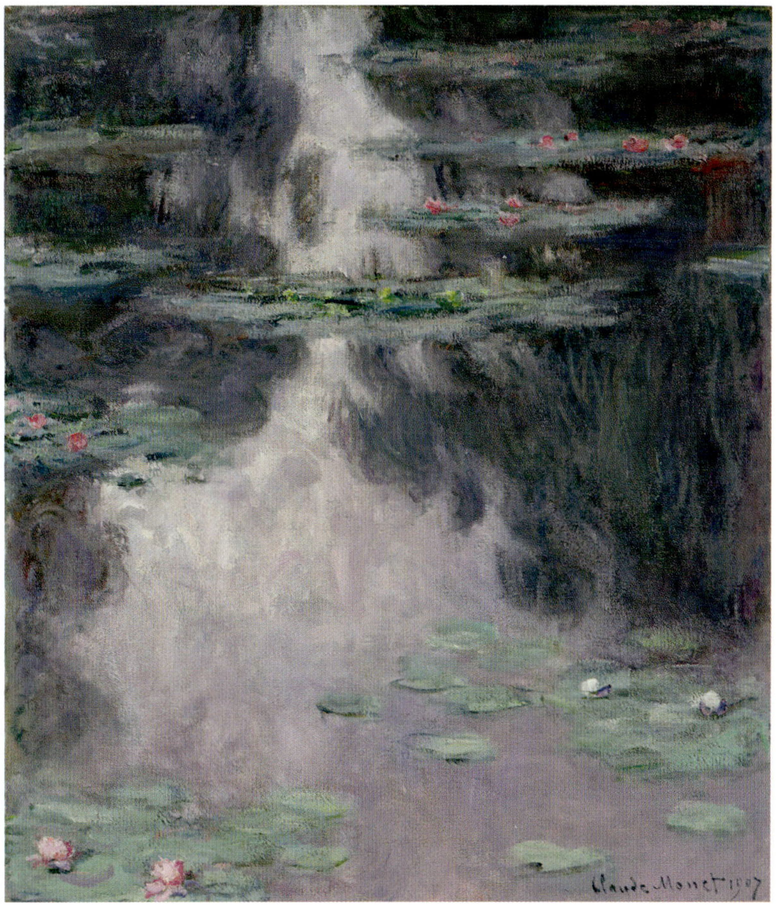

5 | *Water Lilies*, 1907
Oil on canvas, 92.1 × 81.2 cm (36 1/4 × 32 in.)
Museum of Fine Arts, Houston
Gift of Mrs Harry C. Hanszen (68.31)

"I am pursuing my idea of *Grande Décoration*. [...] This is indeed the project I had a long time ago: of water, water lilies, and plants, but on a very large surface."[62] Right away, the artist had the idea of drawing inspiration from the pond to turn it into a continuous décor. There had been talk of such a thing since 1898, before the pond took on its definitive look, "because they are models for a decoration for which he has already

6 | *Yellow Irises*, 1924–25
Oil on canvas, 150 × 130 cm
(59 1/16 × 51 3/16 in.)
Private collection

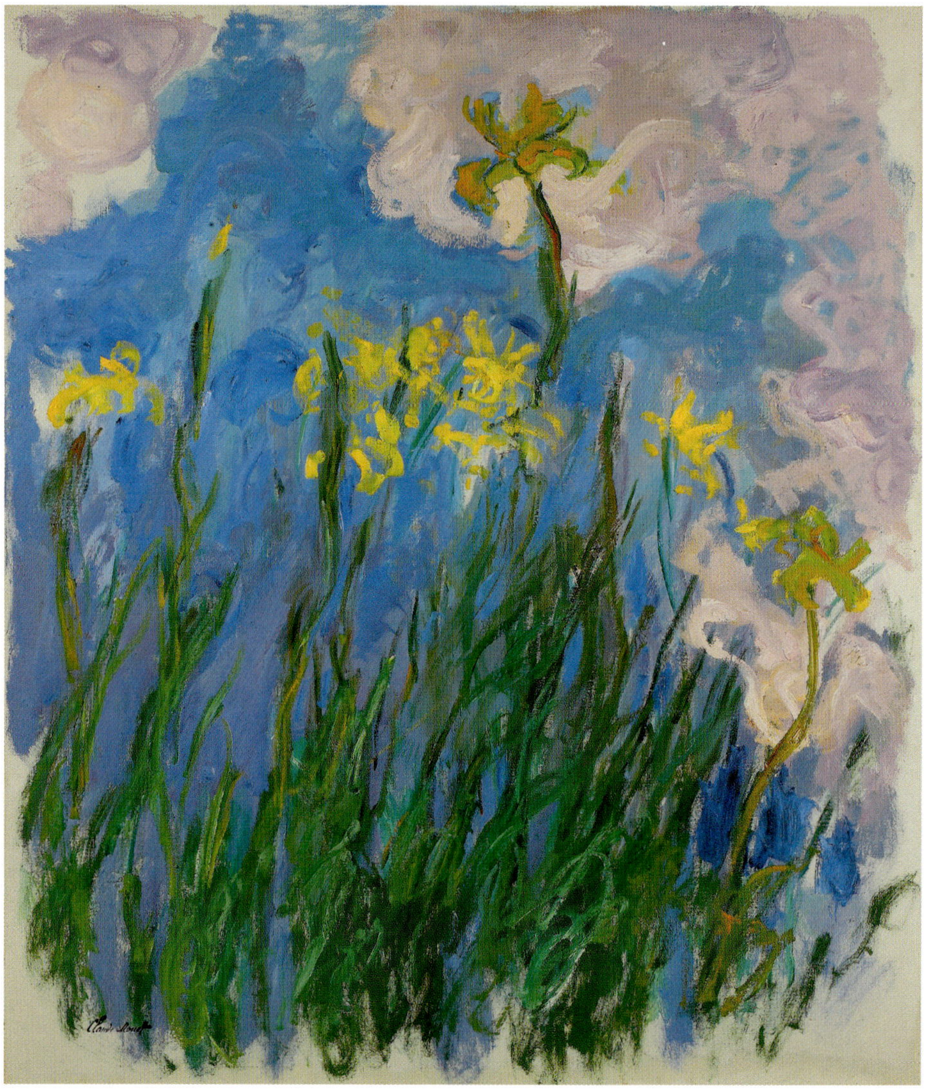

started the studies, large panels which he then showed me in his studio. Imagine a circular room whose walls, down to the skirting-board, would be completely filled by a horizon of water dotted with these plants, walls of a transparency by turns green- and mauve-ish, the calm and silence of the still water reflecting spreading blooms; the shades of colour are imprecise, deliciously subtle, of a dream-like delicacy."[63] The project gathered momentum, for the decorative frieze definitely and considerably exceeded the announced height. "One moment I was tempted to use this water lily theme for the decoration of a living room: borne along the walls, enveloping all the surfaces with its unity, it would have given the illusion of an endless whole, a wave with no skyline or shore; nerves overtaxed by work would be relaxed in front of it, using the restful example of static water."[64] Monet had a long-term view, and his reputation as an artist with an immediate vision does not do him enough justice.
The Orangerie works, installed shortly after the death of the artist, who donated them to the State in 1922 to celebrate the Victory, were the ultimate culmination of a line of thought that had spanned many years. The painter turned his back on easel painting, in favour of the monumental dimensions of large decorative painting, which was a general concern in art circles in 1900 and thereabouts. Monet himself had

shown an interest in this on several occasions, especially when, in 1876, he had embarked on the canvases assigned to decorate Montgeron castle (fig. 2). Nor had he refused to tackle the panels commissioned by Paul Durand-Ruel for his sitting-room on Rue de Rome. Again, he chose one of the pictures painted at Bordighera, *The Villas at Bordighera* (1884, Paris, Musée d'Orsay) to be placed above the door in the reception room of his friend Berthe Morisot.[65] Lastly, he paid much attention to the decoration of his house in Giverny. But the set of water lilies has a quite different dimension. By undertaking such an ambitious project, Monet linked back up with the grand tradition of decorative painting, as exemplified by such as Raphael and Michelangelo. His work could also be placed in the tradition of the great French decorative cycles of the seventeenth century or, closer to him, Pierre Puvis de Chavannes, whose grand décors he must have known about, especially those in the Rouen museum. Later on, Chagall rightly observed that "Monet is the Michelangelo of our time"[66] and his capacity for work and his inventive powers are actually comparable to those of the painter of the Sistine Chapel.

The Giverny Studio

The water lily canvases might express, as the artist wished, a supreme serenity, but the easel pictures painted in around 1920 convey the image of a less harmonious world. The more intense hues, the more dramatic contrasts with the recent views of the Japanese bridge (cat. nos. 24 and 25), the long, dovetailed strokes of the *Weeping Willow* (cat. no. 26), all have often been attributed to the artist's blurred vision. But these aspects, like the brushwork asserted in them, are absent from the *Grand Decorations*, on which Monet was working at the same time. Are the studio works really the result of weak eyesight, or did they remain as such because they were deemed less commercial? Or is it simply that the artist did not see fit to relinquish them? We know that Monet destroyed whatever he was not satisfied with, and perhaps we keep in mind the effects of growing blindness on the painter at that time.

"Everything is wonderful right now and this light blinds me,"[67] he wrote to his friend Clemenceau in May 1922. At that time, his cataract reached its worst point and, early in 1923 Monet had to decide to brave the operation he so dreaded. However, as he himself said, although he was obviously bothered by the cataract, he could still see and was still writing letters. After three operations in a row, the artist was able to announce in November 1923 to Étienne Clémentel, who was worried about the fate of the *Grand Decorations*: "I'm working."[68]

Monet was never one to vent anxiety or suffering, but, in his most private works, he allowed a less optimistic vision show through, a fact which did not escape Paul Valéry. After a visit to Giverny on 7 September 1925, Valéry noted: "He shows us his latest canvases. Strange clumps of roses caught beneath a blue sky. A dark house."[69] When Vuillard and Ker Xavier Roussel paid him a visit in 1926, they asked the artist if, like so many young painters, he had made copies of works at the Louvre. His answer was unexpected: "Very few, unfortunately! When I was very young, I copied the *Flayed Ox*... What a strange idea, isn't it? And a bit of Rubens in one of the decorations for Marie de Médicis... I think that's all."[70] Monet subsequently decided to silence tragedy and to celebrate brilliance. But the willow tree whose modernity still surprises might well be a distant echo of Rembrandt's *Flayed Ox* of 1655.

The water lilies met with mixed reactions; some saw in Monet's late output the failure of an elderly painter, spoilt by fame.[71] Marthe de Fels implied as much in the monograph she wrote on Monet in 1929. That same year, Paul Morand singled out certain scathing comments.[72] But the diplomatic writer's verdict was that of a man in a hurry, and he was, furthermore, far from being the only person to have a linear idea of modernity. Fellow painters were more perceptive, however, as revealed in an indignant letter from Paul Signac to the critic Florent Fels: "Let me tell you that you are quite wrong in your appraisal of Monet's 'studio'. That room where you were received—I know it well—contains not the trivia you refer to, but the most beautiful Monets, of all periods, preserved for their own sake, by the old master. I still want to steal one or two [*sic*]!"[73] A few days after Monet's death, Signac was asked to say something about the oeuvre of the great man. He declined to do so, as he always did for posthumous tributes. "I am still too moved by the loss of this master and friend, whose entire life and work were encouraging examples to me, to hold forth about him, which, incidentally, seems very simple: for anyone who has managed to follow the development of contemporary art, Claude Monet emancipated French painting; there is no painter who is not indebted to him for something."[74] Over and above the friendship and unflagging loyalty of his youthful admiration, Signac, then president of the Salon des Indépendants, was thoroughly versed in the situation of contemporary art in France. He knew that with the exception of the Cubist circles, many younger artists admired Monet's late work, in which they saw far more than a mere version of Impressionism. Some asked to be received in Giverny, as is suggested by a letter from Monet: "If Messrs. Matisse and Marquet would like to choose a day to come for a thoroughly simple lunch."[75] In the 1950s others, such as André Masson, came to the patriarch's defence with much gusto. "Perhaps it was too often said that he was content to record colorful sensations: 'Let the eye live its life'. The truth is that he knew, better than anyone else, 'how to organise sensations' and choose from among this invasion of infinite iridescent forms, one dominant one."[76]

The impact of the series on the founding fathers of abstraction has been pointed out by Michel Hoog,[77] who reminds us about the sudden turmoil in Vassily Kandinsky when, in the winter of 1896/97, in front of a Monet *Haystack*, he grasped the possibility of a painting without representation; and notes a similar epiphany in Malevich's words about Monet's *Rouen Cathedral* in 1929. Today we also know how much the American abstract artists of the 1950s owed to the discovery of the Giverny studio after the war, notably Joan Mitchell and Ellsworth Kelly, whose accounts, painted and written alike, eloquently express that debt. They discovered an extraordinarily novel form of expression, powerful and free, independent of a very lengthy tradition of western painting, as was already made clear back in 1909 by Roger Marx. The rehabilitation of Monet's late works was under way, and artists were backed up by dealers, persuaded, like Katia Granoff, of their modernity. The term "informal art" has been used when discussing the *Grand Decorations*, and it is a fact that the fascinating coloured continuum installed in the Orangerie stems from an unfocussed art where the subject disappears. But if Monet's oeuvre occasionally flirts with the boundaries of "pure painting", we should be cautious about labelling his canvases as abstract. As we have seen, he saw himself as a realist, and drew inspiration directly from a natural ensemble which he had himself created. On several occasions he reminded people that the spectacle of the world was

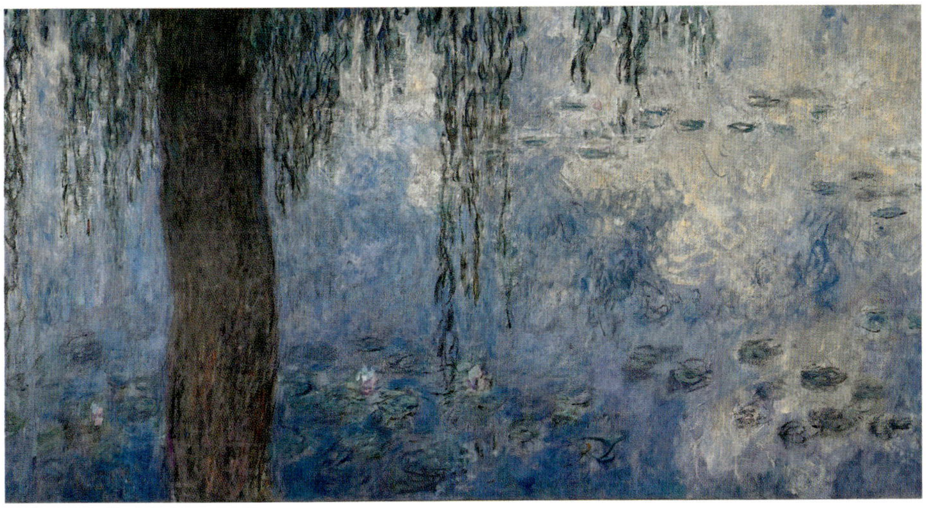

7 | *Water Lilies : Morning with Willows* (detail), 1914–18
Oil on panel, 200 × 127.5 cm
(78 3/4 × 50 3/16 in.)
Musée de l'Orangerie, Paris
Donation Claude Monet, 1922

the source of his art: "The splendour I aspire to springs from nature, upon which I depend; and perhaps originality is reduced, in my work, to the receptiveness of a highly sensitive organism and the convenience of a shorthand typist who projects onto the canvas, as onto a screen, the impression gathered by the retina. If you need momentum, and for the good of the cause, find something to affiliate me with, compare me with old Japanese artists: the rarity of their taste has always entertained me, and I agree with the suggestions of their aesthetic, which evokes presence by way of shadow, the whole by the part; compare me with our eighteenth-century painters, with whom I recognise that I am in close communion, in terms of sensibility and technique. But how much wiser it would be not to isolate me from my era, to which I belong with every fibre of my being! How much better the future would be informed by showing me as the disciple of Courbet and Jongkind, a contemporary of Stéphane Mallarmé and Claude Debussy!"[78] Among his contemporaries, Monet could find no painter to mention, preferring to refer to a poet and a composer.

The wealth and timely relevance of Monet's art drew him close to young painters, but sharing his artistic ideas. "From time to time I have a visit from Bonnard and Vuillard. They are fine painters."[79] It was certainly no coincidence that Bonnard chose to rent *Ma Roulotte*, a house in Vernonnet, a mile or two from Giverny, and the two men saw each other frequently, as neighbours. As emerges from their correspondence, the two men admired and respected each other (p. 135) The letter in which Monet asks Bonnard to come urgently to Giverny is especially significant, because it sets the tone of their exchanges, and shows how the opinion of the younger man counted for Monet. "I would be most happy to see you and if you have a spare moment today, that would suit me very well, because I would like to show you where I am with my big machines" (p. 135). In another letter dated 19 January 1925, Monet tells his friend that he is truly despondent, "with the moment drawing near when I must deliver these panels. I am obsessed by it, and I curse the idea I have to give them to the State" (p. 135). Like Bonnard, Monet was a loyal friend, and they continued seeing each other to the end. Claire Joyes notes that Bonnard had been with Monet a fortnight before his death.[80]

We also know, thanks to Jacques Salomon, that Édouard Vuillard was one of the last to visit the patriarch. On 30 June 1926 they went to Giverny with the painter Roussel and Annette Salomon. The photographs taken on that lovely summer's day (cat. no. 30), and the account of it left by Jacques Salomon in his diary before it was published in 1971 are among the very last reports of the artist. Shortly thereafter Monet passed away, and the funeral was a private affair: "Behind his coffin, drawn by two local men, the painters Bonnard, Roussel, and Vuillard, then a man mute beneath the weight of his grief, Georges Clemenceau."[81]

The excerpts from letters by Claude Monet cited throughout this essay are from Daniel Wildenstein, *Claude Monet, Biographie et catalogue raisonné*, Lausanne and Paris: Bibliothèque des Arts, 1974-91, 5 vol.

1 A rhyming quatrain sent by Stéphane Mallarmé to Claude Monet in 1890; Paris, Bibliothèque Littéraire Jacques Doucet.

2 Abbé Anatole Toussaint and Jean-Pierre Hoschedé, "Flore de Vernon et de la Roche-Guyon", *Bulletin de la Société des Amis des Sciences Naturelles de Rouen*, 1898.

3 Jean-Pierre Hoschedé, *Claude Monet, ce mal connu*, 2 vols.; Geneva: P. Cailler, 1960, p. 57.

4 Genvième Aitken and Marianne Delafond, *La Collection d'estampes japonaises de Claude Monet, Fondation Claude Monet*; Giverny: Fondation Claude Monet/Lausanne and Paris: Bibliothèque des Arts, 2003.

5 Daniel Wildenstein, *Claude Monet, biographie et catalogue raisonné*; 5 vols.; Lausanne and Paris: Bibliothèque des Arts, 1975–91, T. IV, p. 54.

6 Letter from Monet to Paul Durand-Ruel; Giverny 22 July 1883, W366.

7 The various letters and documents concerning Monet's requests are kept in the Archives Départementales de l'Eure, Évreux (18 S 25).

8 Lilla Cabot Perry, "Reminiscences of Claude Monet. From 1889 to 1909", in Meredith Martindale, *Lilla Cabot Perry, an American Impressionist*; Washington, D.C.: The National Museum of Women in the Arts, 1990, p. 116.

9 Apart from three landscapes of Honfleur painted in 1917.

10 Joachim Gasquet, *Cézanne*; Paris: Éditions Bernheim-Jeune, 1926, p. 149.

11 Letters from Monet to Josse or Gaston Bernheim-Jeune; Giverny, 21 December 1900, W1582a and W1582b.

12 Arsène Alexandre, *Claude Monet*; Paris: Bernheim-Jeune, 1921; and Marc Elder, *À Giverny, chez Claude Monet*; Bernheim-Jeune, 1924.

13 Letter from Monet to Paul Durand-Ruel; Giverny, 18 October 1883, W377.

14 *Idem*; 30 October 1883, W378

15 *Idem*; Giverny, 1 December 1883, W383.

16 Letter from Monet to Berthe Morisot; Giverny 11 July 1890, W1064.

17 Lilla Cabot Perry, *op. cit.*, p. 116.

18 Letter from Monet to Théodore Duret; Giverny, 13 August 1887, W794.

19 Duke of Trévise, "Le Pélérinage de Giverny," *La Revue de l'art ancien et moderne*, no. 282, January 1927, pp. 42-50 and no. 283, February 1927, pp. 121–34.

20 René Gimpel, *Journal d'un collectionneur, marchand de tableaux*; Paris: Calmann-Lévy, 1963, p. 348.

21 Roger Marx, "Les *Nymphéas* de M. Claude Monet," *Gazette des Beaux Arts*, June 1909, p. 529.

22 Lilla Cabot Perry, *op. cit.*, p. 116.

23 Lilla Cabot Perry, *op. cit.*, p. 116.

24 Paul Morand, *Venises*; Gallimard, *L'Imaginaire*, 1971, p. 10: "I was already thinking of Venice, I wanted to celebrate that water lily-city, where each street was the Seine."

25 Joachim Pissarro, *Monet and the Mediterranean*; Fort Worth: Kimbell Art Museum, and New York: Brooklyn Museum of Art, 1997, p. 13.

26 Octave Mirbeau, "Claude Monet," *L'Art dans les deux mondes*, 7 March 1891, no. 16, p. 183.

27 Arsène Alexandre, "Le jardin de Monet," *Le Figaro*, 9 August 1901, no. 221, p. 1.
28 Letter from Monet to Alice; Bordighera, 29 January 1884, W394.
29 *Idem*, Bordighera, 5 February 1884, W407.
30 Dossier kept in the Archives Départementales de l'Eure, Évreux, (18 S 25).
31 Gustave Geffroy, *Claude Monet: sa vie, son temps, son œuvre*; Paris: G. Crès, 1922, p. 328.
32 Maurice Kahn, "Le Jardin de Claude Monet," *Le Temps*, no. 15606, 7 June 1904, p. 2-3
33 Duke of Trévise, *op. cit.*, p. 44.
34 Jean-Pierre Hoschedé, *op. cit.*, p. 65.
35 Gabrielle van Zuylen, "The Eye of a Gardener... Claude Monet", p. 39-47.
36 Letter from Monet to Julie Manet; Giverny, 29 May 1900, W1560.
37 *Idem*; Giverny, 31 May 1900, W1561.
38 Robert Herbert, "Method and Meaning in Monet," *Art in America*, September 1979, pp. 90–108.
39 Marianne Alphant, *Claude Monet, une vie dans le paysage*; Paris: Hazan, 1993, p. 573.
40 Gustave Geffroy, *op. cit.*, p. 329.
41 Letter from Gustave de Bellio to Monet, 17 June 1883, quoted in Daniel Wildenstein, "Giverny ou la conquête de l'absolu," *Monet à Giverny: au-delà de l'impressionnisme*: New York: The Metropolitan Museum of Art, 1978; and Paris: Herscher (French ed.), 1983, p. 19.
42 G.-J. [Georges Jeanniot], "Notes sur l'art. Claude Monet," *La Cravache parisienne*, 23 June 1888, p. 2.
43 Maurice Guillemot, "Claude Monet," *La Revue illustrée*, no. 7, 15 March 1898, n. p. [p. 2].
44 Louis Vauxcelles, "Chez les peintres. Un après-midi chez Claude Monet," *L'Art et les Artistes*, no. 9, December 1905, p. 90.
45 Letter from Monet to Paul Durand-Ruel, 12 February 1905, W1764.
46 The film *Ceux de chez nous* made in 1914-15 by Sacha Guitry was shown from 22 November to 5 December 1915 at the Théâtre des Variétés in Paris.
47 Octave Mirbeau, *op. cit.*, p. 184.
48 Monet to Evan Charteris, Giverny, quoted in Sylvie Patin, *Monet*, Paris, Gallimard, 1991, p. 152–53, W2626.
49 Arsène Alexandre, *op. cit.*, p. 1.
50 Françoise Heilbrun, "The Patriarch of Giverny in front of the Camera," pp. 31-37.
51 Octave Mirbeau, *op. cit.*
52 Louis Vauxcelles, *op. cit.*, pp. 85–90.
53 Duke of Trévise, *op. cit.*, pp. 121–34.
54 Letter from Monet to Nickolas Muray, Giverny, ca. July 1926, W2627.
55 "I feel almost ready to try painting again," letter from Monet to Gustave Geffroy, 6 March 1913, W2060.
56 Letter from Monet to Félix Fénéon, around 1 June 1914, W2119.
57 Duke of Trévise, *op. cit.*, p. 134.
58 Jean-Paul Riopelle, quoted by Jean-Dominique Rey, *Galerie-Jardin des Arts*, July/August 1974, p. 26.
59 Roger Marx, *op. cit.*, p. 524.
60 Monet to Gustave Geffroy, 11 August 1908, W1854.
61 Charles F. Stuckey, *Claude Monet (1840–1926)*; The Art Institute of Chicago; London: Thames and Hudson, 1995, p. 9.
62 Letter from Monet to Raymond Koechlin; Giverny, 15 January 1915, W2142.
63 Maurice Guillemot, *op. cit.*, n. p. [p. 3].
64 Roger Marx, *op. cit.*, p. 529.
65 Julie Manet, *Journal (1893-99)*; Paris: Klincksieck, 1969; Giverny, 30 October 1893 W378.
66 Pierre Schneider, *Les Dialogues du Louvre*, Paris: Denoël, 1972, p. 42.
67 Letter from Monet to Georges Clemenceau; Giverny, 22 May 1922, W2498.
68 Letter from Monet to Étienne Clémentel, 7 November 1923, W2541.
69 Paul Valéry, *Cahiers*, 2 vols.; Paris: Gallimard, 1974, p. 948.
70 Jacques Salomon, "Chez Monet, avec Vuillard et Roussel," *L'Œil*, no. 197, 19 May 1971, p. 24.
71 For all the different reactions caused by the *Grand Decorations*, see Sylvie Patin, *Regards sur les Nymphéas, de Paul Claudel à André Masson*, Paris: Éditions de la Réunion des Musées Nationaux, 2006.
72 Paul Morand, "Vétheuil et Giverny," *L'Art vivant*, 1 September 1929, p. 669.
73 Letter from Paul Signac to Florent Fels, 31 October 1925; Archives Fels, copy kindly made available at the Archives Signac.
74 Letter from Paul Signac to an unidentified recipient, 14 December 1926, *Catalogue d'autographes, dessins, portraits*; Paris: Librairie Jean-Claude Vrain, Paris, no. 188, repr.
75 Letter from Monet to the brothers Gaston and Josse Bernheim-Jeune; Giverny, 1 May 1917, W2229.
76 André Masson, "Monet le fondateur," *Verve*, 7, nos. 27–28, December 1952, p. 68.
77 Michel Hoog, "Le cheminement vers l'abstrait," in *Les Nymphéas de Claude Monet au musée de l'Orangerie*; Paris: Musée de l'Orangerie, 1984, new ed. 1989, p. 71.
78 Roger Marx, *op. cit.*, p. 528.
79 Florent Fels, "Claude Monet," *Nouvelle Revue Française*, 1925, p. 17.
80 Claire Joyes, *Claude Monet et Giverny*; Paris: Chêne, 1985, p. 123. The presence of Bonnard and Vuillard at the burial was confirmed by Jacques Salomon, *op. cit.*, p. 24.
81 Marthe de Fels, *La Vie de Claude Monet*; Paris: Gallimard, 1929, p. 214.

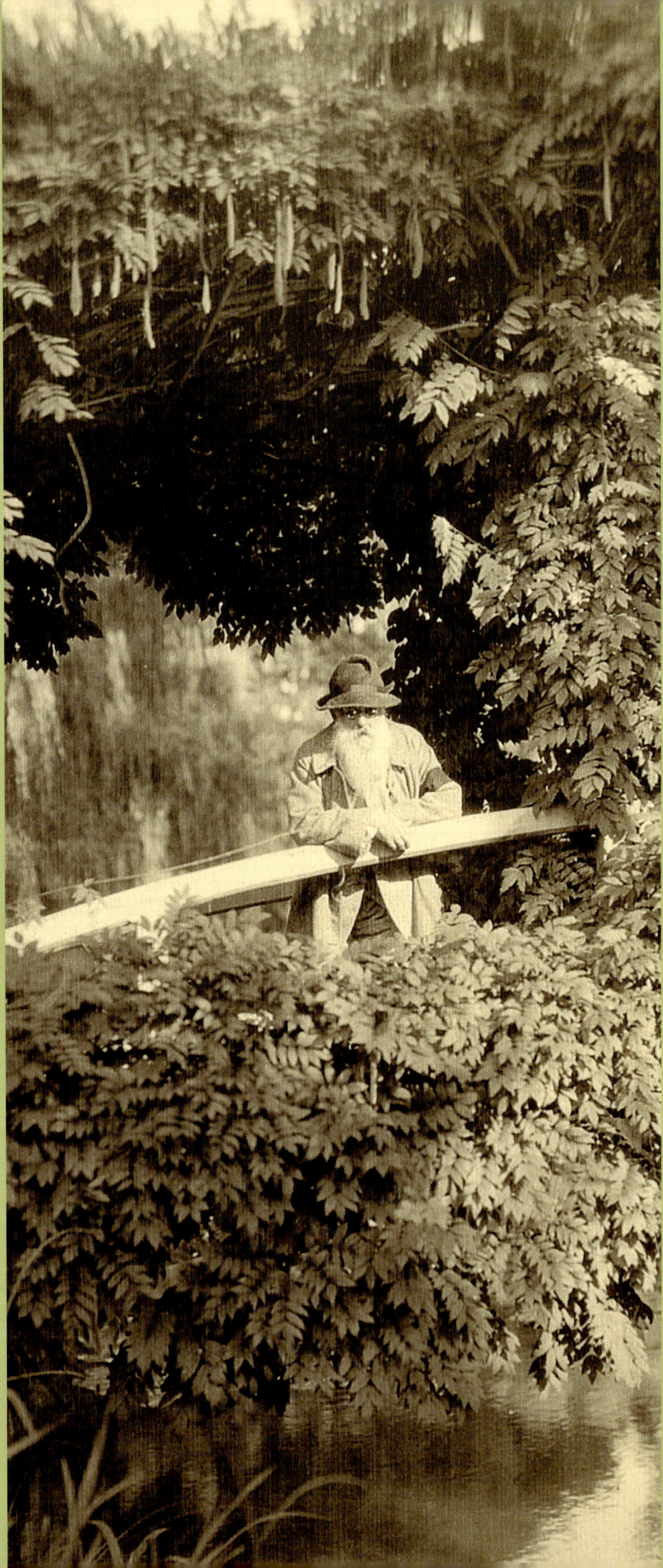

Françoise Heilbrun

The Patriarch of Giverny in front of the Camera

"Paris with all its excitement... did not suit a man
given to stubborn contemplation...
He lives in the country in a carefully chosen landscape;
the *plein air* is his only studio, and [in it] he is creating
the finest and most significant works of this era."
Octave Mirbeau, 1889

"Apart from painting and gardening, I'm no good at anything."[1]
Claude Monet

In the wake of his exhibition at the Galerie Georges Petit in 1890 and the leading part he played in the acquisition of Manet's *Olympia* by the Musée du Luxembourg, Claude Monet had become a celebrity, not only in the eyes of the cultured élite, but also in the eyes of ordinary people. An indication of this being his portrait[2] reproduced in the Félix Potin collection which presented inexpensive illustrations of the photographed faces of statesmen, artists, writers and athletes of renown (cat. no. 31). In 1905, after transforming the land he purchased on the banks of the river Epte into a water garden, Monet happily let himself be photographed in that lovingly created and tended Garden of Eden, which he rightly regarded as a work of art in itself, and the source of inspiration for his painting. Well aware of the need to get his work known, he nevertheless dreaded—as he observed in different interviews—that there might be confusion between his public life and his private life. He strove, to the end, to restrict the distribution of these pictures to his nearest and dearest. Though he did agree to the publication in certain gardening and nature magazines of the photographs taken by the horticulturist Georges Truffaut,[3] his intent being to entertain at Giverny only those persons who had a keen interest in his art. Yet he was much in demand. At the turn of the century, the inventions of the Viennese Karl Klič, which turned heliogravure[4] into a standardized industrial process,[5] had transformed the press by making it possible to print magazines in large editions —something which became common practice in the 1920s. With guaranteed outlets, there were suddenly photographers aplenty, as well as agencies specialising in artwork reproduction.

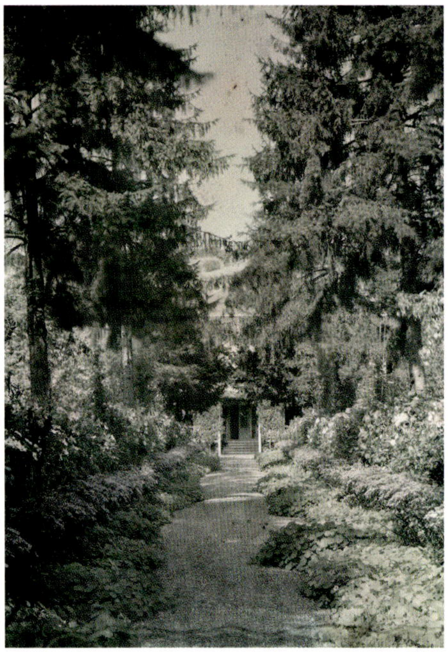

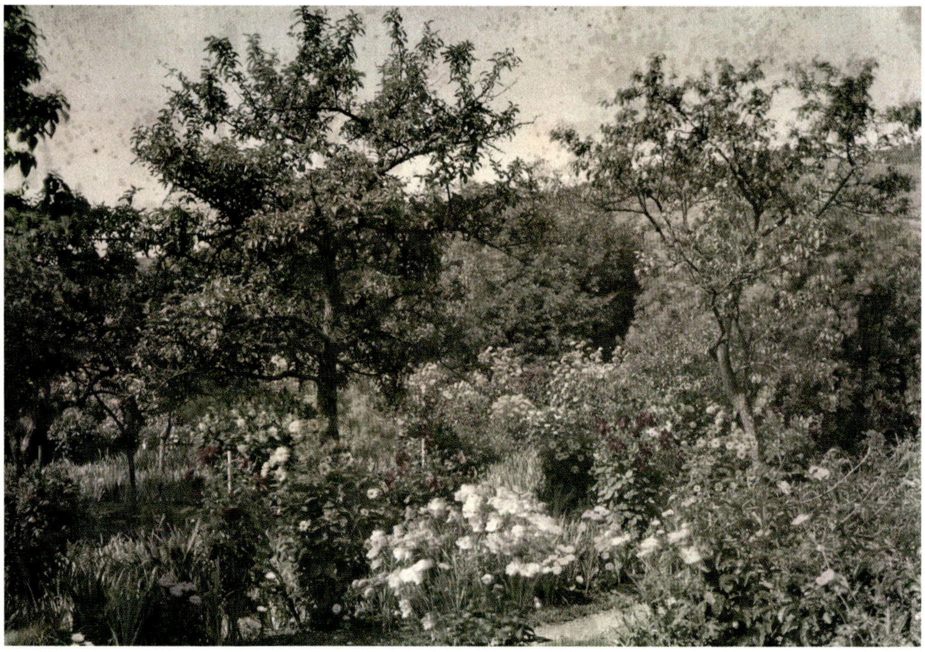

page 30:
Thérèse Bonney, *Claude Monet on the Japanese Bridge in his Garden in Giverny* (detail), see cat. no. 55

1 | *Giverny, the Path with the Spruce Trees*, ca. 1900
Autochrome, 18 × 24 cm (7½ × 9⁷⁄₁₆ in.)
Musée Marmottan Monet, Paris

2 | *Giverny, View of the West Part of the Garden*, ca. 1900
Autochrome, 18 × 24 cm (7⅛ × 9⁷⁄₁₆ in.)
Musée Marmottan Monet, Paris

Jacques-Ernest Bulloz [1858–1942]

An article by Louis Vauxcelles, on a visit to the master with the German Impressionist painter Félix Borchardt, appeared in *L'Art et les Artistes* in December 1905. It was illustrated with photographs by Jacques-Ernest Bulloz showing Monet, posing lord-like in his garden in Giverny, near the pond, on the Japanese bridge, and in his studio-*cum*-sitting room. Was this done to rectify the impression given by the delightful photograph taken by the painter Theodore Robinson, in which the master appeared as a peasant-painter,[6] on the cover of the March 1898 issue of *La Revue Illustrée* (cat. no. 32)?
Bulloz was known to Monet. He had trained at Braun, the art publisher, then in 1897 opened his own company in Paris, specialising in the reproduction of works of art. He was interested not only in ancient art, but also in the avant-garde,[7] working for Auguste Rodin, Gustave Moreau, the Impressionists, and the Postimpressionists. Bulloz spent every summer in Giverny, and wrote in his memoirs how he met Monet one day, in a boat laden with canvases. Monet invited Bulloz to visit him with the photographs of his paintings belonging to Durand-Ruel. Subsequently, Bulloz often saw the painter, and photographed both his work and the artist in person near the water lily pond.[8] After Vauxcelles' article, few illustrated pieces showing Monet in his garden appeared until after his death.

Pierre Choumoff [1872–1936]

Édouard, Duke of Trévise (1883–1946), an art-lover and collector, went twice to Giverny in 1920 with the photographer Pierre Choumoff. The visit on 14 November coincided with the artist's eightieth birthday. Choumoff,[9] who had worked for Rodin and Léonce Bénédite, took a series of photographs in the garden and in the house (a view of Monet near the Japanese bridge and the pond (cat. no. 35), another of him in his sitting room, and a close-up portrait).[10] But these pictures would not be published until 1927[11], in the duke's valuable articles which appeared after the painter's death in the January and February issues of *La Revue de l'Art ancien et moderne*.[12]

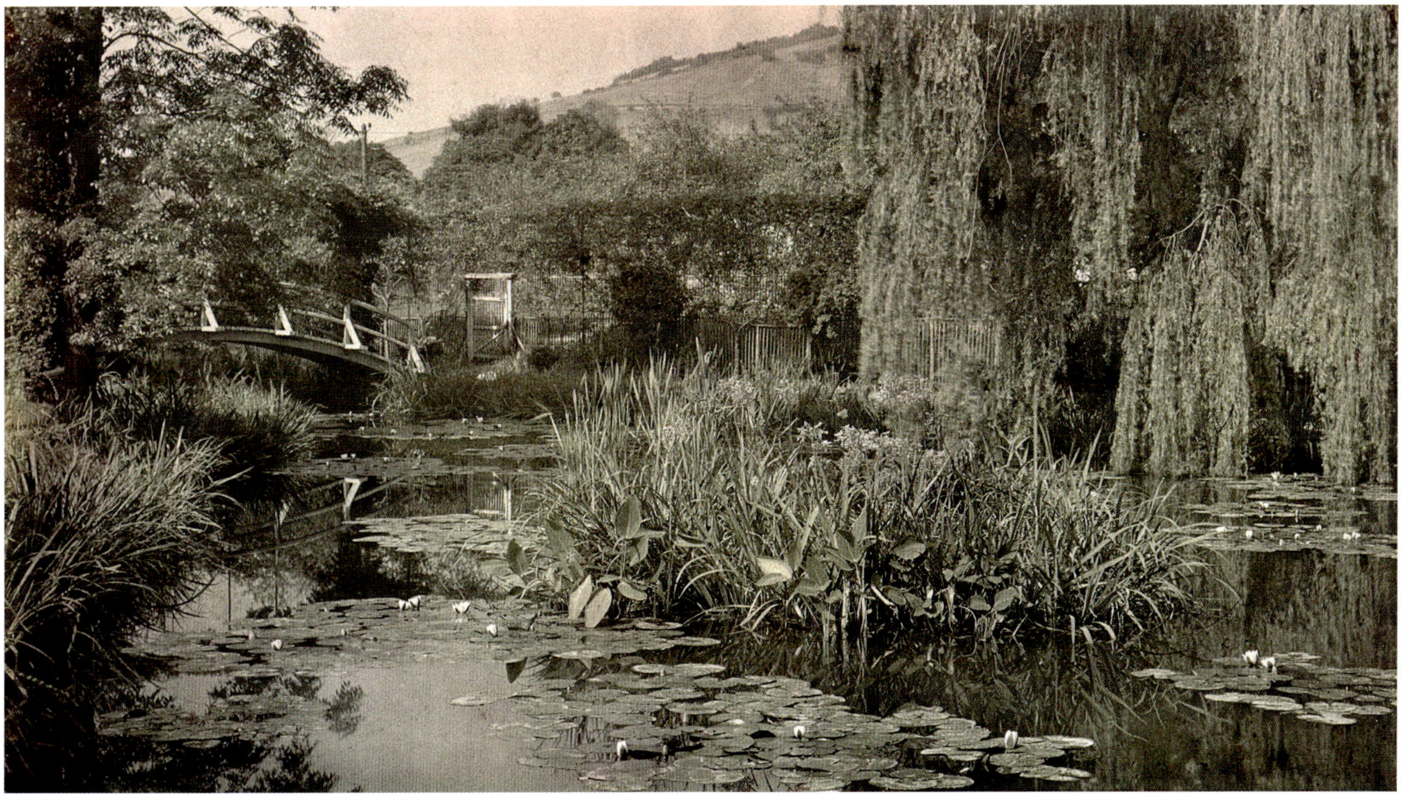

3 | *Giverny, the Pond and the Japanese Bridge*, ca. 1900
Autochrome, 18 × 24 cm (7 1/8 × 9 7/16 in.)
Musée Marmottan Monet, Paris

Thérèse Bonney [1894–1978]

The photographs of Monet taken by Thérèse Bonney probably date from some time after May 1925, because in them Monet is wearing his glasses and the armband he had worn since Marthe's death (cat. nos. 54-55). Thérèse Bonney was a powerful personality. Born in the United States, she had settled in Paris, where she had been a brilliant student of literature before opening the first American photographic agency in Europe, in 1923.[13] Her major interest lay in design and contemporary French architecture, which she helped to acquaint people with on the other side of the Atlantic. But she also produced some very beautiful portraits of artists, in addition to those of Monet and Pierre Bonnard, Raoul Dufy, Sonia Delaunay and, above all, Alexander Calder.[14]

The Appearance of Colour

The Giverny garden beseeched color, and color techniques had just been invented in photography. In 1868, the principle based on the selection then the addition of three complementary colours, blue, yellow and red, had been invented independently by Ducos du Hauron and Charles Cros. The Lumière brothers carried out the first application of the process, patented in 1904 (after ten years in the making) and marketed only in 1907. They had had the idea of using as filters tiny grains of potato flour, dyed with one of the primary colors and mixed in such a way as to make an even coat. The whole thing, covered with a panchromatic gelatine-silver bromide emulsion, was then sandwiched between two hermetically sealed sheets of glass. The positive image, one-off and obtained by reversal, was then projected onto a screen. It could also be printed on paper, but it had to be retouched in order to achieve a satisfactory result. Industrially manufactured autochrome plates were used by thousands of amateurs and one or two seasoned photographers, giving rise to an initial aesthetics of color in photography, with the grain created in the image by the tiny coloured grains of potato flour, evoking the technique practised by the Neoimpressionist painters. The magazine *L'Illustration*, in whose salons, in 1907, the public launch of the autochrome had been staged, did not publish any colour photographs of Monet's garden before his death, contenting itself with reproducing some of his paintings with this procedure. In the 15 January 1927 issue of this magazine, Monet's obituary penned by René Delange was illustrated with several autochromes, including three original plates taken in the spring of 1921,[15] when the garden was in full bloom (cat. nos. 44 to 46), and held in the magazine's archives, which were acquired in 2006 by the Musée d'Orsay. The large format and excellent quality of the plates suggest the work of a professional. Étienne Clémentel's heirs have informed us that he did not take autochromes of this format, and Thierry Gervais, curator of the exhibition devoted to Léon Gimpel at the Musée d'Orsay, also believes that the pictures cannot be by Gimpel.[16] Nathalie Boulouch, a color photography specialist, suggests François Vizzavona as their possible author, he, too, happening to run a company specialising in artwork reproduction.[17] Dominique de Font-Réaulx, for her part, suggets the names of Emmanuel Sougez and Jules Gervais-Courtellemont, both having worked for *L'Illustration*.[18] Oddly enough, there are no photographic credits for these photos, which is unusual when professionals are involved. The autochromes of the same quality and format, bequeathed by Michel Monet to the Musée Marmottan, (figs. 1 to 3) became part of the collections as anonymous works at a time when, it is true, little importance was attached to photographers' identities. In the book accompanying the exhibition of photographic treasures at the Institut de France, Arnaud d'Hauterives entertains the idea that these autochromes might have been taken by Monet himself,[19] which seems unlikely, as far as our current knowledge permits us to know. It is possible that Monet, who was so proud of his garden, had it reproduced in a technique doing justice to all its subtleties, for the pleasure of keeping the evidence in his own possession. But for the time being the author of these photographs remains a mystery.

Étienne Clémentel [1864–1936]

In 1916 Étienne Clémentel, then Minister of Agriculture, met Monet through Georges Clemenceau, and the two men became close friends. Monet's letters to Clémentel, held in the Department of Graphic Arts at the Musée du Louvre,[20] shed light on the generosity and devotion shown to Monet by this politician, a cultured man who loved the arts,[21] and who himself dabbled in painting and photography as an amateur. Despite shortages brought on by the war, he always made sure that the painter of the *Water Lilies* had enough coal to heat his home, and enough oil to paint with. He was often asked to lunch in Giverny, when Monet did not travel to Versailles, where the minister lived.[22]

Clémentel's autochromes, donated by his heirs to the Musée d'Orsay, are small, and were not meant for publication. They were taken with a Richard *Vérascope*, making it possible to take two views from a slightly different angle, these views then being superposed and giving a feeling of three-dimensionality when they were viewed as transparencies in a device specially designed to that effect. Two of them depict the Giverny garden, offering us quite a comprehensive view of it (cat. nos. 42-43).

Amateur Photographs

At the turn of the century, the Eastman-Kodak company—among others—revolutionized the practice of photography by greatly simplifying how photos were taken (the snapshot), then developed and printed. Photography came down quite simply to "pressing a button," as declared by the advertisement. As many amateurs, Bonnard, Édouard Vuillard and Felix Édouard Vallotton all captured moments of their private and family lives on film. Where Monet was concerned, it would seem that he used a Kodak camera at least once to reproduce the shadow of his head reflected in the water lily pond (cat. no. 34).[23] Another print of the same format, whose publication its owner withheld, shows him in the path, clutching the small camera. In another photograph (cat. no. 33), we see Claude and Michel Monet carrying a camera with a stand[24] in one of the garden's paths. It can be assumed that it was Michel who took the pictures, and that he was, in particular, the author of the snapshot taken of Claude Monet shortly after his cataract operation (cat. no. 53). In 1926 it would be Jacques Salomon's turn, during his visit to Monet in the company of Vuillard and Ker Xavier Roussel (cat. no. 57), to photograph the group outdoors. The pictures would not be printed until 1971, when they appeared in the magazine *L'Œil*. Attributed to Henri Martinie and showing Monet and Clemenceau (during a visit from the great collector Matsukata), the pictures are, by virtue of their very subject, among the most touching (cat. nos. 47 and 51), especially the one in which the two men are seen from behind, walking somewhat unsteadily along. In one of these photographs, reproduced by Pierre Georgel as being by Count Sanji Kuroki,[25] the men are featured with Lili Butler on the Japanese bridge.

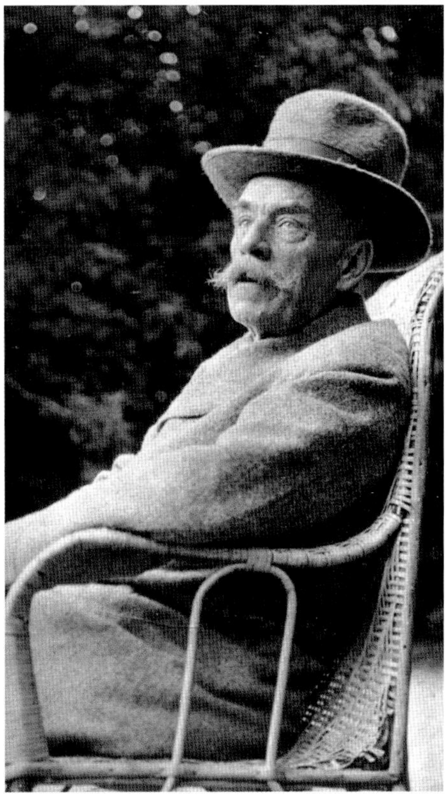

4 | Sacha Guitry, *Octave Mirbeau*

Photographer-*cum*-Artist: Midway between Amateur and Professional

"Amateur" photographers were also able to acquire the experience of a professional. This was the case with Baron Adolf de Meyer, an upper-class international dandy, and an excellent photographer, to boot. He had bolstered his social status by marrying the beautiful Olga Caracciolo, presumed daughter of the future King Edward VII, and his talent as a photographer by being noticed in 1903 by Alfred Stieglitz among the members of the Linked Ring Brotherhood, before immortalising Nijinsky in the ballet *Afternoon of a Faun* in 1912. When he visited Monet in 1905 with Joseph Durand-Ruel,[26] it was not just as a photographer, but also as a collector curious to meet the author of the two canvases he had just acquired that same year from the dealer he was with, *The Thames, Waterloo Bridge, Effect of Sun* (1903) and *The Cliffs at Pourville, Morning* (1897). It is likely that the exhibition at the Grafton Galleries, paid for by Durand-Ruel in London the year before had attracted de Meyer's interest, London being where he resided when he was not in Paris or Venice. The portraits he took of Monet are outstanding for their layout, their extremely luminous quality,[27] and the excellence of their printing (cat. nos. 37 and 38). He published at least one of them, a third version, in *Vanity Fair*, in March 1921.[28] Sacha Guitry, for his part, numbered among Monet's friends, and was often entertained in Giverny, the artist having first known his father, the great actor Lucien Guitry. Monet, who was usually reluctant to stop working, often went to Paris to see his plays.[29] At first he refused to appear in Guitry's film, *Ceux de chez nous*, but, fortunately, he let himself be persuaded, and duly featured in one of the best scenes, shot near the pond. The film dates from 1915, with the photographs coming, it would seem, a little while later. Guitry was as able a photographer as he was a film-maker, producing more sober portraits than Baron de Meyer's, but no less powerful (cat. nos. 39 and 41). He is attributed with taking the photograph showing Monet and Gustave Geffroy (cat. no. 40), but it would seem also justifiable to regard him as the author of the photograph of that other close friend of Monet, the writer Octave Mirbeau, sitting outside in an armchair, so similar to the portrait of Monet (cat. no 41 and fig. 4) is the layout against the distant backdrop of greenery.

I wish to express my special thanks to Marina Ferretti-Bocquillon who invited me to write this article, as well as all those who assisted me in my research: Sébastien Baschet, Anne Cook, Flavie Durand-Ruel, Valérie Joxe, Vanessa Lecomte, Lise Lentignac, Gregory Leroy, Philippe Piguet, and Marie Robert.

1 Claude Monet in Maurice Kahn, "Au jour le jour : Le Jardin de Claude Monet," *Le Temps*, no. 15606 (June 7, 1904), p. 3.

2 Taken when the artist was 28.

3 In September 1908 in the magazine *Fermes et Châteaux*, in October 1913 and in November 1924 in *Jardinage*.

4 A technique making it possible to permanently reproduce a photograph.

5 The image is first inserted in the typed text by means of a grid; the printing is then greatly speeded up by the use of rotary presses; these two inventions were the brainchild of the Viennese Karl Klič Cf. M. Frizot "Les procédés photomécaniques" in Françoise Heilbrun (ed.), *La Photographie au musée d'Orsay*, Paris: Musée d'Orsay-Skira Flammarion, 2008, pp. 195–99.

6 Certain passages in Louis Vauxcelles' article suggest as much.

7 On Jacques-Ernest Bulloz, see Marie Garet's doctoral dissertation prepared at the École du Louvre in 2007.

8 Garet, *ibid*, p. 47, excerpt from Bulloz' memoirs, reproduced, fig. 20, two variants of the portrait of Monet near the water lilies, carbon prints held in the Archives Photographiques du Fort de Saint-Cyr.

9 In 2007, Clémence Carette wrote a Master I thesis at the Université de Paris I, Panthéon-Sorbonne, about Pierre Choumoff, *Pierre Choumoff et la photographie de sculpture*.

10 A fourth, showing him in the large studio with the *Water Lilies*, was sold in Geneva in 2003, reproduced in Galerie Koller, Geneva, no. 6 May 2003, cat. no. 129.

11 The Duke of Trévise published an article on 25 January 1921 in *La Vie au Champs*, on "Les quatre-vingt ans de Claude Monet".

12 The Duke of Trévise, "Le pèlerinage de Giverny," *La Revue de l'art ancien et moderne*, no. 282, January 1927, pp. 42–50, and no. 283, February 1927, pp. 121–34.

13 Cf. Lisa Schlansker Kolosek, *L'Invention du chic, Thérèse Bonney et le Paris moderne*, Paris: Norma, 2002.

14 Her archives are held at the Cooper-Hewitt Museum in New York, whose director, Paul Warwick Thompson, wrote the preface to the book by L. Schlansker. Oddly enough, Thérèse Bonney claimed not to be especially interested in photography, which did not prevent her from collecting nineteenth century prints, some of which were donated by the Fondation Kodak-Pathé to the Musée d'Orsay.

15 See Dominique de Font-Réaulx, "Nouvelles acquisitions," *48/14 La Revue du musée d'Orsay*, 2006. The photos are actually much earlier than 1927.

16 One of the best photographers working for *L'Illustration*.

17 Active between 1898 and 1958; his collection which includes autochromes, including some reproductions of Monet paintings, is held at the Archives du Fort de Saint-Cyr.

18 Jules Gervais-Courtellemont was another photographer working for *L'Illustration*, which would seem to rule him out, because his work has been studied extensively.

19 Arnaud d'Hauterives, "Évocation des autochromes conservés au musée Marmottan Monet : le jardin de Claude Monet à Giverny," in *Éclats d'Histoire, les collections photographiques de l'Institut de France* Arles/Paris: Actes Sud/Institut de France, 2003, pp. 250-53.

20 "It extended to 1926 and was first published by Daniel Wildenstein, *Claude Monet, biographie et catalogue raisonné* (5 vol.), Lausanne and

Paris: Bibliothèque des Arts, 1974-91, then by P. Gassier, "Monet et Rodin photographiés chez eux en couleurs", *Connaissance des arts*, April 1975, pp. 92–97.

21 "Étienne Clémentel et les arts," cf. P. Arizzoli-Clémentel, *Revue de l'Histoire de Versailles et des Yvelines*, vol. 89, 2006–07, pp. 85–98. The latter reminds us that Madame Clémentel entertained at Versailles an intellectual and artistic élite, and, in particular, the dealer Ambroise Vollard.

22 Clémentel was incidentally very close to Rodin and played a decisive part in the 1916 donation to the State of the sculptor's works. The autochromes by Clémentel depicting Rodin were donated by his heirs to the Musée Rodin. See Hélène Pinet, *Couleurs du temps, les photographies d'Étienne Clémentel*, Paris: Musée Rodin, 1988.

23 The print's format is recognised as being that of the "Pocket Kodak" used by Vuillard, Bonnard and Maurice Denis, available in shops in 1895.

24 This was probably one of his 9 × 12 cm ($3^1/_2$ × $4^3/_4$ in.) format plate cameras, which were quite light, and used by Degas in 1895. Several anonymous prints in this same format are held in the Philippe Piguet collection.

25 Pierre Georgel, *Monet : le cycle des Nymphéas*, Paris: RMN, Musée de l'Orangerie, 1999, p. 48, fig. 55.

26 Flavie Durand-Ruel found in the archives signs of these pictures; she also found the two pictures that de Meyer would sell to Durand-Ruel in 1912 and 1914. See Daniel Wildenstein, *op. cit.*, vol. V, p. 429, nos. 234 and 238, who published the letters written by Durand-Ruel to Baron de Meyer in 1911 and 1912, about the purchase of the paintings.

27 Attributable to the Pinkerton Smith lenses that de Meyer had bought in 1903, which produced a precise focus in the middle of the image and a more diffused one at the edges, due, too, to the systematic way in which de Meyer lit his subjects from behind. See Anne Ehrenkranz, *A Singular Elegance, The Photographs of Baron Adolph de Meyer*, San Francisco: Chronicle Books/New York: ICP, 1994.

28 Reprod., *ibidem*, p.102.

29 See Sylvie Patin, *Monet "un œil... mais, bon Dieu quel œil!"*, Paris: Gallimard who published on p. 149 a scene reproduced in *Vu* in 1918 from Sacha Guitry's play *Histoire de France*, portraying Clemenceau and Monet. In 1916 Monet went to Paris to see *Faisons un rêve* by Guitry himself.

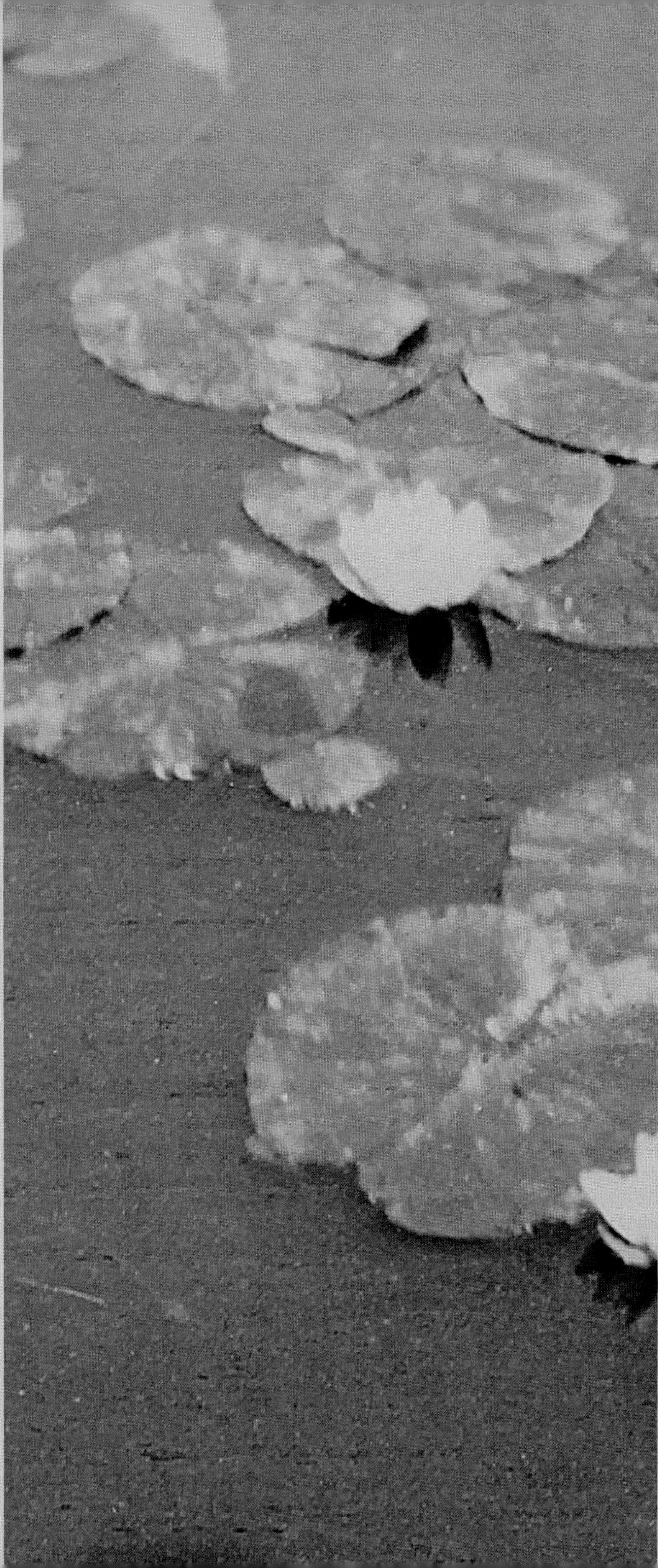

Gabrielle van Zuylen

The Eye of a Gardener... Claude Monet

Giverny is a painter's garden, created by the father of Impressionism, whose dedication was such that he often said that nothing in the world interested him but his painting and his flowers. All the themes that were to obsess Monet until his death at Giverny in 1926 were present in the garden: flowers massed in groups of solid colours, water to reflect the changing sky, and the water lilies which inspired his late great series of paintings, *The Grand Decorations* (fig. 7 p. 27).

But Giverny is also a *gardener*'s garden. Monet was both a great painter and exceptional gardener. Toward the end of his life, he recounted that he had learned gardening as a *métier* in his youth, to console himself when unhappy, and added that the love of flowers might even be the reason why he had become a painter.

As a painter-gardener, Monet was influenced by the styles and tendencies of his period, and above all by a capacity for observation cultivated in the course of his long life. The nineteenth century was a period of change, an era of stylistic diversity in the art of the garden. The English had been first to return to a simpler planting of flowers inspired by their rural cottage gardens as an ecological protest to the materialism of the Industrial Revolution. This tendency was carried further by Ruskin's Arts and Crafts movement in the 1870s and was spearheaded by William Robinson's proposal to restore the native flora of fields and woods to the garden. The widely read French writer and botanist Édouard André spread this doctrine, which both influenced and corresponded to Monet's own tastes as a landscape painter who had always preferred the country to city life.

During his self-imposed exile in England during the war of 1870, Monet had spent much time observing gardens closely, and actually painted some of the landscaped public parks, which later inspired Baron Haussmann's transformation of Paris. The planting and landscaping of the new parks and garden squares of Paris was the work of Jean-Charles Adolphe Alphand, though in a more distinctly French style, with a lavish layout of plants and flowers, both native and exotic. Monet knew Paris well, and had lived near to the Parc Monceau, which he had often painted. The gardens he designed before moving to Giverny were influenced by all he had seen (fig. 1).

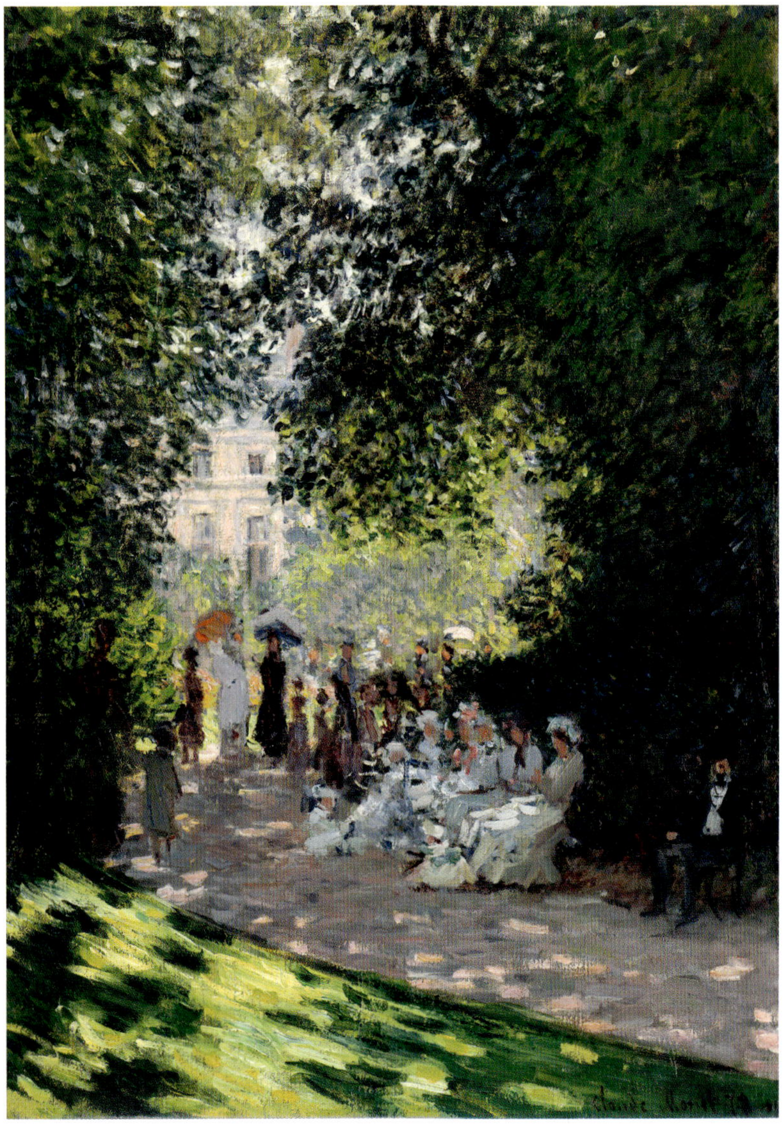

page 38:
Self-Portrait on the Surface of the Water Lily Pond, Giverny (detail), see cat. no. 34

1 | *The Parc Monceau*, 1878
Oil on canvas, 72.7 × 54.3 cm (28⁵/₈ × 21³/₈ in.)
The Metropolitan Museum of Art, New York
The Walter H. and Leonore Annenberg Collection (59.142)

In 1872, after his return to France, marked by his fortunate London encounter with the art dealer Paul Durand-Ruel, Monet was able to afford a move from Paris to a house on the Seine at Argenteuil with a large space to plant a garden. Although close to the city, it was still a rural village.

The first garden at the house he rented at Argenteuil (fig. 2), backed by the river, showed a certain affiliation to the new park and garden transformation of Haussmannian Paris under Napoléon III, with its formal beds of raised bedded plants, bordered by Monet's blue and white Dutch pots. There were the typical paths and geometrical borders, but always backed with more natural tall and colourful plants: a profusion of wild plants loosely mixed with gladioli, spreading nasturtiums and other favourites. Monet's first garden became a source of great pleasure, relaxation, comfort and inspiration; the subject for many paintings—even the flowers cut from their beds were used for commissioned still-lifes (cat. nos. 1 and 2).

It was also here that he began his long and close friendship with Gustave Caillebotte, a fellow Impressionist and gardener. His good and generous friend, the affluent painter Caillebotte aided Monet not only financially but also inspired him by his own garden on the other side of the Seine and as a giver of gardening advice. This was a vibrant and generous friendship, as would become those with Georges Clemenceau, Octave Mirbeau and Gustave Geffroy, with whom there would be exchanges of plants, visits and much "garden correspondence."

Monet's discovery of a place to live in the quiet valley of the Epte marked a turning point in his life, at a time when he was beset by financial worries and critical failure, and was grieving the death of his first wife. The small village of Giverny is spread out along the low hills facing the valley of the Seine, where two streams, the tiny Ru and the Epte, divide the Île-de-France from the province of Normandy.
Monet became increasingly attached to "this beautiful land"[1], and it was a perfect home for a painter fascinated by light and water: "The subject is of secondary importance to me: what I want to reproduce is what exists between the subject and me."[2] The ever-changing soft light of the river valley was the real subject, and Giverny was the place in which to capture it.

In the summer of 1884, during the first years at Giverny, Monet had much to do in the house and to begin the garden with small means and had little help apart from his large extended family. He also began to explore the region; as he explained to Paul Durand-Ruel, "It always takes time to familiarise oneself with a landscape."[3] He wrote not only as the painter who created the series *The Haystacks* and *The Poplars* (cat. no. 7) but with the eye of a gardener who understands the importance of the bordering climate, terrain and views to link the borrowed landscape to where he lives.

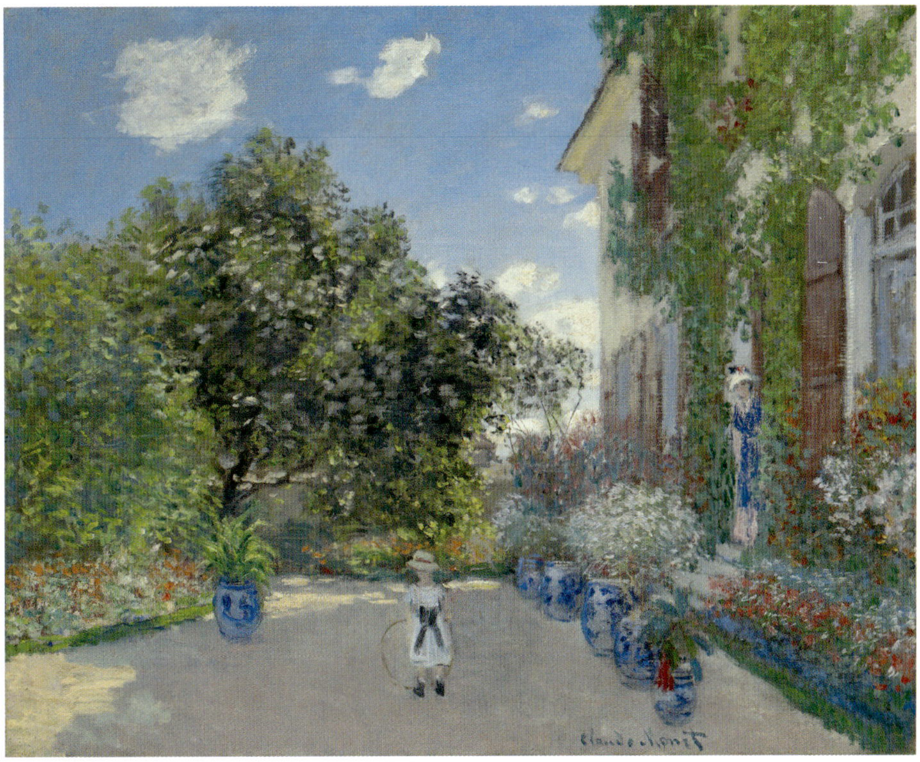

2 | *The Artist's House at Argenteuil*, 1873
Oil on canvas, 60.2 × 73.3 cm
(23¹¹/₁₆ × 28⅞ in.)
The Art Institute of Chicago
Collection of Mr. and Mrs. Martin A. Ryerson
(1933.1153)

Monet was fifty years old in 1890 when he managed to borrow enough money—almost ruining Durand-Ruel his dealer in the process—to buy Le Pressoir, the house he had already lived in for seven years. The long rough pink house with an exotic air had belonged to a merchant from Guadeloupe. The property covered two and a half acres sloping down to the Chemin du Roy, the road at the end of the village. A small local railway ran along the edge of the road at the foot of the walled orchard. The garden as it existed was heavily planted with dark yews and overgrown box trees, and was depressingly bourgeois. Monet, who hated all formality, at once removed the box, and only allowed the two yews in front of the house to remain as a concession to his second wife, Alice. The plan of the garden remained geometrical, with a broad central avenue leading straight from the house to the front gate set in the bottom wall. Nasturtiums spilled on to the gravel paths. Several smaller parallel paths lined either side of the garden—with rectangular beds to the left to the house below the barn, and a series of square beds to the right of the central avenue. But the straight lines were soon to disappear under Monet's lavish planting.

In 1886 an invitation to see the bulb fields close to The Hague had enthralled him (cat. no. 5). The enormous fields in full bloom made a mosaic of strong, luminous colours, the inspiration for future blocks of massed flowers.

The year after buying Le Pressoir, Monet wrote to the poet Stéphane Mallarmé, "I have much to do, a quantity of new painting to finish. And moreover, I must confess, I leave Giverny with difficulty, above all now that I'm fixing up the house and the garden to my taste."[4] Monet was busy erecting a light metal framework over the wooden balcony in front of the house and raising metal archways over the central avenue. He had all the metal-work throughout the garden painted a bright leaf green, the same Impressionist colour he used for the doors and shutters on the outside of the house, to harmonise with the greens of the garden.

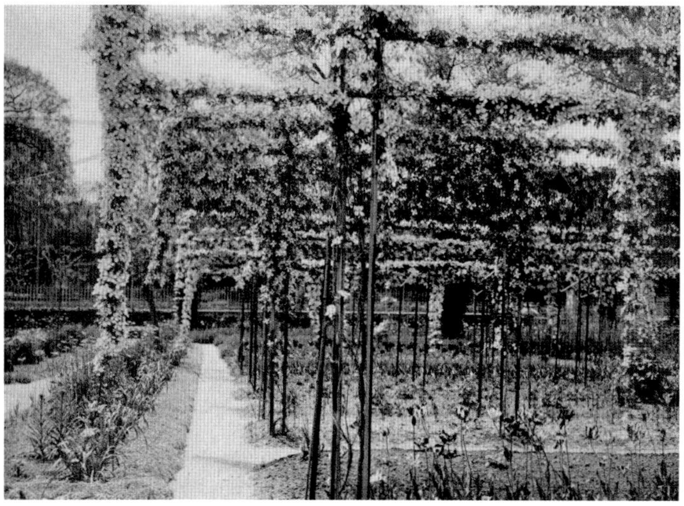

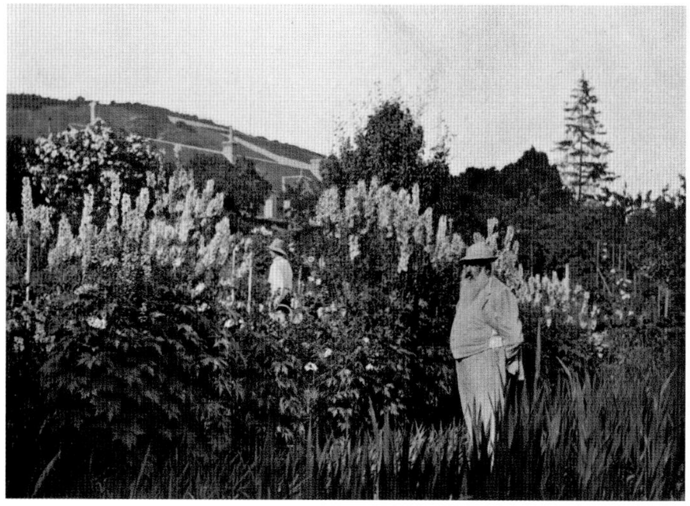

3 | Gouthière, "A charming use of the white-flowered Clematis and its pink-flowered variety, on high trellises, in the Giverny gardens," excerpt from Georges Truffaut, "Le jardin de Claude Monet," *Jardinage*, no. 87, November 1924, p. 58, Truffaut, Évry

4 | "At Giverny, Mr. Claude Monet in his garden near clumps of larkspur," excerpt from Jean-Claude-Nicolas Forestier, "Le jardin de M. Claude Monet," *Fermes et Châteaux*, no. 39, 1 September 1908, p. 13
Musée des Impressionnismes, Giverny

Monet worked alone in the garden, except when helped by his children. His days were long, starting at five o'clock every morning, when he walked through the garden, obsessively inspecting and dead-heading the plants in the early light before taking his canvases and paints over to the left bank of the Epte, where he was painting a series of studies of light on the poplar trees. By 1892 improved finances and a further loan from Durand-Ruel enabled him to hire a head gardener, Félix Breuil, who was recommended to him by his friend Octave Mirbeau, the writer and art critic. Soon Breuil was joined by five assistants (cat nos. 73 and 88). Three greenhouses were built below the barn used by Monet as his studio, and were a source of great delight to him, for he continued to collect plants throughout his life; but they were also a cause of anxiety, as when both he and his wife spent a cold winter's night assuring themselves that the new heating system was working properly. The old orchard was abandoned, and instead Monet planted Japanese flowering cherries and apple trees on the lawn near a path bordered with his favourite bearded iris and oriental poppies. Clematis were grown on high metal supports (fig. 3), and roses covered the central arches over the nasturtium bordered central avenue. Monochromatic groups of strong-coloured flowers were planted throughout the garden, alternating with beds of paler flowers. Details were unimportant—massed colour and texture dominated the garden. Every season brought new colour and new compositions: golden daffodils were followed by bright red tulips underplanted with forget-me-nots; lilacs, wisteria and irises brought mauve and purple into the garden. In June the lilies, delphiniums, peonies, lupins and Canterbury bells came into flower and massed asters, glowing dahlias, sunflowers and graceful Japanese anemones filled the garden from September until the first frosts. Roses flowered everywhere: dazzling swatches of colour hung over the central walk, standard bushes dominated the beds and climbers wreathed special metal supports, throwing colour into the air. Monet's only prejudice was against plants with variegated leaves—colours must remain solid and true.

Marcel Proust much later described his impression of the Clos Normand (cat. no. 4) garden, now almost as well known as the artist, in 1907 in the *Figaro* newspaper, having only seen Monet's paintings.

"I feel sure that I shall see something that is not so much a garden of flowers as of colors and tones, less of an old-fashioned flower garden than a color garden, so to speak, one that achieves an effect not entirely nature's, because it was planted so that only the flowers with matching colors will bloom at the same time, harmonise in an infinite stretch of blue or pink [...] The garden itself is a real transposition of art, rather than a model for a painting, for its composition is right there in nature itself and comes to life through the eyes of a great painter."[5]

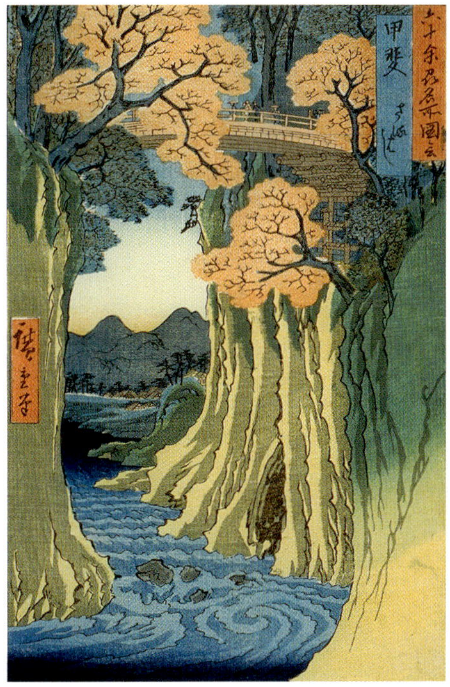

5 | Utagawa Hiroshige,
The Monkey Bridge in Kai Province
Wood engraving, 32.8 × 22 cm
($12\frac{15}{16} \times 8\frac{5}{8}$ in.)
Fondation Claude Monet, Giverny

On Tuesday, 1 February 1883 Monet went to Paris to see an exhibition of Japanese prints at the Durand-Ruel gallery. He had already been collecting them over ten years (fig. 5), having discovered his first prints wrapped around objects he bought in Amsterdam during a trip to Holland, and had long been influential in spreading the Japanese influence among his contemporaries. By chance he met his friend Camille Pissarro at the Durand-Ruel exhibition, but while Pissarro was carried away by the economy and strength of line in the exhibits, Monet was fascinated by the images of exotic plants, still water, and Japanese bridges. Coincidentally, four days later he signed the final papers giving him ownership to the strip of land on the other side of the railway, bought to make a second garden, the water garden.

Time was lost getting permission to make changes in the terrain. Whilst at Rouen painting the *Cathedral* series, Monet was forced to write to the Prefect of the Eure to ask permission to renew the water in the pools to be dug. "In view of the cultivation of aquatic plants, I would like to install a *prise d'eau* in the Epte. [...] I plan to build two small bridges in light wood over the stream."[6]
In mid-July he sent a second letter to the Prefect, justifying his project in some detail: "I want you to know that the aforementioned 'culture of water plants' is less ambitious than the phrase implies, as it concerns only an object of amusement to please the eye, and also to provide inspiration for my painting; in fact I will grow only plants such as water lilies, reeds and various irises in the pool, plants that grow naturally along our river, and there is no question of polluting the water."[7]

Monet was still in Rouen when his stalemate with the local authorities ended, and permission was given to begin work (figs. 2 and 3 p. 50). Overjoyed, he rushed to see the director of the Jardin des Plantes at Rouen, Émile Varenne, and was offered coveted plants from the municipal greenhouses and precious advice on how to establish them at Giverny. He also made time to visit all the local nurseries and sent home baskets of plants.

The latter part of the year was occupied in preparing the new garden and building the two bridges. The larger curved Japanese bridge, over the pool, inspired by his collecting of prints first appeared in a painting finished in the winter of 1895, before Monet left for a two-month trip to Norway. Worried by the news of a cold spell seizing the countryside around Giverny, Monet wrote a concerned and touching letter home: "I imagine the skater's joy, but I tremble for the garden. Are you sure the pool is free of ice? It would bee too sad if all the plants perished."[8] A second letter to his wife followed: "I am appalled by the news about my poor roses, and await more disasters. Have you though about covering the Japanese peonies, at the very least it would amount to murder if you have not already done so."[9] Every gardener will

6 | "When the large-flowered tree peonies come into flower, Master Claude Monet shows off his garden to Mr. Georges Truffaut," excerpt from Georges Truffaut, "Le jardin de Claude Monet," *Jardinage*, no. 87, November 1924, p. 56
Truffaut, Évry

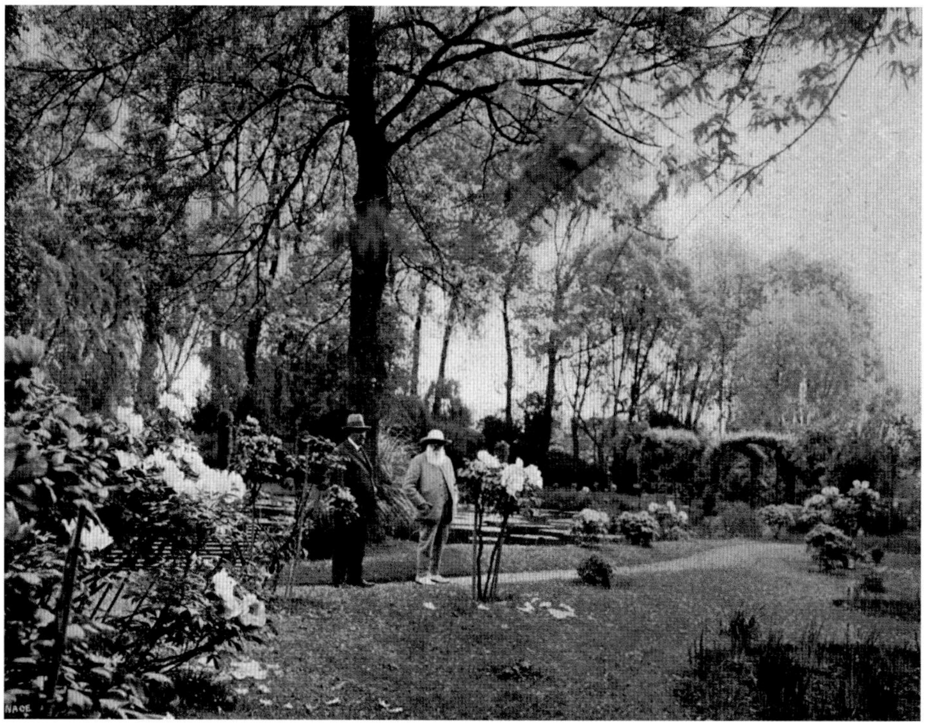

recognise Monet's anguish. The Japanese peonies were special treasures, some a present from Japanese friends, others ordered directly from Japan to grow around the pool in the new water garden. From this period on, Monet sold paintings primarily in order to pay the increasing cost of the garden and allow himself the luxury of buying new plants. Monet's close friend Geffroy described the new garden in his book *Claude Monet : sa vie, son temps, son œuvre*, published in Paris in 1922: "Monet designed the garden and laid out the plants, the willows unfurling their green tresses, the bamboo springing forth, the massed rhododendrons bordering the paths; and he sowed the pond with water lilies, whose free roots float in the waters, spread with large pads bursting forth with white, rose, mauve and green flowers. Monet comes to stand on the wisteria-covered Japanese bridge and judge the painting he created."[10]

The originality of the water garden was that it was laid out like a painting; the sky seems present only in water, the changing reflections deepening the colours or lightening the surface of Monet's mirror. Two years later, Georges Truffaut described the completed garden in an article written for the review *Jardinage* (fig. 6):
"a vast pond fed by clear, rapid-flowing water [...] He planted a framework of Babylon willows with golden boughts lightly skimming the waters.
On one shore, forming a backdrop, there is a cluster of briary plants among which ferns, kalmia, rhododendrons, and holly predominate. Shade along the water's edge is provided by hardy rose trees or roses climbing along existing trees [...] Every known variety of water lily was planted in the pond [...] There are abundant irises of all varieties along the edges of the pond. In the spring there are *Iris siberica* and *virginica* with their long, velvety petals; later, Japanese iris (*Iris kaempferi*) abound and impart an oriental touch, which is further enhanced by such plants as Japanese tree peonies [...] At some places on the water's edge, the bamboo wood is hidden by

plants with enormous leaves, *Petasites*, and at one celebrated spot, for it has often been painted by the master, a Japanese bridge, marvelously decorated with mauve wisteria at the top and white wisteria with long clusters at the bottom, spans the pretty river [...] At the water's edge, there are beds of meadow rue with leaves as lacy as those of some ferns, with pink and white fluffy flowers; multi-stemmed wisterias; inulas; and numerous types of avens, some of which form borders of a charming slate pink. There are also vanhouttei spiraea, with white flowers mingling with tamarisks [...] Roses predominate; roses in all shapes and sizes; varieties of cluster roses (even stemmed ones), bush roses, standard roses. But hardly any long-stemmed roses that have been grafted onto eglantines are to be found in Claude Monet's garden."[11]

Paul Cézanne passed through Giverny in November 1894, before the water garden showed its full promise. He visited the front garden, the Clos Normand, and saw Monet's latest paintings. A man of few words, he observed, "Monet is but an eye... but, good God, what an eye!" Clemenceau, had early become aware of an evolution and change in Monet's painting of Nature. He later wrote in 1895: "When I saw Monet, with his four canvases in the field of poppies, change his palette as the sun continued on it's course, I sensed a study more precise of the light than of the subject ; the mobility of luminosity. This affirmed an evolution, a new way to see, to feel, to express: a revolution."[12]

The interaction between Monet's painting and his garden, his two obsessions, gradually increased with in time to become the conscious center of his art and work space and fill his canvasses. Now the two gardens, the Clos Normand and the water garden with added lily pond, had expanded over time and thanks to the increasing financial freedom to hire gardeners to work with him and buy more and more plants, shrubs and trees in the endless development, expansion and transformations of his land. A microcosm of nature. He no longer depended on the seasons and the weather to be able to paint. All the subjects and motifs, he held in his memory, were now close at hand as well as his beloved family at Giverny. He had created a great and beautiful garden using his eye and perfect knowledge of the art of garden design—"a paradise", declared his wife, Alice. He alternated between work *en plein air*, his studios, greenhouses and the comfort of home. Monet increasingly used the pool as an extension to his failing eyesight. He continued to paint details in the water garden—a group of day-lilies, irises, the branches of the weeping willows touching the water—but his dominant obsession remained the juxtaposition of the sky reflected in water and the water lilies.

Monet started the *Water Landscapes* in the water garden where were concentrated all that he had loved: the sky and water, flowers and leaves. They were the continuation of the first studies of reflected landscapes in the 1850s and the paintings of gardens in the 1860s. He explained that he could accept his growing loss of sight, even blindness sustained by the memory of the beauty of nature.

On 11 August 1908 he wrote to Geffroy: "These landscapes of water and reflected light have become an obsession. It's beyond my old man's strength; nevertheless I want to express what I feel."[13]

Monet's life became progressively sadder and more difficult. His wife died in May 1911. The death of her husband, Monet's son Jean, in 1914 was a shattering blow, as was the horror of the Great War but his dear daughter-in-law Blanche remained with him. Worse still, Monet began to suffer increasingly from cataracts. It became harder for him to work outside in the garden, so instead, urged on by his great friend Clemenceau, he built a large new studio to the right of the house and began painting the giant canvases, donated to France in April 1922 as *The Grand Decorations*. These vast, almost abstract masterpieces were painted from memory rather than observation. Proust paid homage to Monet's great talent: "Flowers of the earth, also flowers of the water, these tender water lilies which the master has painted so sublimely."[14] Clemenceau called the water garden his friend's studio, but by now the painter's eye had no use for the reflecting mirror across the Chemin du Roy.

Claude Monet died early in December 1926. Clemenceau was with him to pay a final farewell to his friend. Finding Monet's coffin draped with the traditional black pall, he tore away the offensive cloth and seized a bright multi-coloured shawl to cover the coffin, saying "Pas de noir pour Monet."

Blanche Hoschedé-Monet stayed on at Giverny after Monet's death, keeping the house and the garden as they had been during the painter's life. Monet's heir, his second son Michel, had always had a difficult relationship with his father, which in part explains why he never lived in the house and did nothing to keep it up or save the garden when his sister-in-law died after the war. But, by willing the property to the Académie des Beaux-Arts, he unknowingly brought about the rebirth of Giverny. Gerald van der Kemp's acceptance of the curatorship was the key element in this miracle. By this time Curator of Versailles, van der Kemp hesitated before agreeing to his colleague's request, for Michel Monet left no financial provision for restoration or upkeep. But his admiration for Monet, coupled perhaps with the fact that he too was a painter and a gardener, persuaded him to undertake the task. Thanks to his energy and dedication and to the help of his American wife, Florence, the long sad years of neglect ended. Gilbert Vahé, a brilliant student at the École Nationale d'Horticulture, became head gardener, and valuable help was given by all those who had known the garden in Monet's lifetime. All the available documents, including bills for plants and photographs of the garden, were used to restore the work of Monet, and the Académie des Beaux-Arts opened Giverny to the public. But Giverny was never really a "private" garden: Monet opened it to the world with the first paintings he made in his beloved garden, filling it with splendid colour, just as colour invaded and overflowed on to his canvases.

Gardens and man are subject to the fourth dimension of Time: growth, change and decay. Monet's art created his garden and preserved it in his paintings for all mankind. His last years, beset by the anguish of the increasing loss of sight, and the fear of total blindness and death, brought a revolution to the world of art. He reversed the laws of the universe, a new way of seeing the world, the infinitely small and the infinitely large, the boundless depth and space of the earth reflected in a pond with only his brush and remembered light and colour. The sublime

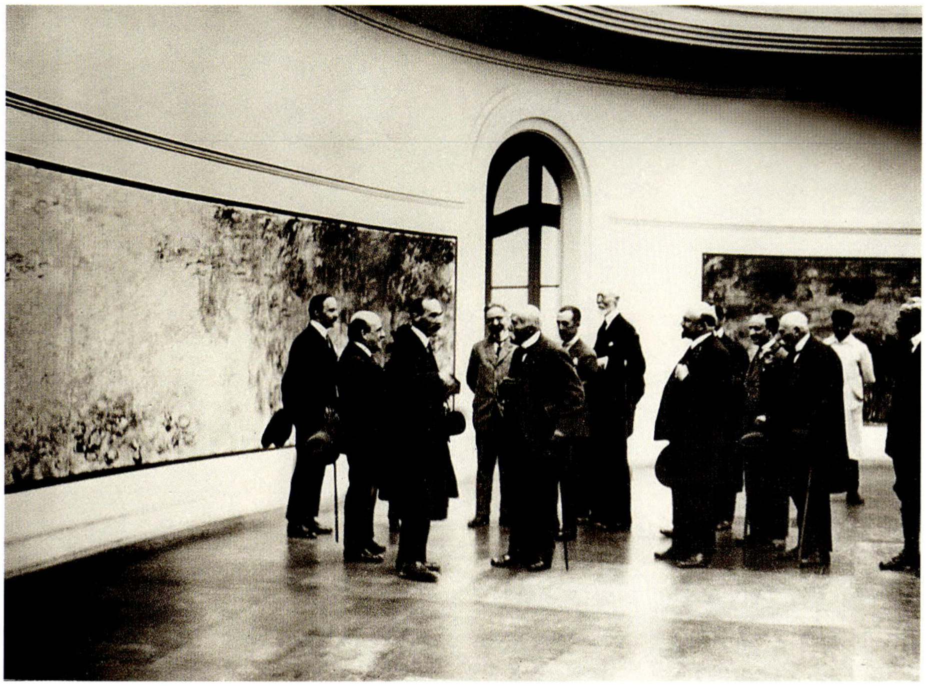

7 | *Clemenceau inaugurating the Water Lilies room at the Orangerie in the company of Paul Léon and Mr. Verne, Monday 16th May, 1927*
Musée Clemenceau, Paris

painting of the *Grand Decorations* at the Orangerie des Tuileries in Paris were taken from his studio, where he had refused to part with them, and inaugurated on 17th May, 1927, the year after his death (fig. 7).

The excerpts from letters by Claude Monet cited throughout this essay are from Daniel Wildenstein, *Claude Monet, Biographie et catalogue raisonné*, Lausanne and Paris: Bibliothèque des Arts, 1974-91, 5 vol.

1 Monet to Paul Durand-Ruel, 27 October 1890 (W1079).

2 Monet quoted in *Dagbladet*, 4 April 1895, reprinted in Daniel Wildenstein, *Claude Monet, Biographie et catalogue raisonné*, vol. 3, Lausanne and Paris: Bibliothèque des Arts, 1974-91, p. 65.

3 Monet to Paul Durand-Ruel, 3 July 1883 (W 362).

4 Monet to Stéphane Mallarmé, 28 July 1891 (W1121).

5 Marcel Proust, "Les *Éblouissements* par la Comtesse de Noailles," *Le Figaro*, 15 June 1907, translated in English in Charles F. Stuckey, "Splendors," *Monet. A Retrospective*, New York: Hugh Lauter Levin Associates, 1985, p. 250.

6 Monet to the Prefect of Eure, 17 March 1893 (W1191), Évreux: Archives Départementales de l'Eure (18 S 25).

7 Monet to the Prefect of Eure, 17 July 1893 (W1219), Évreux: Archives Départementales de l'Eure (18 S 25).

8 Monet to Alice Monet, Christiania, 13 February 1895 (W1268).

9 Monet to Alice Monet, Sandvika, 17 March 1895 (W 1284).

10 Gustave Geffroy, *Claude Monet : sa vie, son temps, son œuvre*, Paris: G. Grès, [1922] 1924, pp. 328-29.

11 Georges Truffaut, "Le Jardin de Claude Monet," *Jardinage*, no. 87, 14 November 1924, pp. 55-56, reprinted and translated in English in Stuckey, *op. cit.*, pp. 314-16.

12 Georges Clemenceau, "Révolution de Cathédrales," *La Justice*, 20 May 1895, p. 1, quoted in Michel Winock, *Clemenceau*, Paris: Éditions Perrin, 2007, p. 531.

13 Monet to Geffroy, 11 August 1908 (W1854), in Geffroy, *op. cit.*, p. 238.

14 Proust, *op. cit.*, p. 250.

Vanessa Lecomte

Chronology: Monet's Garden in Giverny (1883-1927)

The excerpts from letters cited throughout this chronology are from the following sources:
Daniel Wildenstein, *Claude Monet, biographie et catalogue raisonné*, 5 vols. Lausanne and Paris: Bibliothèque des Arts, 1974–91 (Claude Monet's letters)
Octave Mirbeau, *Correspondance avec Claude Monet*. Tusson: Du Lérot Éditeur, 1990
Jacqueline and Maurice Guillaud (eds.), *Claude Monet au temps de Giverny*, exhib. cat., Paris, Centre Culturel du Marais, 1983 (letters from Alice Hoschedé to Germaine Hoschedé-Salerou, Philippe Piguet Collection)
Archives Départementales de l'Eure, Évreux (letters from Claude Monet and Octave Mirbeau to the Prefect of the Eure)
Documentation du Musée d'Orsay, Paris (unpublished letters from Claude Monet to Gustave Caillebotte).
Special thanks to Philippe Piguet, Véronique and Philippe Perdrix, and Robert Sheldon, whose contributions have been crucial to the writing of this chronology.

1883
29 April: Claude Monet settles with Alice Hoschedé in a property in Giverny. From Louis Joseph Singeot he rents the property situated in the part of the village known as Le Pressoir, bounded by the Rue du Haut or du Village and the Chemin du Roy, leading from Gisors to Vernon. In front of the house is a vegetable garden and an orchard, the so-called Clos Normand, accurately described by Jean-Pierre Hoschedé in *Claude Monet ce mal connu: intimité familiale d'un demi-siècle à Giverny de 1883 à 1926* (Geneva: Pierre Cailler, 1960):
"[...] a large orchard with, in front of the house, just some flowerbeds and two long borders on each side of the central path, the entrance to which is on the Chemin du Roy. [...] They were planted down the centre with spruce and cypress, and lined with pruned box, as well as the flowerbeds. None of this was to Monet's liking, save for the two beautiful yews, in front of the house, which were kept at the end of the walk... The box borders were removed swiftly. As for the spruce and cypress, Monet did not like them, because they did not go with his flower plantings. He considered cutting them down, but my mother, who loved all cypress, was against the idea. There was something epic about it. On the one hand, Monet knowing very well what he wanted to do, and, on the other, my mother refusing any tree felling. [...] The duel was a long one, but mutual concessions were made. Firstly, it was decided to pull out the cypress trees. They were replaced by metal arbours straddling the path, which were in no time covered with climbing roses. They are still there, despite their age. Then it was agreed to prune the spruce, and their lower branches were removed. [...] the spruce were cut half way up, which left just a part of their trunks... Roses quickly grew up them, but one after the other the trunks rotted at the base, so they were removed. All that remained was the arbour...
After the house's immediate surroundings, it was the orchard's turn. The west side became an English-style lawn. [...] On that large lawn, here and there, Monet had groups of irises and oriental poppies planted. The dead fruit trees, and those pulled up, were replaced, in lesser numbers, by flowering trees—Japanese cherry and apple trees. The east side was planted with successive "patches", each one with plants of different species: gladioli, larkspur, phlox asters, large daisies, etc. ... Over them all, light structures were installed, so that *Montana rubens* clematis could grow on them. Almost all the garden's flowerbeds were surrounded with large borders filled with every variety of iris, which Monet was especially fond of. [...] [The garden] had no massive, inelegant beds, [it was] planted with canna lilies, surrounded by extra-double French marigolds, ageratum and bear's ear, and scattered with stiff zinnias, with lovely hues, indeed, but their stiffness suggested they were made of zinc.[...] A railing running the whole length replaced stones. Nasturtiums... climbed over it."
5 June: Monet to Paul Durand-Ruel:
"...then I had gardening to do, which took up some of my time, picking a few flowers to paint when the weather turned bad."
Monet also mentions the installation of a shed on the Île aux Orties, to house his boats and canvases **(p. 134)**.
September–December: Monet works "like a man possessed" on the panels for Durand-Ruel's large reception room in his apartment at 35 Rue de Rome **(cat. nos. 1 and 2 and fig. 1)**.
Second half of December: Monet travels with Auguste Renoir on the Riviera. They call on Paul Cézanne at L'Estaque.

1884
17 January: Monet goes alone to Bordighera where he paints the famous garden of the collector Francesco Moreno **(cat. nos. 3-4)**.
September–November: Monet produces the first depictions of the Haystacks.
17 November: with Paul Durand-Ruel as go-between, Octave Mirbeau meets Monet for an article which he publishes on **21 November** in *La France*.

1885
Ferdinand Deconchy introduces the American painter Theodore Robinson to Monet.

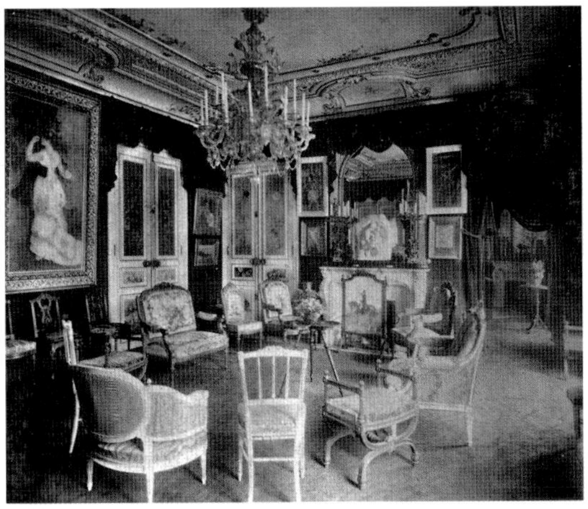

1 | *View of Paul Durand-Ruel's Living Room, Rue de Rome*, n. d.
Archives Durand-Ruel, Paris

March: Monet works on the panels commissioned by Durand-Ruel, and delivers several of them to Paris on **2 April**.
15 May: inauguration of the 4th International Exhibition at the Galerie Georges Petit, in Paris.
27 May: Monet to Paul Durand-Ruel:
"So I decided to tend to the garden and prepare some beautiful flower motifs for the summer."
[Linda Schädler, "Biography", in Christoph Becker, *Monet's Garden*. Zurich: Kunsthaus, 2004, p. 175.]
During the summer: visit from Renoir.
August: visit from Berthe Morisot.
Late summer: visit from John Singer Sargent, who depicts Monet painting one of his early *Haystacks* [*Claude Monet Painting at the Edge of a Wood*], London, Tate Gallery.
24 November: Monet writes to Alice, from Étretat:
"And the garden, are there still flowers? I'd love it if there were still chrysanthemums when I get back."
December: Enlargement of the studio at the west end of the house.

1886
Mid-January: The construction of the studio is completed.
15 June: inauguration of the 5th International Exhibition at the Galerie Georges Petit.
2 October: at Belle-Île, Monet meets Gustave Geffroy, the art critic for *La Justice*.
14 October: Monet writes to Alice, from Kervilahouen:
"For the dahlias, I really don't think it's time to bring them in yet, but they could perhaps be labelled, because if there's a frost, it's impossible to know which colour they are; lastly, I'm counting on you to do all the things I unfortunately haven't been able to tend to; I'd also like someone to collect a few sunflower seeds for me. [...]. The damage to the garden you describe doesn't surprise me."
10 November: Monet to Alice:
"So tell me if the chrysanthemums I sowed are flowering; if so, and there are some pretty ones, please mark them with a bit of wool."

1887
22 April: visit from Théodore van Gogh.
8 May: Monet takes part in the 6th International Exhibition at the Galerie Georges Petit.
June: visit from Sargent and Auguste Rodin.
24 June: visit from Robinson, with whom Monet strikes up a friendship; the two would carry on an active correspondance.
June–July: Monet works on a series of girls in a boat on the Epte River **(cat. no. 6)**, outdoor figures "made like landscapes" and a series devoted to the garden **(cat. no. 9)**.

1888
3 April: Monet to Alice, from Antibes:
"I forgot to tell you that for the chrysanthemums it would be a good idea to replant them in the vegetable garden, spaced well apart, so that they can grow, and on my return we'll plant them out; if a few hollyhocks have survived, look after them."
23 June: the article written by the painter Georges Jeanniot relying on the interview he conducted in Giverny appears in *La Cravache parisienne*: "Monet works only on the effect he has chosen (even if it lasts no more than ten minutes) and always works from life. [...] He never retouches anything in the studio."
[Daniel Wildenstein, "Monet's Giverny", in *Monet's Years at Giverny: Beyond Impressionism*. New York: The Metropolitan Museum of Art / Harry N. Abrams, [1978] 1995, pp. 20–21.]

1889
20 June–29 October: Lilla Cabot Perry with her family at the Hôtel Baudy. From 1890 to 1898, the Perrys spend summers in several rented houses, including Le Hameau, adjacent to Monet's property **(figs. 7 and 8)**.
21 June–21 September: "Monet-Rodin" exhibition at the Galerie Georges Petit.
Mid-July: visit from the American collector James Sutton.

1890
[Ca. 1890]: Mirbeau writes to Geffroy that on his latest visit "Monet was gardening furiously".
Mid-May: Mirbeau to Monet:
"I've found a wonderful orchid in the forest, which compares with all the beautiful exotic specimens. I'll try to make a collection for you. There are twenty-two species. If you can send me a few more dahlias, yes, I would like that. And next year I'll make you a collection of chrysanthenums I have, which are all wonderful, with mad shapes, and beautiful colours, absolutely choice. I found them at a brilliant gardener's in Le Vaudreuil [François Marc], whom I've mentioned to you."
22 June: Monet to Geffroy:
"I have taken up things impossible to do: water with plants moving at the bottom. [...] It's wonderful to look at, but the desire to render it is maddening. After all, I always attack things like this."
[Charles F. Stuckey (ed.), *Claude Monet 1840–1926*, exhib. cat. Chicago: The Art Institute of Chicago, 1995, p. 219.]
On **13 July**, visit from Berthe Morisot, Eugène Manet and Stéphane Mallarmé.
Mid-July: Mirbeau to Monet:
"I will prove to you as clear as day that I am as far from you intellectually as my garden is from yours—from a floral point of view".
27 July: visit from Geffroy and Georges Clemenceau. Monet is at work on the series of *Poppy Fields*.
Ca. 27 September: Mirbeau to Monet:
"I'm very glad that you're bringing Caillebotte [30 September]. We'll talk gardening, as you say, because as for art and literature, it's all humbug. There's nothing but the earth. As for me, I've reached the point of finding a lump of soil marvelous, and I spend whole hours contemplating it. And humus! I love humus the way one loves a woman."
[Robert Gordon and Andrew Forge, *Monet*. New York: Harry N. Abrams, 1983, p. 221.]
27 October: Monet writes to Paul Durand-Ruel asking for financial assistance to purchase the house which he has been renting for seven years:
"[...] I shall have no option but to ask you for quite a lot of money, being on the verge of purchasing the house I'm living in, or else leaving Giverny, which would

2 | *Receipt of authorization to take water from the arm of the Epte known as the "communal arm", signed by Claude Monet,*
24 July 1893
Archives Départementales de l'Eure, Évreux (18 S 25)

3 | *Receipt of authorization to build two footbridges signed by Claude Monet,*
24 July 1893
Archives Départementales de l'Eure, Évreux (18 S 25)

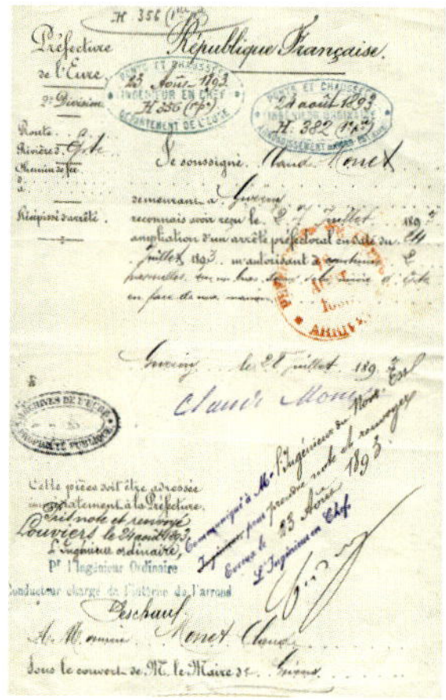

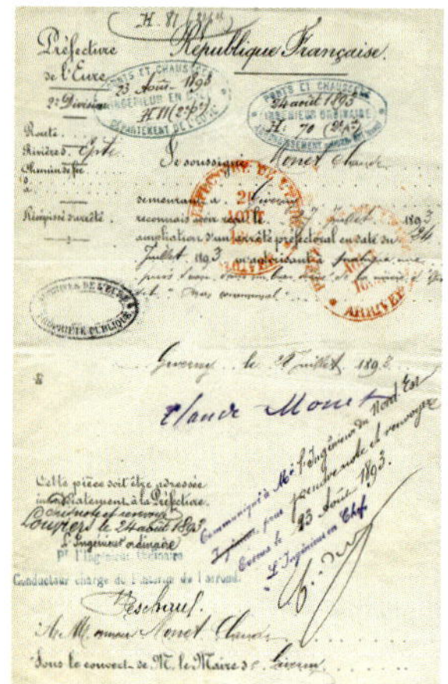

greatly upset me, because I'm sure I would never find anywhere similar in such a beautiful spot."

19 November: Monet signs the purchase agreement for his property at Le Pressoir in the office of Me Grimpard, notary at Vernon: "...house consisting of four ground floor rooms, four bedrooms on the first floor, two attic rooms and a loft above, and a cellar below; painter's studio in the wing at one end of the house; large woodshed, small shed and toilets forming the other wing; another house consisting of a kitchen and two other ground floor rooms, then stables, two bedrooms and toilet room above, attic beneath the roof, cellar over which is an attic not included in the sale; the whole built on a plot with courtyard, garden and shed, entirely walled, containing in all eighty six ares and twelve centiares approximately, and delimited by, in front, the Gisors to Vernon road, and behind the Rue du Haut or du Village... for the sum of 22,000 francs."

1891

[Ca. 1891]: Monet writes to Gustave Caillebotte:
"Here is the name of the Japanese plant that I get from Belgium: *Crythrochaete*. Try to speak of it to M. Godefroy and give me some information on how to grow it."
[Robert Gordon and Andrew Forge, *Monet*. New York: Harry N. Abrams, 1983, p. 221.]

7 March: Mirbeau publishes an article on Monet in *L'Art dans les deux Mondes*, the fleeting magazine founded by Durand-Ruel and Yveling Rambaud. It describes the garden's three seasons with abundant flowers:
"It is springtime.
The wallflowers are exhaling the last of their flagrance; the peonies—the divine peonies—are fading; the hyacinths are dead. The nasturtiums are already showing their young bronze greenery, the eschscholtzias, their long, tapered leaves of a delightful acid green; in the wide beds that they border, against a background of flowering orchards, the irises raise their strange, curling petals, frilled with white, mauve, lilac, yellow, and blue, streaked with brown stripes and crimson-purple markings. Their elaborate depths evoke mysterious analogies, dreams of temptation and perversity, like those that emanate from the disturbing orchids... From the tops of their supple stalks, the day lilies bow their fragrant calyxes; and the poppies on their villous stems open wide vermilion cups and wind around their horizontal stakes. The great blossoms of the clematis spangle the surrounding greenery, the sky of their immaculate, white corollas touched with a mere breath of azure and pink. And the summer plants, between the brightening borders, everywhere prepare for the joy of coming into bloom."
[Octave Mirbeau "Claude Monet", *L'Art dans les deux Mondes,* March 7, 1891 reprinted and translated by Charles F. Stuckey, *Monet. A Retrospective*. New York: Hugh Lauter Levin Associates, Inc., 1985, pp. 157–58.]

18 March: death of Ernest Hoschedé, in Paris.

3 April: Monet to Caillebotte:
"I would ask you, should you see Mr. Godefroy, to reorder my consignment of lis and include me as a subscriber to his publication, then what would please me is if he would get from England some hardy sunflowers, which I don't have and are not to be found in Paris. Here incidentally are the names of those I do have:
Helianthus Latiflorus
— Multiflorus
— Orgyalis
— Rigidus Hospalinus

11 April: Monet to Caillebotte:
"[...] I shall be as happy as can be when Mr. Godefroy has got me the sunflowers I'm waiting for. I'm expecting large *Helianthus Maximiliani*, do you know it[?] Today I sent you at the Argenteuil station a small hamper containing some *Helianthus Latiflorus*. This is one of the most beautiful, growing to almost 10 feet. It spreads hugely. Three or four plants together make fine clumps."

4–16 May: Monet shows the series of *Haystacks* and the two *Studies of Figures:Women with Parasols at* the Galerie Durand-Ruel.

24 May: Monet to Caillebotte: "I have seen the flower show in Paris, some magnificent things. There I met your friend Godefroy.
We must let him know when we will go to see him with Mirbeau.
Can you tell me where I would be able to find seedlings of annual flowers, I saw some superb ones at the show, but is it too late to plant, especially chrysanthemums—and layias with yellow flowers, maybe you would have a few yourself, anyway try to find out."
[Robert Gordon and Andrew Forge, *Monet*. New York: Harry N. Abrams, 1983, p. 221.]

9 June: Monet tells Paul-César Helleu about the arrival of a Japanese gardener.

28 July: Monet to Mallarmé:
"And I must also admit that I am reluctant to leave Giverny, especially now that I am redesigning the house and the garden as I want them."
[Linda Schädler, "Biography", in Christoph Becker, *Monet's Garden*. Zurich: Kunsthaus, 2004, p. 177.]

2 August: auction by the village of the poplars along the Epte River at Limetz. Monet's attempts to obtain a stay are in vain, so he makes an agreement with a wood merchant for the poplars to be left standing long enough for him to finish his canvases.

8 October: Monet purchases the Île aux Orties.

1892

29 February–10 March: exhibition of the series of *Poplars on the Banks of the Epte* at the Galerie Durand-Ruel.

Ca. 20 April: Mirbeau sends the information requested about Achille Savoir, a gardener whom Monet is thinking of employing:
"Lucien, my gardener knows Achille Savoir well. Here is what he told me:
'He's someone out to impress you. To hear him speak, he'll do everything, take up any combat, and he does not know a whole lot. He is not meticulous, nor conscientious, and he is extremely lazy. What is more, *he drinks*. Through negligence, he loses things he plants out under glass, because he cannot be bothered to shade them. His garden is poorly tended. Very often, he would come and ask my advice, for quite commonplace things. In a word, to be honest, I cannot recommend him, because one

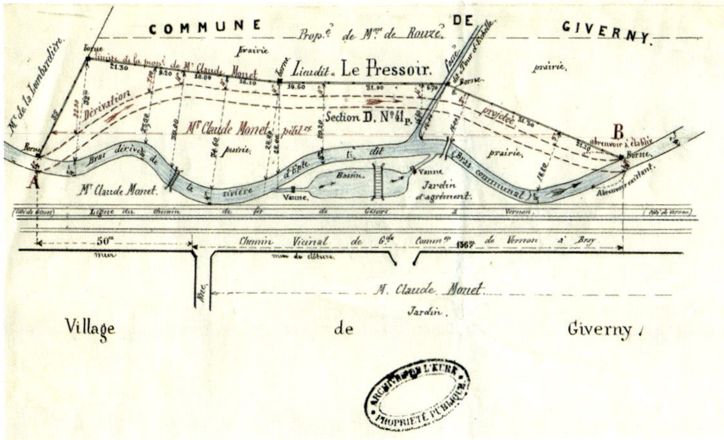

4 | Plan of the first pond project by the engineer of the Ponts et Chaussées [Civil Engineering Department] of the Department of the Eure, 22 June 1893
Archives Départementales de l'Eure, Évreux (18 S 25)

cannot be satisfied with him. Where respectable jobs are concerned, he has actually worked solely for Mme Pellissier. He has worked for horticulturists, but to what end?
[...] To the request I made to him, whether he knew of a gardener, he replied in these words: 'I do know one, Louis Arnoux, who will be leaving his job on the 25th of this month. He is working for Mr. Levé, at Saulseuse castle, near Vernon. He is an excellent gardner, and a most honest man. He is leaving his job because he cannot get along with the watchman. At Saulseuse, he earns fifteen hudred francs, plus beverages. And he certainly earns his money. He is a very peaceful man.You could ask Mr Levé for further information, because he will only have good things to say—he is very unhappy about his gardener leaving."
11 June: Monet to Caillebotte:
"I looked for you at the flower show. I also thought I'd see Godefroy, but met no one. I was banking on seeing you both and I had things to ask you, particularly with regard to a greenhouse, having never had one, and not knowing which manufacturer to turn to, nor if it is better to take a greenhouse with double glazing, or made of wood or metal, or just single glazing, I would be most grateful if you could find such information and write me a word about it. My plan is to have quite a large cold or temperate greenhouse, with a lesser part of it used as a hot house.
Despite this appalling weather, the garden has been magnificent all through May. I kept wanting to see you, but I have been permanently interrupted, the first flowering is now over and we'll have to wait for the summer flowers, as long as everything is not scorched by the heat. I'll let you know, and you must come and see me, and I must also visit you in Gennevilliers.
As far as Godefroy is concerned, he's a strange fellow, he still has not sent me his famous dahlia (lady [illegible]); has he given it to you [?]"
Late June: Mirbeau contributes anonymously to two of the periodicals (*Le Jardin* and *L'Orchidophile*) produced by Godefroy-Lebœuf, horticulturist in Argenteuil, whom he mentions in a letter to Monet:
"I am going to fetch the begonias Godefroy is sending me. It seems they are ready to flower, like the ones we saw at the Show [...]
[...] I have just seen a Japanese catalogue he sent me [probably the catalogue of a horticulturist at Yokohama, Louis Boehmer], which had some black lilies... Tee hee!... We'll have to get some of those."
16 July: Monet weds Alice at Giverny in the presence of Caillebotte, Helleu and Robinson.
20 July: wedding of Suzanne Hoschedé and the American painter Theodore Earl Butler.
Monet takes on Félix Breuil as head gardener on Mirbeau's recommendation. (Félix Breuil's father was the writer's father's gardener at Rémalard).
Construction of greenhouses.

1893
5 February: Monet signs the purchase agreement for a plot of land of 1,268 sq.m. [13,500 sq.ft.] situated below his property, between the Vernon-Gisors railway line and the Ru, a small arm of the Epte. He starts creating a water garden on the new plot.
16 February: while working in Rouen on the series of *Cathedrals*, Monet visited Émile Varenne, director of the Botanical Gardens. He writes to Alice:
"... After work this morning I was able to make my vist to Monsieur Varenne at the Botanical Gardens. He's a very kind man, Monsieur Varenne, and I hope to obtain quite a lot of things from him; he offered me a cutting from that lovely climbing begonia which I'll bring back on Sunday. We visited all greenhouses, really superb, what orchids! They are gorgeous. As for plants for the young botanists, he's going to introduce me on my next visit to the head gardener who is only allowed to give plants away on Monsieur Varenne's orders, but he tells me that if it would be a good idea if the children were to draw up some kind of list with the priest. He gave me quite a lot of good advice on a lot of things; he's worth knowing in short. He told me I could go anywhere I wanted and feel at home..."
[Catherine Hug and Monika Leonhardt, "Claude Monet the Gardener" in Christoph Becker, *Monet's Garden*. Zurich: Kunsthaus, 2004, p. 131.]
7 March: Monet tells Alice about the dispatch of plants purchased from gardeners in Rouen:
"I've finally found some wallflowers. There are some very good gardeners here. So, the day after tomorrow, in the morning, several baskets will come to Vernon, because I had to go two of them to get the number I wanted. In one of the baskets, which will have to be carefully opened, there will be other plants, hardy varieties, then some passion flowers for the temperate greenhouse, as well as two very pretty yellow flowers and two odd little nasturtiums; all for the greenhouse, apart from ther hardy plants."
17 March, through the good offices of the journalist Ch. F. Lapierre, Monet requests authorization from the Prefect of the Eure, Mr. Pointu-Nores, to install a diversion in the Epte and to have two small footbridges built to have access to the land on the other bank **(fig. 4)**.
"I have the honor to inform you that I am the owner of a piece of land situated between the Pacy-Gisors railroad and the left bank of a branch of the Epte, and tenant of the land forming the opposite bank of this branch. In order to renew the water of the ponds that I am going to dig on the land I own, for the purpose of growing aquatic plants, I should like to install a water feeder in the Epte by means of a small trench whose ends will be open on the right bank of the Epte and provided with a small sluice gate 60 or 70 cm wide. Nothing would be installed in the bed of the stream that could modify the level or flow of the water. It would, in short, be nothing but a small intermittent diversion whose water volume, insignificant in relation to the output of the stream, would be restored to it after watering my plants. I believe that my project lies within the limits of the usage rights belonging to riverside owners, and I hope you will be willing to grant me authorization as soon as possible for the installation of the water feeder that I would like.
In addition, in order to pass from my land to the land that I rent on the other bank and vice-versa, I plan to install over the stream of the Epte two small, light, wooden footbridges. As far as the width and height

5-6 | *Delivery slip from the Latour-Marliac Nursery to Claude Monet, 15 May* [1894], nos. 261 and 262
Latour-Marliac Sarl, Le Temple-sur-Lot

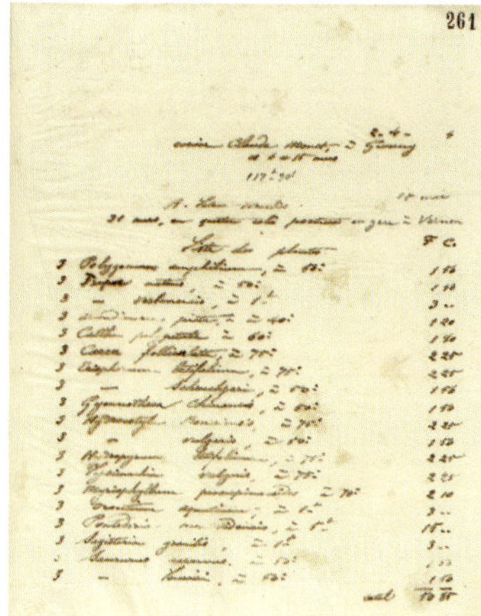

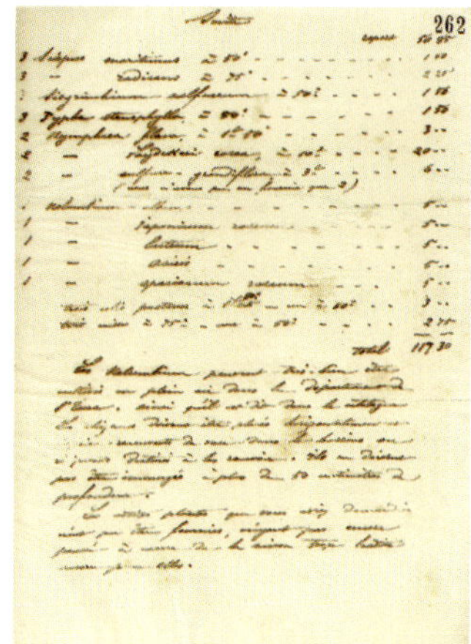

at both ends of these footbridges are concerned, I will conform to the instructions that you will be kind enough to give me in the authorization that I request in order to build them."
[Robert Gordon and Andrew Forge, *Monet*. New York: Harry N. Abrams, 1983, p. 208.]
The correspondence from Monet to Alice describes the open opposition shown by the village council and certain inhabitants of Giverny, maintaining that "aquatic plants might be harmful to the water and alter its quality."
20 March: Monet to Alice:
"I'm upset about these new difficulties. I was completely involved in my painting and fairly pleased. This enrages me and I want no longer to have anything to do with... all those people in Giverny; no more engineers, no more diggers, etc. There is nothing but trouble ahead and, believe me, I give it up completely. I am not writing to the prefect, I'm going to wire Lagrange not to send anything. Don't rent a thing, don't order any lattice, and throw the aquatic plants in the river; they'll grow there. I want to hear no more about it, I want to paint. Shit on the natives of Giverny, and the engineers.
I give the land to whoever wants it."
[Robert Gordon and Andrew Forge, *Monet*. New York: Harry N. Abrams, 1983, pp. 208-09.]
21 March: Monet to Alice:
"This morning I met Lapierre who is seeing to it that my request finds its way to the Prefect's own hands. So I shall write it this evening, before I retire to bed. [...] So much bother for so little. I hope at least that Picard is still busy though; there are still terraces to be made. Nobody has any right to stop my earth-moving, as long as I don't dig beyond a certain depth. I should also very much like to know if Father Colomb is doing what I told him to, and if the trellis fencing will finally be erected; then there is the Quéruel solution.
I'm much afraid of the cold, especially for the tiger flowers and the last onions planted; I must talk to Eugène and find out what the temperature is at night."
24 April: birth of James (Jimmy) Butler, son of Suzanne and Theodore Earl Butler.
15 July: visit from Mirbeau. It was probably on this particular day that he decided to make overtures to the Prefect of the Eure in a letter dated two days later:
"You have shown me such kindness, and this encourages me to ask another service of you. My friend, the great painter, Claude Monet, who lives in Giverny, near Vernon, is waiting on your decision to obtain the permit to divert water from the Epte, which runs beside his property.
He has had a pool, or rather a pond, dug, where he grows wonderful water lilies and dreamlike Japanese irises. This pond poses a threat to no one, and in no way adversely affects the river. But local farmers have protested, with their customary mischief, against this diversion being made. I do not have to teach you anything about the thousand and one scenes of the rural comedy. You are better acquainted with them than I. The arguments of those protesting do not stand up. They are protesting, what is more, against something that they themselves do day in day out, but with this one difference: they do it without ever asking for permission.
I am therefore taking it upon myself, Sir, to earnestly request that you grant this permit for my friend Claude Monet. You will afford me much pleasure, in so granting it, on his behalf, first of all, with his passion for those flowers, and then for myself, because when I go to Giverny, it is a joy to see this enchanting spot.
Were there any danger whatsoever, I would make no such request, being totally respectful of other people's rights. But, in truth, this is nothing but mischief being raised by bad neighbours, cantankerous peasants jealous of accommodating a bourgeois person who is, however, the most liberal and peace-loving of people."
17 July: Monet sends a reminder to the Prefect of the Eure, explaininhg the reason for his request, pursuant to the committee of inquiry dealing with his project to grow aquatic plants.
"I have the honor of submitting to you a few observations regarding the opposition raised by the municipal council and several inhabitants of Giverny concerning the two inquiries made relative to the request which I have had the honor of addressing to you, in view of obtaining the authorization to create a duct to draw water from the Epte River to feed a pool in which I intend to cultivate aquatic plants.
I would like to point out to you that, under the pretext of public salubrity, the aforementioned opponents have in fact no other goal than to hamper my projects out of pure meanness, as is frequently the case in the country when Parisian landowners are involved; that, for the rest, these opponents, whose number is small in relation to our population, are composed of people whom I do not or no longer employ, such as Mme. Serrurier etc., and that they are acting out of spite and petty vengeance. I dare to hope, *Monsieur le Préfet*, that you will take these reasons into consideration and respond favorably to my request.
I would also like you to know that the aforementioned cultivation of aquatic plants will not have the importance that this term implies and that it will be only a pastime, for the pleasure of the eye, and for motifs to paint; and finally that I am cultivating in this pool only plants such as water lilies, reeds, different varieties of irises which generally grow in a natural state along our river, and that there is absolutely no danger of poisoning the water.
If the villagers remain unconvinced, I am prepared to promise to renew the water of this pool only during the night, when no one is using the water.
I hope that after these explanations you will understand the situation and that you will be able to grant me a favorable response.
You will please pardon the liberty I take in asking you, *Monsieur le Préfet*, to accept the expression of my most distinguished sentiments."
[Michel Hoog, *The Nymphéas of Claude Monet at the Musée de l'Orangerie*. Paris: Éditions de la Réunion des Musées Nationaux, 1990, p. 107.]
24 July: two prefectural decrees grant Monet the right to make a diversion in an arm of the Epte River, known as the "communal arm", and build two footbridges **(figs. 2 and 3)**.
30 October: visit from Berthe Morisot and Julie Manet. This latter notes in her diary that the greenhouse is filled with chrysanthemums and that a "Japanese-looking" bridge spans the pond **(fig. 8)**.

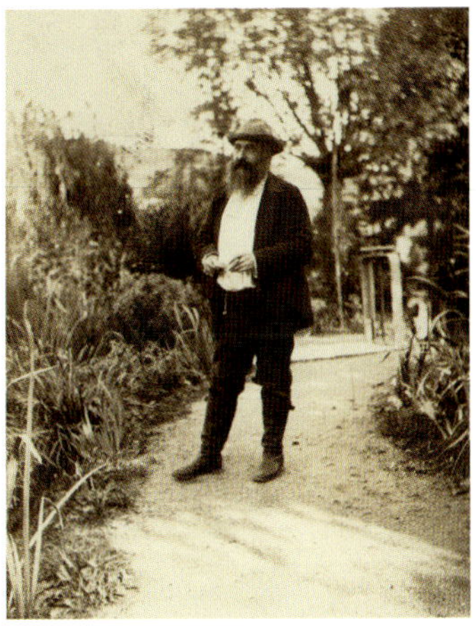

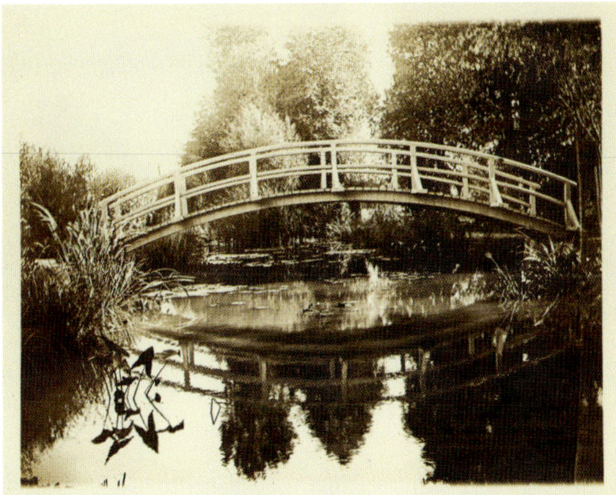

7 | [Lilla or Margaret Cabot Perry?], *Claude Monet at Giverny*, between 1899 and 1909
Photograph, 12 × 9 cm (4³/₄ × 3⁹/₁₆ in.)
Archives of American Art, Smithsonian Institution, Washington, D.C. Courtesy Lilla Cabot Perry photographs, ca. 1889–1909

8 | [Lilla or Margaret Cabot Perry?], *Bridge at Giverny*, between 1899 and 1909
Photograph, 10 × 13 cm (3¹⁵/₁₆ × 5¹⁵/₁₆ in.)
Archives of American Art, Smithsonian Institution, Washington, D.C. Courtesy Lilla Cabot Perry photographs, ca. 1889–1909

1894

Late January: Monet plans the construction of a new kitchen and the extension of the house westwards to set up his first studio.

15 May: delivery of four packages to Vernon railway station, the first certified order from the Latour-Marliac Nursery **(figs. 5 and 6)**. Joseph Bory Latour-Marliac gives the following instructions: "The *Nelumbium* can be very easily grown outdoors in the Department of the Eure, as noted in the catalogue. The rhizomes should be laid horizontally and covered with mud in the ponds or receptacles earmarked to hold them. They should not be put at a depth of more than 50 centimetres [20 inches]."

11 October: Alice Butler, daughter of Suzanne and Theodore Earl Butler, born in Giverny.

28 November: Mirbeau, Rodin, Geffroy and Clemenceau travel to Giverny where they meet Cézanne.

1895

6-12 January: Monet produces the first known depictions of the water garden.

[27] February: Monet to Alice, from Sandviken:

"I am incidentally still hoping to be able to take them a few plant specimens from here, which a gentleman has promised to obtain from a botanist in Christiania. It would seem that there are quite a lot of special plants in Norway."

April: the dispute about the sale of Giverny's communal marshland is reported by the press, in particular in *Le Rappel de l'Eure*. Monet is against the installation of a factory and Mirbeau envisages using his personal connections. Monet's offer of 5,500 francs for "the improvement of the marshland" is eventually accepted on **9 February 1896.**

10-31 May: Monet's show at the Galerie Durand-Ruel, including in particular the series of *Cathedrals*.

Mid-November: Mirbeau to Monet:

"It would be most kind of you to send me two beautiful clumps of *multiflorus maximus*, because I think it is high time they were planted.

As soon as the phlox cuttings have taken, as well as the cuttings of a few dahlias which you found pretty, I shall send them to you. I shall also have some *superbus* carnations to let you have, the one you so liked last year We planted them out yesterday."

1896

Summer: Monet starts work on the series of *Mornings on the Seine*, near Giverny **(cat. no. 8)**.

November: Monet works on a series of pictures of flowers **(fig. 4 p. 21)**.

1897

Monet has the second studio built, its ground floor, reserved for the gardeners, subequently turned into a garage and dark room.

On the advice of Émile Varenne, Monet has a second hothouse constructed.

9 and 10 June: wedding of Jean Monet and Blanche Hoschedé.

August: visit of the journalist Maurice Guillemot, whose report appears on **15 March 1898** in *La Revue Illustrée*:

"The master has a passion for flowers, and he reads more catalogues and horticultural price lists than articles by aesthetes, for which he can not be blamed. On the large panels he glimpsed in the studio, he says: One must imagine a *circular room* whose wall-space, *below* the baseboard, is to be entirely occupied by a horizon of water dotted with plant life, walls of transparency tinged with some green here, some mauve there, the calm and the silence of still waters reflecting the spreading vegetation."

[Michel Hoog, "The Series of Water-Lilies", *The Nymphéas of Claude Monet at the Musée de l'Orangerie*. Paris: Réunion des Musées Nationaux, 1990, p. 36.]

1898

Publication of "Flore de Vernon et de la Roche-Guyon" by Jean-Pierre Hoschedé and Abbé Anatole Toussaint, *Bulletin de la Société des Amis des Sciences Naturelles de Rouen*.

1st June-July: Claude Monet show at the Galerie Georges Petit, including the series of *Cathedrals*, *Mornings on the Seine*, and *Chrysanthemums*.

Summer: Monet, dissatisfied, destroys some of his canvases.

16 June: *Le Gaulois* devotes a supplement to Monet and publishes an anthology of criticism.

1899

6 February: death of Suzanne Hoschedé-Butler.

During the summer: Monet starts the series of *Water Lily Ponds* **(cat. no. 12)**.

Early December: Claude and Alice Monet are photographed in Paul Nadar's studio in Paris **(cat. no. 59)**.

1900

Monet starts work on a series of views of the flower garden, near the central path **(cat. no. 13)**.

[February]: Monet gives his instructions to the gardener:

Sowing. Around 300 pots Poppies—60 Sweet pea—around 60 pots white Agremony—30 yellow Agremony—Blue sage—Blue water lilies in beds [greenhouses]—Dahlias—Iris Kaempferi.

From the 15th to the 25th, lay the dahlias down to root, plant out those with shoots before I get back. -Don't forget the lily bulbs. - Should the Japanese peonies arrive plant them immediately if weather permits, taking care initially to protect buds from the cold, as much as from the heat of the sun. Get down to pruning: rose trees not too long, except for the thorny varieties. In March sow the grass seeds, plant out the little nasturtiums, keep a close eye on the gloxinia, orchids, etc., in the greenhouse, as well as the plants under frames. Trim the borders as arranged; put wires for the clematis and climbing roses as soon as Picard had done the necessary. If the weather's bad, make some straw matting, but lighter than previously. Plant cuttings from the rose trees at the pond around masure in the hen huts. Don't delay work on tarring the planks and plant the Helianthus latiflorus in good clumps right away. If anything's missing such as masure, pots etc., ask Madame if possible on a Friday so as to have it on Saturday. In March force the chrysanthemums along as the buds won't open in damp conditions; and don't forget to put the sulphur sheets back over the greenhouse frames.

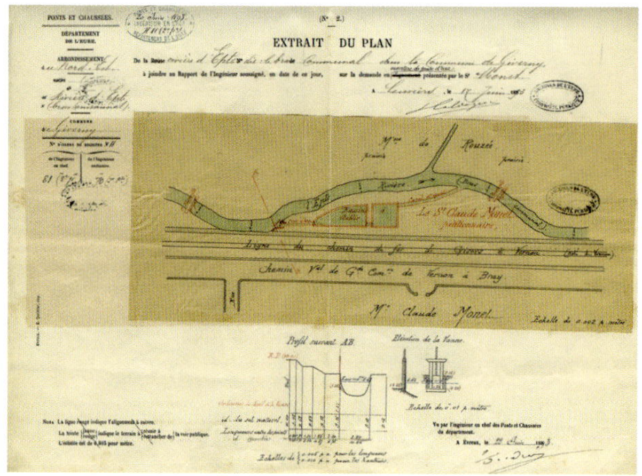

9 | *Plan of the pond with diversion project from the arm of the Epte known as the "communal arm", report of the subdivisional foreman*, 8 October 1901
Archives Départementales de l'Eure, Évreux (18 S 25)

[Catherine Hug and Monika Leonhardt, "Claude Monet the Gardener" in Christoph Becker, *Monet's Garden*. Zurich: Kunsthaus, 2004, p. 143.]

9 March: Monet to Alice from London:

"I hope you found the house and the garden, and the greenhouse, all in good order; it would be good if you could keep an eye on everything from time to time; and that Pascal gets a bit used to having an eye kept on him, too; likewise, it would be good to know what is happening at the Florimond garden, see if the vegetables are in good shape, and know what has been planted. Eugène ought to go there twice a week; it would be a good idea to find out and go there the day he is there."

In the spring and during the summer: Monet produces the second series of the *Water Lily Ponds* **(cat. no. 14)**.

29 May Monet to Clemenceau :

"This is the perfect time, you will see a splendid garden, but make haste. Do you wish to come on either Sunday or Monday? If you leave it much later, everything will have flowered. See what Geffroy says and write to me. I am counting on you. I have a lot of new canvases. With my very best regards
Give Geffroy a good shake and come."

Summer: visit from the American collector Desmond FitzGerald.

July: visit from Joseph Durand-Ruel who takes a series of photographs in Monet's studio.

31 October: wedding of Theodore Earl Butler and Marthe Hoschedé in the presence of Paul Durand-Ruel, Anna Bergmann, Abbé Toussaint, Pierre and Jeanne Sisley, and Fernand Haundorff.

22 November–15 December: exhibition "Œuvres récentes de Claude Monet" at the Galerie Durand-Ruel. First public showing of the series of the *Water Lily Ponds*.

23 November: Arsène Alexandre publishes an article on Monet in *Le Figaro*:

"We are told that Mr. Monet has flooded a part of his garden at Giverny, to sow water lilies, and that he will build a bridge with Japanese lines across this pond, which is as flower-filled as it is improvised.
The idea was delightful, but perhaps the artist failed to make the effects diverse enough, and the series is not without certain similarities. What is more, for pictures of this size, the motif is possibly a little simple and of secondary interest. Often, however, Mr. Monet has disguised these shortcomings beneath the splendour of his symphony. Nobody excels in presenting festivals of flowers the way he does. A garden view, without water lilies but with a dazzling carpet of lilac blossoms, is a thing of quite novel wealth."

Late December: Monet becomes associated with Joseph (Josse) Bernheim-Jeune and Gaston Bernheim.

1901

10 May: Monet to Paul Durand-Ruel:

"[...] Sadly I am doing nothing for the time being; the weather is not good and the spring flowering has simply not happened, no blossom on the apple trees, and I am wondering if I will have any irises, everything is so behind."

The same day: Monet signs the purchase agreement for a new plot of land on the other side of the Ru, in Me Grimpard's office, for 1,200 francs. A sale clause reveals his intention to retrace the pond's shape.

Summer: visit from Arsène Alexandre who writes in *Le Figaro* of **9 August**:

"Indeed, what is most remarkable about Monet's garden is not the plan but the planting [...]
The garden is divided into tidy "squares" like any truck garden of Grenelle and Gennevilliers. [...]
He also wants, perhaps above all, his flower palette before him to look at all year round, always present, but always changing. Everything is designed in such a way that the celebration is everywhere renewed and ceaselessly replaced. If a certain flower bed is stilled in a certain season, borders and hedges will suddenly light up. [...]"
Sometimes he works in the garden, exhilarating his eyesight and his imagination with the elusive glints that play on this marquetry of great full-blooming flowers and [the reflections colored like] molten metals. Sometimes, more often, he works in the large studio set amidst his flowering truck garden, like a combination market stall and observatory.
[Arsène Alexandre, "Monet's Garden", *Le Figaro*, 9 August 1901, reprinted and translated in Charles F. Stuckey, *Monet. A Retrospective*. New York: Hugh Lauter Levin Associates, Inc., 1985, pp. 220–22.]

13 August: Monet writes to the Prefect of the Eure, requesting authorization to divert a small arm of the Epte, known as the "communal arm", within his property **(p. 132)**.

8 October: the subdivisional foreman of the Civil Engineering Department [Ponts et Chaussées] of Gisors sends a favourable report to the Prefect, accompanied by a plan of the place **(fig. 9)**. This matter would nevertheless be submitted to a 20-day committee of inquiry.

13 November: the village council convenes in an extraordinary session to examine Monet's request, and authorization is granted on condition that the water inlet and outlet are made "using grids letting the water flow freely and not by means of sluice-gates, without reducing the rate of flow."

26 November: the sub-Prefect of Les Andelys addresses the Prefect of the Eure:

"The purpose of his request concerns quite simply the growing of aquatic plants, as he is already doing in his current pond, but on a larger scale, and because such plants constantly need the same water level, as well as water that is warmer than running water, it would be impossible to cultivate them if the pond were fed by anything other than sluice gates."

11 December: Letter from the Prefect of the Eure sent to Claude Monet in care of the sub-Prefect of Les Andelys authorizing him to divert the small communal arm **(p. 133)**.

1902

Work starts on diverting the Ru and enlarging the pond.

21 January: Monet writes to the Prefect of the Eure:

"I am pleased to ask you to be kind enough to grant me the permit to enclose, by means of a trellis fence, a part of the land that is included in the property I own at Giverny, situated beside the Vernon-to-Gisors

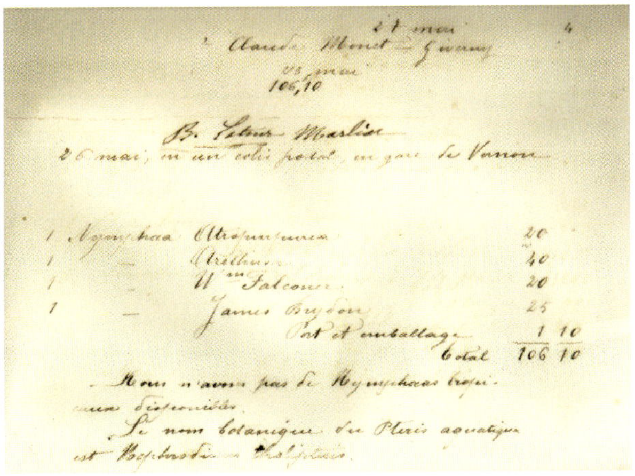

10 | *Delivery slip from the Latour-Marliac Nursery to Claude Monet*, 27 May 1904
Latour-Marliac Sarl, Le Temple-sur-Lot

railway line, and to this effect to have the alignment accorded to me by the relevant person."

"I am hereby sending you a request for an alignment of part of the land situated beside the Vernon-to-Gisors railway line, which I should like to be able to enclose with a trellis fence as soon as possible. Through the good offices of our mutual friend Mr. Olivier Sainsère, I am taking the liberty of asking you to act in such a way that this permit be granted as swiftly as possible, and to this effect, I should be most grateful to you."

8 February: Monet to his son Jean Monet living in Rouen:

"I am writing to ask you if you could obtain for me the different chemical fertilisers, as itemised below. If so, please kindly dispatch them forthwith and by express mail to Vernon railway station. Thank you in advance, with tender kisses for you both. Your father. Here is the list:
100 kg pulverised ferrous sulphate
20 kg mineral superphosphate
4kg potassium sulphate
10 kg of dried blood
I do hope you will be able to provide me with all of the above
P.-S. -Now I must ask my little Blanche something, namely whether she could please go to a gardener on the Rue Verte whose name, I believe, is, Marie, and ask him if he still has the famous hardy little nasturtium that we grow every year on the fence.
It was from him that I got a pot a while ago, and that scatterbrain Florimond lost them all for me, or more or less. In a word, if she can find some at Marie's, please get this latter to send me two by express mail to Vernon railway station."

11–25 February Monet exhibits at the Durand-Ruel Gallery in New York.

15–28 February: exhibition "Œuvres récentes de Camille Pissarro et nouvelle série de Claude Monet *Vétheuil*" at the Galerie Bernheim-Jeune, Paris.

21 February: Monet tells Alice about the works for enlarging the pond:

"What is more, in every respect, my presence is helpful here, because, with this persistent frost, despite splendid days, nothing can be planted inthe pond, and, although the work is progressing, there is still some way to go, and I'm afraid there will be a mess for a while. This is getting on my nerves quite a bit."

In a second letter to Alice Monet, dated **27 February**, Monet announces that planting has started:

"And yesterday I was busy in the pond planting things, as I am today, which is why I am telegraphing to say I won't be able to be away more than five days."

28 June: Monet receives authorisation to use a trellis fence to enclose part of the land on his property beside the railway line.

28 July and **11 August**: an exchange of plots of land is signed and sealed with the Compagnie des chemins de fer in the office of Me Texier, notary at Vernon.

12 November: wedding of Germaine Hoschedé and Albert Salerou in the presence of Abbé Toussaint, Jeanne Sisley and Auguste Rémy **(cat. no. 83)**.

1904

27 May: delivery from the Latour-Marliac Nursery in one package of *Nymphaea Atropurpurea, Nymphaea Arethusa, Nymphaea W Falconer, Nymphaea James Brydon* to Vernon railway station **(fig. 10)**.

7 June: Maurice Kahn publishes a major article in *Le Temps*: "Au jour le jour: Le Jardin de Claude Monet":

"Look there," Monet said: "that was once an orchard. The trees were all dead or had been lopped off."

The fruit trees have been replaced by groupings of the most sumptuous and varied species of flowers, irises, tulips, Japanese peonies. Blue, violet, yellow, and pink flowers are blended together in clumps of dazzling tones among the green of leaves and stems. There are no plots of grass, no baskets, no fenced flower beds—none of those arrangements that are held to be the summit of the gardener's art and that give flowers the artificial appearance of bouquets or parlor knickknacks. [...]

[...] All around the pond are water irises, and behind them are azaleas, tamarisk trees, a weeping willow. The overall aspect of the garden—and particularly the little green bridge—has caused it to be named the "Japanese Garden." Mr. Hayashi, the Japanese commissioner at the 1900 World's Fair, was also struck by the resemblance, which Monet maintains is quite unintentional. [...]

In the summer, sitting beneath his vast parasol at the edge of his pond, bent over his beloved water lilies, he attempts to capture the shimmer of the water, the reflections of the broad leaves, the capricious play of the light.

"Aside from painting and gardening," he said to me, "I'm good for nothing."

After having seen Claude Monet in his garden, one has a better understanding of why such a gardener is also such a painter. This great man is an unabashed lover of life. And painting is for him a way to create living beauty.

[Maurice Kahn, "Claude Monet's Garden", *Le Temps*, June 7, 1904 reprinted and translated in Charles F. Stuckey, *Monet. A Retrospective*. New York: Hugh Lauter Levin Associates, Inc., 1985, pp. 243–45.]

1905

Views of the pond show the Japanese bridge surmounted by an arch designed to support wisteria plants.

27 October: visit from Joseph Durand-Ruel and Baron Adolf de Meyer, who made several portraits of Monet **(cat. nos. 37 and 38)**. Alice Monet writes about their visit to her daughter Germaine Salerou, on **9 February 1906**:

"I have just sent you 2 photos of Monet [...] you will, like us, I think, admire, in addition to the likeness, the beauty of the process and the paper. I cannot recall if you were still here when the person who took them came: Baron Meyer, an Englishman brought by young Durand as an art lover, but whose real purpose was to photograph Monet. I am delighted because he was successful [...] For the photo, Monet recommends not to make it smaller, nor to cut the precious Japan paper, which bears the signature [...]"

December: in *L'Art et les Artistes*, Louis Vauxcelles publishes an article illustrated by seven photographs of Monet's garden by Jacques-Ernest Bulloz **(cat. no. 36)**.

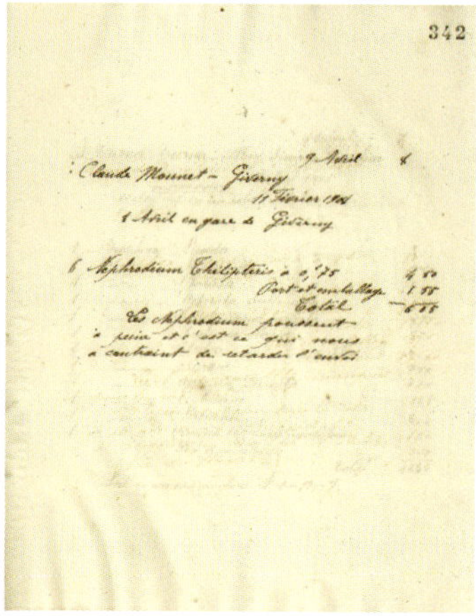

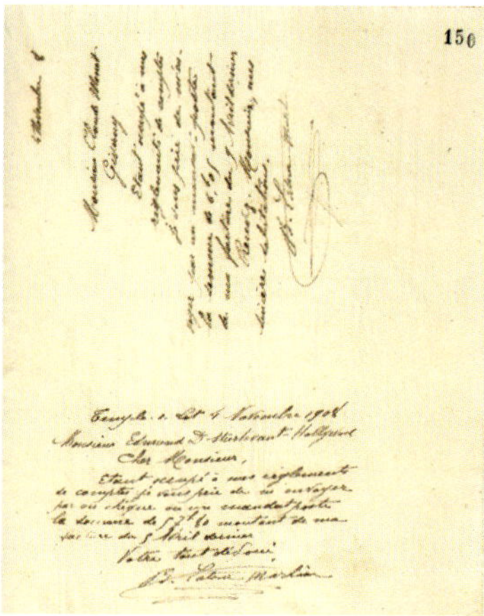

11 | *Order form from Claude Monet to the Latour-Marliac Nursery*, 9 April 1908, no. 342
Latour-Marliac Sarl, Le Temple-sur-Lot

12 | *Request for payment sent to Claude Monet by Latour-Marliac*, 4 November 1908
Latour-Marliac Sarl, Le Temple-sur-Lot

"However, because it was already four in the afternoon, and because "the water lilies close before five in the summertime," he led us down to the second garden. You know that, after having purchased a large field across the road from his property, Monet had flooded a part of it to create a river. He sprinkled a profusion of water lilies across that river. The leaves lie flat upon the surface of the water, and from among them blossom the yellow, blue, violet, and pink corollas of that lovely water flower. [The pond is spanned by] an arched wooden bridge painted green, near which Monet sets up his easel. Weeping willows and poplars abound, and on the banks of the stream he has planted hundreds of flowers—gladioli, irises, rhododendrons, and some rare species of lily whose petals are tipped with brown. The whole thing comes together to create a setting that enchants us rather than inspiring our awe, a dreamlike setting that is extremely oriental."
[Louis Vauxcelles, "An Afternoon Visit with Claude Monet", *L'Art et les Artistes*, December 1905, reprinted and translated in Charles F. Stuckey, *Monet. A Retrospective*. New York: Hugh Lauter Levin Associates, Inc., 1985, p. 246.]

1906

20 February: letter from Alice to Germaine Salerou:
"Monet is now busy planting large bamboos being put in the pond, and he's not going anywhere. Oh how I'd love to see him working, like that poor Renoir, but his garden is taking up too much of his time!"
12–24 March: exhibition "Œuvres de Claude Monet 1894-1905" at the Galerie Bernheim-Jeune.
27 March: Letter from Alice to Germaine Salerou:
"[...] Monet is in despair, his bamboo plantings, so dear to him, are in danger [...]"
15 October–3 November: exhibition at the Galerie Bernheim-Jeune.

1907

21 April: the Giverny village council deliberates on Monet's proposal to have the village's two main streets asphalted. Of the 2,800 francs estimate, Monet offers to pay 1,200 francs, the remainder being covered by a subscription plus an amount to be levied from the communal coffers; the council shows reservations on this latter point.
Letters from Alice Monet to Germaine Salerou attest to the damage caused in the garden by bad weather.
17 May: "[...] What dreary weather, added to Monet's devastation at seeing his garden wrecked by that downpour. [...]"
5 June: a letter from Alice to Germaine Salerou reveals that the asphalting will commence on **10 June.**
15 June: Marcel Proust publishes "*Les Éblouissements* par la Comtesse de Noailles" in the *Le Figaro* literary supplement.
13 July: Alice to Germaine Salerou:
"[...] Monet is back at work, but without any zeal. The water lilies have really suffered from the recent cold snap. He can no longer find any purpose [...]"

1908

15 March: visit from Joseph Durand-Ruel who takes several photographs of Monet's studio.
9 April: delivery from the Latour-Marliac Nursery to Vernon railway station **(figs. 11 and 12)**.
27 May: Alice to Germaine Salerou:
"[...] he has decided that we will go next Friday to Brunoy to see a horticulturist who grows just irises and orchids [...]"
11 August: Monet to Geffroy :
"The landscapes of water and reflections have become an obsession. It is beyond my old man's powers, but nevertheless I want to render what I sense. I have destroyed some [...] and I began some again [...] and I hope that something will come from so many efforts."
[Charles F. Stuckey (ed.), *Claude Monet 1840–1926*, exhib. cat.. Chicago: The Art Institute of Chicago, 1995, p. 240.]
September: Jean-Claude-Nicolas Forestier, curator at the Jardins de Paris, whom Monet had received in Giverny, publishes a detailed description of the garden in the magazine *Fermes et Châteaux*: the Clos Normand, the bridge and the rose arcades, and the water lily pond **(fig. 4 p. 42)**.

1909

4 March: Alice to Germaine Salerou:
"[...] Snow, and more snow, there is at least 4 inches, and it is freezing, it is starting to get us down and Monet is full of sighs because Félix Breuil, [head gardener] says that "everything is lost". In any event, lots of frozen roses and the poor tulips and hyacinths which were just coming up are all definitely damaged. Well, it's a disaster [...]"
On **26 March**: Alice to Germaine Salerou:
"[...] Though late, after such a long, cold winter, the garden is starting to come to life. There are beds full of pretty crocuses, then pretty primroses, Bizy hybrids [from a forest close to Vernon] are in full flower, which is most pleasing [...]"
6 May–5 June: exhibition "*Les Nymphéas*, series de paysages d'eau par Claude Monet" at the Galerie Durand-Ruel, organized with the Bernheim brothers, including 48 canvases in the second series of *Water Lilies*. The show was a great success and extended until **12 June**.
8 May: Arsène Alexandre publishes "Un paysagiste d'aujourd'hui et un portraitiste de jadis" in *Comœdia*:
"The painter would have wished to have a circular room to decorate, of modest, carefully calculated dimensions. All around, up to the middle of a person's stature, there would have reigned, passing through all possible modulations, a painting of water and flowers like the radiant series we see at Durand-Ruel's. Nothing else. No furniture. Nothing but this central table of this room, which would be a dining room."
1 June: Roger Marx publishes an article on the exhibition in the *Gazette des Beaux-Arts*, in which he offers his ideas to Monet:
"I was tempted to use as the decoration of a Salon this *Water Lilies* theme: carried along the walls, swathing all the surfaces with its unity, it would give the illusion of an endless whole, a horizonless, shoreless wave; nerves overtaxed by work would find relaxation there, as with the restful example of still water, and, for anyone living there, this room would offer the haven of peaceful contemplation in front of a flower-filled aquarium."

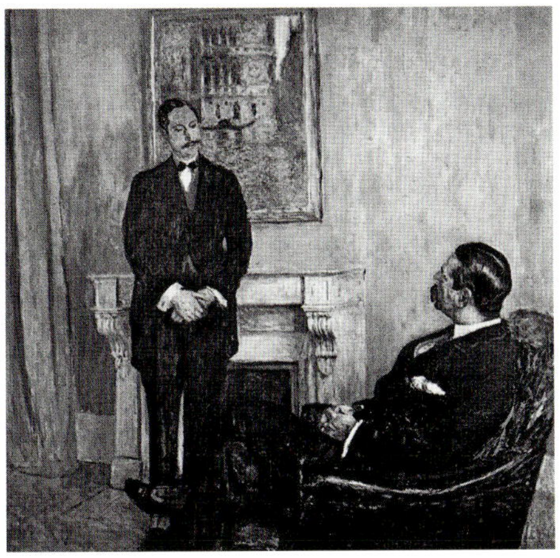

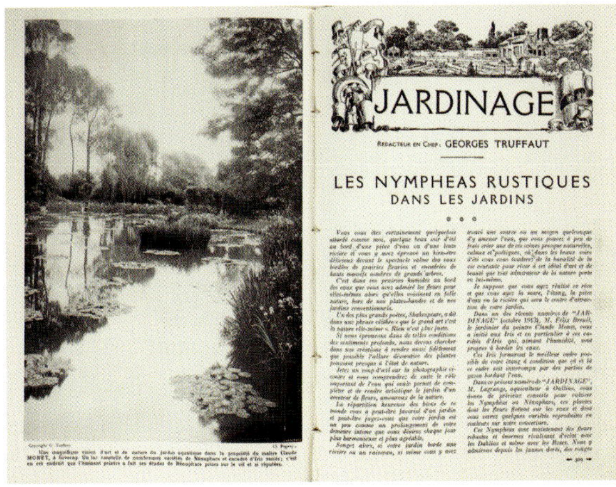

JARDINAGE

Rédacteur en Chef: GEORGES TRUFFAUT

LES NYMPHEAS RUSTIQUES DANS LES JARDINS

13 | Édouard Vuillard, *Gaston Bernheim de Villers and Joseph (Josse) Bernheim-Jeune*, 1912, oil on canvas, 157 × 159 cm (61 13/16 × 62 5/8 in.), Courtesy of Galerie Bernheim-Jeune, Paris

14 | Pogany, "Water garden in the property of the painter Claude Monet in Giverny", taken from M. Lagrange, "Les nymphéas rustiques dans les jardins" *Jardinage* magazine, no. 28, May 1914, pp. 308–9, Truffaut, Évry

4 June: letter from Alice to Germaine Salerou: "What weather we had last night! Monet is also upset about his asphalting, as the road was already bad, there's a real river of tar flowing down the hill and if any cars pass it will be horrible. But the road cannot be left permanently blocked, it has been for 4 days. Then the poor garden which was in full bloom is quite damaged."

6 June: Alice describes Clemenceau's visit to Germaine Salerou: "Clemenceau came to pay us a visit after lunch and stayed until five o'clock! [...] He was so amazed by the garden, and the water lilies, that he said to his daughter as he left: "You know, on the way home we're going to sell Bernouville [Clemenceau's property near Gisors, some 20 miles from Giverny], there's nothing more to be done after seeing Monet's garden!" Monet and he looked so happy to see each other again, and they even embraced each other; it was a pleasure to behold, and his visit was perfectly timed because Monet was most upset by the damage to the garden, and as you see that didn't stop him from admiring it."

1910

Refurbishment of the sitting room-*cum*-studio.

Terrible floods ravage the pond and the garden. Monet is deeply distressed.

28 January: Alice to Germaine Salerou:

"In front of the pond there's more than three feet of water! It's heartbreaking to see the poor pond, with just large brambles showing; the rhododendrons and azaleas are in the water, the little bridges are afloat, held by chains, and there is a danger the large bridge will be swept away. You see what a state Monet is in."

December: Monet offers the City of Le Havre three canvases, including the *Water Lilies* **(cat. no. 15)**, for the token sum of 3,000 francs.

1911

19 May: death of Alice in Giverny.

1912

28 May–8 June: the exhibition "Monet. Venice" at the Galerie Bernheim-Jeune is a great success **(fig. 13)**.

July: Monet discovers that he is suffering from a double cataract.

5 August: more damage in the garden. Monet writes to Gaston or Josse Bernheim-Jeune: "My weeping willows of which I was so proud, devastated with branches torn off... a real grief for me."

1913

July, Georges Truffaut, the famous horticulturist, has a chance to visit Monet's garden. In **October** he publishes in the magazine *Jardinage* an article about Monet's irises by Félix Breuil, Monet's head gardener **(cat. nos. 73 and 86)**.

Summer: Small series of *Flower Arbours*.

Sacha Guitry visits Giverny with the American singer Marguerite Namara, whom he photographs with Monet **(cat. no. 49)**.

1914

Monet starts work on the construction of a third studio. The works span two years.

15 January: André Arnyvelde publishes "Chez le Peintre de la Lumière 'Je sais tout' interviewe Claude Monet" in *Je sais tout*. Several photographs show Monet in a garden path looking at the water lilies in his pond, in the old studio turned into a sitting room, and in his studio, finishing one of the canvases in the series of *Flower Arbours*.

9 February: death of Jean Monet in Giverny. His weadow Blanche Hoschedé-Monet moves in to the Monet home.

2–21 March: retrospective exhibition at the Galerie Durand-Ruel.

May: Mr. Lagrange, an aquiculturalist at Oullins (Rhône), publishes "Les nymphéas rustiques dans les jardins" in the magazine *Jardinage*. He offers lavish advice for growing water lilies and illustrates his article with two views taken in Claude Monet's water garden **(fig. 14)**.

1915

15 January: Monet to the collector Raymond Koechlin: "I'm working on my *Grande Décoration* idea... As you guessed, this is indeed the project I had in mind a long time ago: water and water lilies, but on a very large surface."

1–16 February: exhibition at the Durand-Ruel Gallery in New York.

17 June: Mirbeau, Geffroy, Lucien Descaves, Léon Hennique, J. H. Rosny and possibly Paul Margueritte, members of the Académie Goncourt, visit Monet's studio. Descaves tells of seeing "huge canvases, about two metres high by three and half meters long", adding that a studio earmarked for the *Grand Decorations* is under construction. On how long the work would take, Monet reckons: "About another five years".

21 June: visit from Édouard Vuillard and Pierre Bonnard.

5 July: a sub-prefectural decree authorises the construction of the new studio, to the northwest of the property. Prior demolition work on the different shacks and sheds would be carried out by Maurice Lanctuit, a builder in Vernon. The cost of the demolition, the construction of the studio, and the installation of a water tank with pipes all comes to 35,677,51 francs. The height of the glass roof rises to 15 metres [50 feet] and the base measured 23 metres by 12 [75 × 40 feet].

8 July 1915: a photograph shows Monet painting beside the pond under a huge parasol with Blanche and Nita Salerou at his side.

Summer: for the film *Ceux de chez nous*, Guitry shoots a sequence showing Monet painting by the pond.

22 November–5 December: screening of Guitry's film at the Théâtre des Variétés.

December: Monet and Renoir exhibition at the Durand-Ruel Gallery in New York.

1916

Work finishes on the large studio.

26 April: Monet invites Bonnard to see his *Grand Decorations* **(p. 135)**.

1917

30 April: Monet receives Étienne Clémentel, Minister of Trade and Industry, and Albert Dalimier,

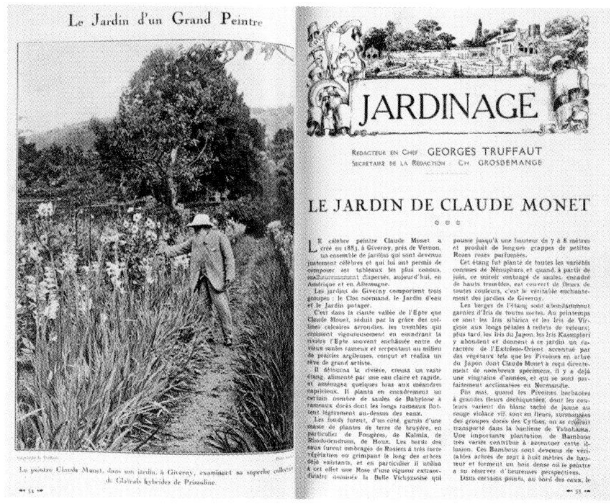
Le Jardin d'un Grand Peintre

JARDINAGE

GEORGES TRUFFAUT

LE JARDIN DE CLAUDE MONET

15 | Gouthière, "Claude Monet, in his garden in Giverny, examining his superb hybrid Gladiolus," taken from Georges Truffaut, "Le jardin de Claude Monet," *Jardinage* magazine, n° 87, November 1924, pp. 54-55. Évry, Truffaut

Under-secretary of State for Fine Arts, to discuss a carpet.
10 May: Monet invites Albert Marquet and Henri Matisse to lunch.
11 November: On their visit to Giverny, Monet authorizes Georges and Joseph Durand-Ruel to take views of the large studio with the series of large panels of *Water Lilies*.

1918
Spring–summer: Monet starts the series of *Japanese Bridges* **(cat. nos. 24 and 25)**.
19 August: first visit from the collector René Gimpel accompanied by Georges Bernheim-Jeune. Gimpel notes in his diary: "The interior consists of a single, immense room with a glass roof, and there we encounter an astonishing artistic sight; a good dozen canvases standing on the floor, arranged in a circle, side by side, each of them roughly two meters long and one meter twenty high; a panorama of water and water lilies, of light and sky. Water and sky have neither beginning nor end and in this infinite vastness." [Linda Schädler, "Biography", in Christoph Becker, *Monet's Garden*. Zurich: Kunsthaus, 2004, p. 186.]
12 November: to celebrate the Armistice, Monet decides to donate to the State two of the large panels he is finishing. Clemenceau persuades Monet to enlarge this gift to the whole project, but where it is to go still has to be decided.
I am just about to finish two decorative panels that I want to sign with the date of the Victory, and I am asking you to offer them to the State by your intermediary. It is not very much, but it is the only way I have of taking part in the Victory. I would like these two panels to be placed in the Musée des Arts Décoratifs and would be pleased if they could be chosen by you. [Michel Hoog, "The Series of Water-Lilies", *The Nymphéas of Claude Monet at the Musée de l'Orangerie*. Paris: Editions de la Réunion des musées nationaux, 1990, p. 38]

1919
18 January–late January: "Monet-Rodin" show at the Bernheim-Jeune gallery.
1-17 May: exhibition "Recently Imported Works by Claude Monet" at the Durand-Ruel Gallery in New York.
24 June: Monet writes to Josse Bernheim that all his gardeners have resigned:
"For a moment I thought I would have to abandon the garden in Giverny."

1920
February : As a pre-condition to his donation to the State, Monet stipulates the acquisition of his *Women in the Garden;* this purchase was made in **February 1921**
22 March: visit from François Thiébault-Sisson, art critic for *Le Temps*.
4 June: visit from Joseph Durand-Ruel with the American collectors Mr and Mrs Martin A. Ryerson and Mrs Charles Hutchinson.
Early August: Arsène Alexandre goes to Giverny to prepare the book published by Bernheim-Jeune in 1924, *À Giverny, chez Claude Monet*.
27 September: initial prior agreement for the donation between Monet and Paul Léon, director of the Académie des Beaux-Arts. Monet appoints Louis Bonnier as architect for the pavilion to be built in the main courtyard of the Hôtel Biron.
October: *Le Temps* publishes an article by François Thiébault-Sisson on the **14th;** the piece by Arsène Alexandre does not appear in *Le Figaro* until the **21st**.
27 November: second visit from Kuroki in presence of Clemenceau.

1921
21 January–2 February: Monet retrospective at the Galerie Bernheim-Jeune.
June: visit from Mrs. Kuroki, a great Japanese friend, and Clemenceau **(cat. no. 47)**.
December: Bonnier is removed from the project, and replaced by a new architect, Camille Lefèvre.

1922
Gustave Geffroy publishes the book *Claude Monet: sa vie, son temps, son œuvre* with G. Grès, which brings together his memoirs and includes an anthology of critical writings. He devotes a chapter to Monet's garden : "À Giverny - Une autre œuvre de Monet: sa maison et son jardin".
12 April: signature of the official certificate of donation for the *Grand Decorations*.
May: Monet's eyesight worsens.

1923
On **10 January**: the cataract operation is carried out at the Ambroise Paré clinic in Neuilly **(cat. no. 53)**.
February: Muriel Ciolkowska publishes in *International Studio* an article illustrated by photographs taken by Harry B. Lachman in Monet's studio in early July of the previous year, in which can be seen Marguerite Namara, Monet, Blanche Hoschedé, Theodore and Alice Butler, Marthe Hoschedé, and Lachman.
18 and 26 April: letters from Moser & fils to Monet announce the arrival of a nursery representative in Giverny, and the preparation of an order for the **autumn**.

1924
Marc Elder publishes *À Giverny, chez Claude Monet* with Bernheim-Jeune.
"-Where, my dear master, did you get this liking for water lilies?
- There was a stream, the Epte, flowing from Gisors, bordering my property. I had a trench dug to fill a small pond dug out in my garden. I love water, but I also love flowers. That is why, once the pond had been filled, I dreamed of garnishing it with plants. I took a catalogue, made a choice in a haphazard fashion, and that's all.
in Robert Gordon and Andrew Forge, *Monet*. New York: Harry N. Abrams, 1983, p. 208.
-I thrice changed and thrice enlarged my ponds by diverting the Epte... My garden is a slow work, pursued with much love...
[...]
-It has taken me some time to understand my water lilies, said Claude Monet. I planted them for the pleasure; I grew them with no thought of ever painting them... No landscape can imbue you in just one

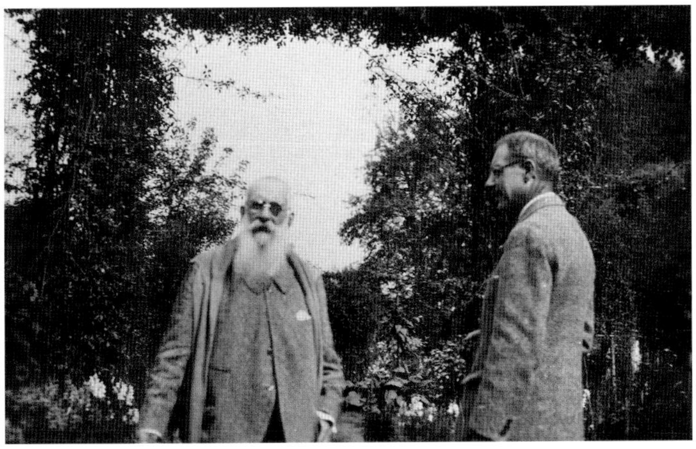

16 | Reine Natanson, *Pierre Bonnard and Claude Monet in Giverny*, 1926
Private collection

day... And then, all of a sudden, I had the revelation about the spells cast by my pond. I took up my palette... And since then I've hardly ever used any other model."
17 February: visit from Jeanne Baudot and Maurice Denis.
Early September: visit from Jean Ajalbert, winner of the Prix Goncourt, and his wife.
9 or 10 October: at the request of Joseph Durand-Ruel, Monet receives a visit from the art critic Henri Saulnier-Ciolkowski, with his young wife, the journalist Edward Verrall Lucas and a photographer.
15 October–7 November: exhibition of a small number of paintings by Claude Monet at the Galerie Paul Rosenberg.
November: Truffaut publishes in the magazine *Jardinage* a report on Claude Monet's gardens, which "include three groups: the Clos Normand, the water garden, and the vegetable garden". Truffaut concludes: "Claude Monet's finest work is, in my opinion, his garden". **(fig. 15, fig. 3 p. 42, fig. 6 p. 44 and cat. no 87)**

1925
First half of the year: Visit from Florent Fels with Maurice de Vlaminck.
7 May: death of Marthe Hoschedé-Butler.
7 September visit from Paul Valéry on holiday at Le Mesnil where he is staying with Henri Rouart and Julie Manet:
"He shows [us] his latest canvases. Strange clumps of pinks caught beneath a blue sky. A dark house... We go to the studio with the water lilies on the water. Vast pure poetry."
Late October–early November: visit from Étienne Moreau-Nélaton accompanied by Helleu and his daughter Paulette [Paulette Howard-Johnston].

1926
14 June: wedding of Alice Suzanne Marie Butler and Roger Louis Ferdinand Toulgouat.
30 June: visit from Ker Xavier Roussel and Vuillard, with his daughter Annette and her husband Jacques Salomon **(cat. no. 57)**.
Late June: study of the water garden by the photographer Nickolas Muray **(cat. no. 58)**.
25 October: wedding of Alice Hoschedé's granddaughter, Simone Salerou, and Robert Piguet **(cat. no. 84)**.
Ca. 20 November (?): visit from Bonnard, Thadée Natanson and his wife **(cat. no. 56 and fig. 16)**.
21 November: Clemenceau lunches with Monet, as reported by Thiébault-Sisson in an article published in *Le Temps on* **8 January 1927:**
"He had told me that he had just received an entire stock of lily bulbs from Japan, the flower he loved best of all, and that he was waiting for two or three cases of very expensive seeds that would produce beautifully colored blossoms. 'You will see all of this in the spring," he told me, "I will no longer be here'."
François Thiébault-Sisson, "About Claude Monet", *Le Temps*, January 8, 1927, reprinted and translated in Charles F. Stuckey, *Monet. A Retrospective*. New York: Hugh Lauter Levin Associates, Inc., 1985, p. 349.
5 December: Monet dies at his property in Giverny at the age of 86. Clemenceau is with him.
8 December: the burial takes place in Giverny cemetery in the presence of a few close relatives and friends, including Clemenceau, Blanche Hoschedé-Monet, Jean-Pierre Hoschedé, K. X. Roussel, Georges Durand-Ruel, Pierre Durand-Ruel, Theodore Earl Butler, James Butler, Joseph and Gaston Bernheim-Jeune, and Thadée Natanson.
21 December: Paul Léon, Messrs. Guiffrey and Masson, curators at the National Museums, and Camille Lefèvre visit Michel Monet. Arrangements are drawn up for the transfer of the *Grand Decorations*.

1927
January and February: the Duke of Trévise, who went to Giverny on **14 November** 1920, publishes in *La Revue de l'Art ancien et moderne*, two detailed reports titled "Le pèlerinage de Giverny", illustrated with photographs by Pierre Choumoff **(cat. no. 35)**.
16 May: inauguration of the *Water Lilies* at the Orangerie, in the presence of Clemenceau, Paul Léon and Michel Monet **(fig. 7 p. 74)**, prior to the official inauguration on **17 May** in the presence of Édouard Herriot, Minister of Public Education and Fine Arts, and the opening to the public on **20 May**.

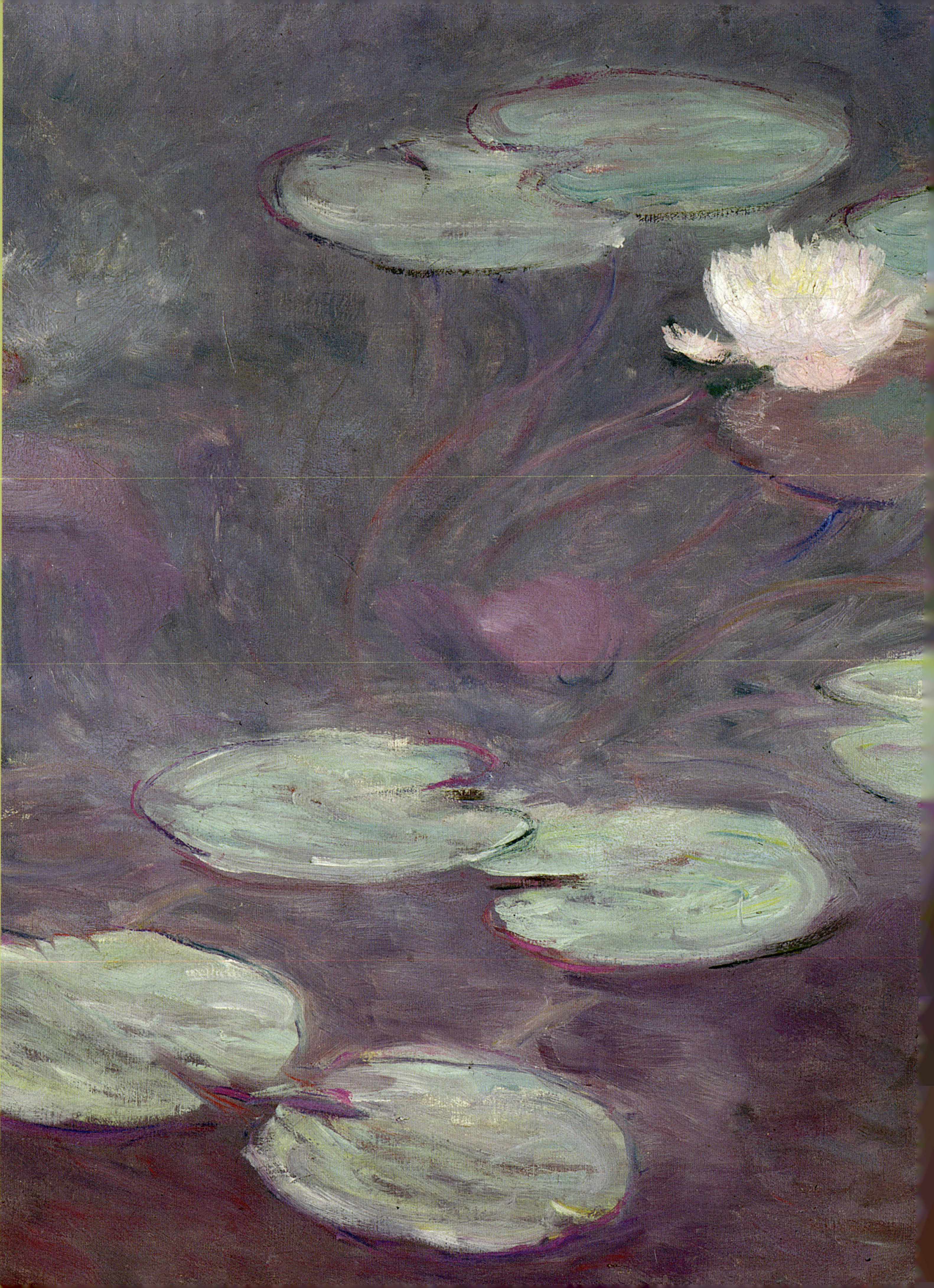

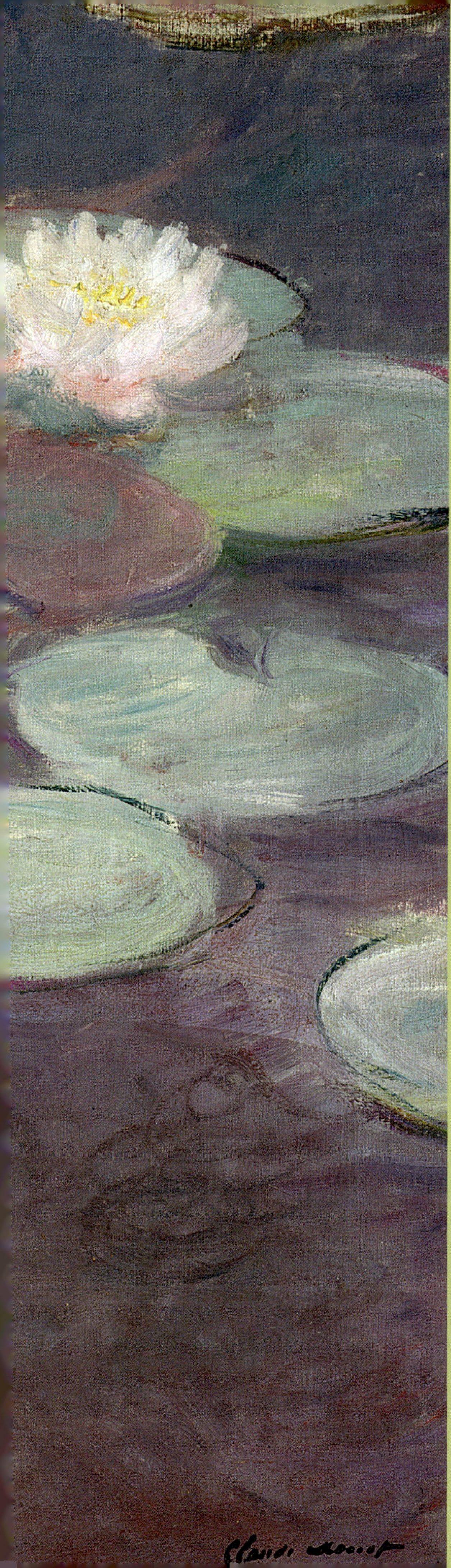

Catalogue

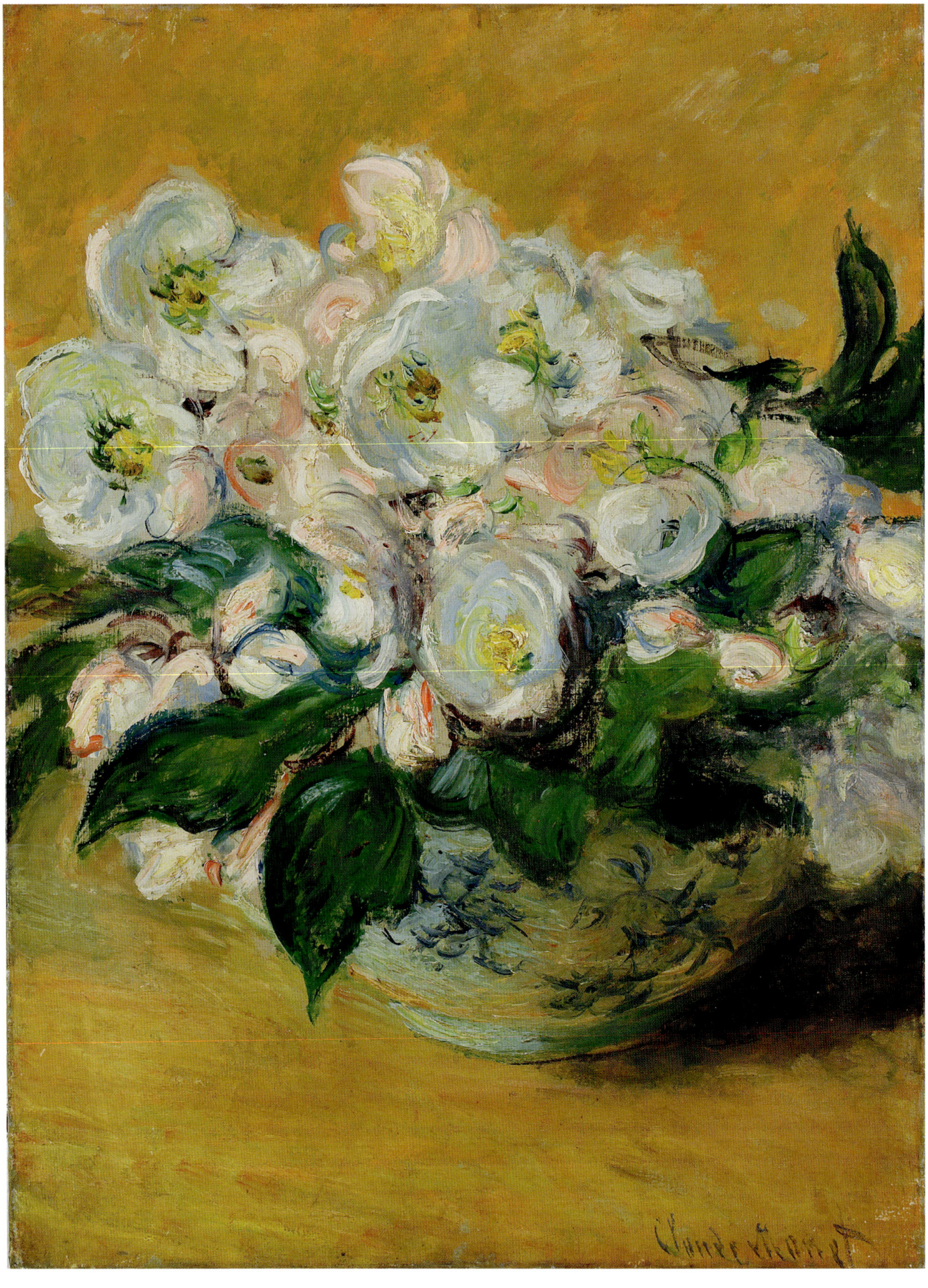

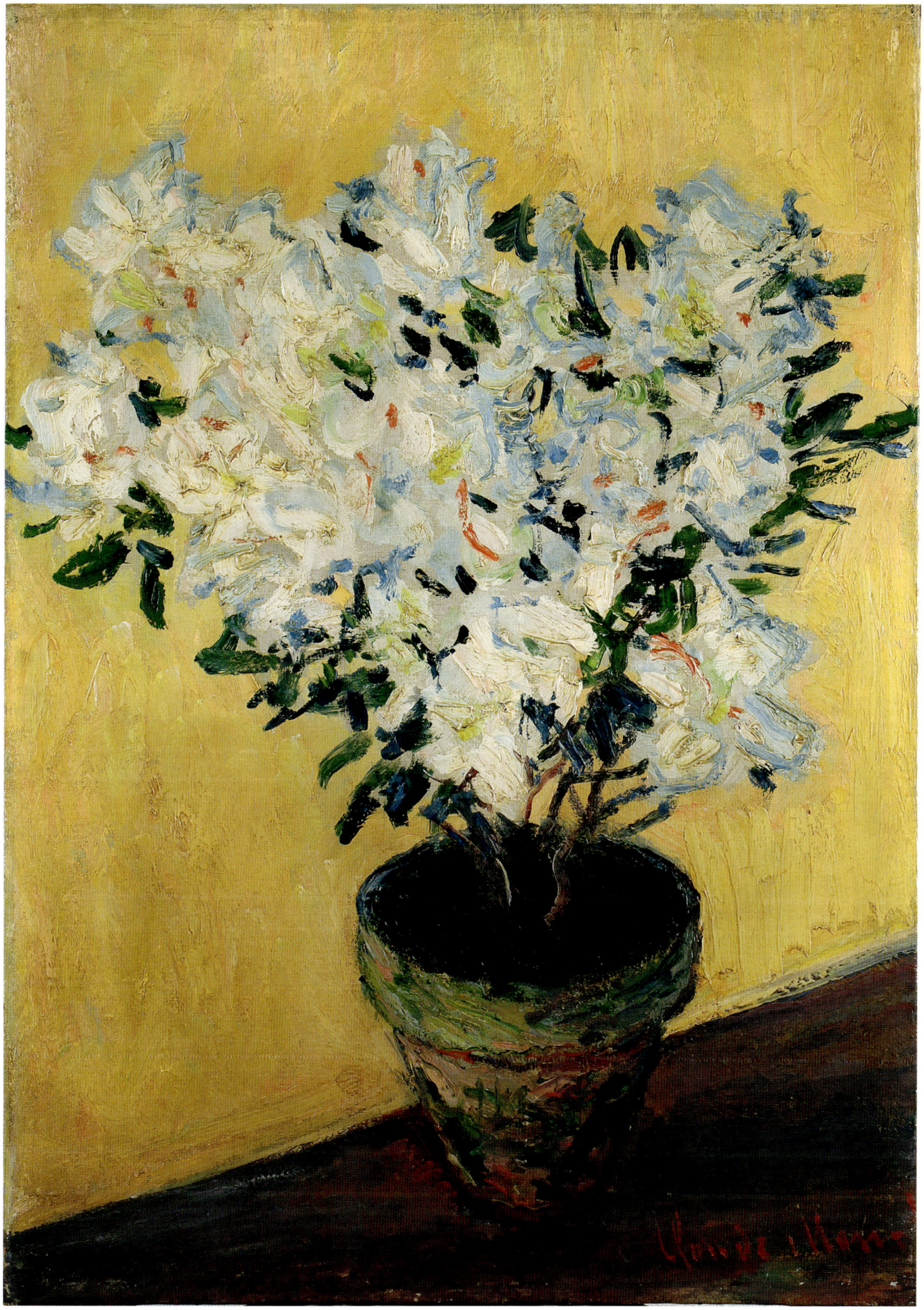

1 | *Christmas Roses*, 1883
Oil on canvas, 50.5 × 37 cm (19⅞ × 14$^{9}/_{16}$ in.)
Private collection (Ph 101717)

2 | *Pot of White Azaleas*, 1885
Oil on canvas, 50.5 × 37 cm (19⅞ × 14$^{9}/_{16}$ in.)
Private collection

3 | *A Palm Tree at Bordighera*, 1884
Oil on canvas, 61.3 × 74 cm
(24⅛ × 29⅛ in.)
Private collection

4 | *Under the Lemon Trees*, 1884
Oil on canvas, 73.5 × 60.5 cm
(28$^{15}/_{16}$ × 23$^{13}/_{16}$ in.)
Ny Carlsberg Glyptotek, Copenhagen

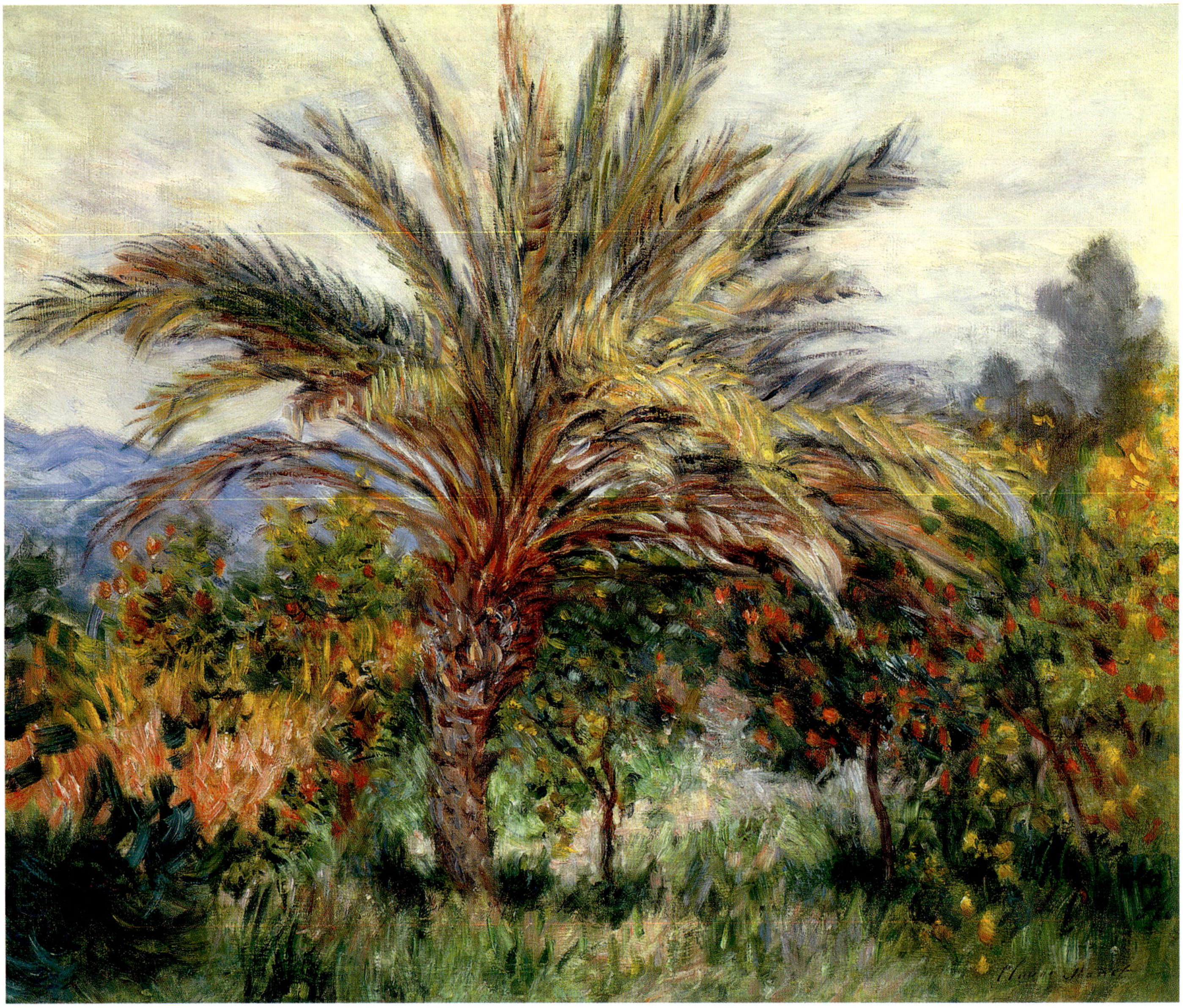

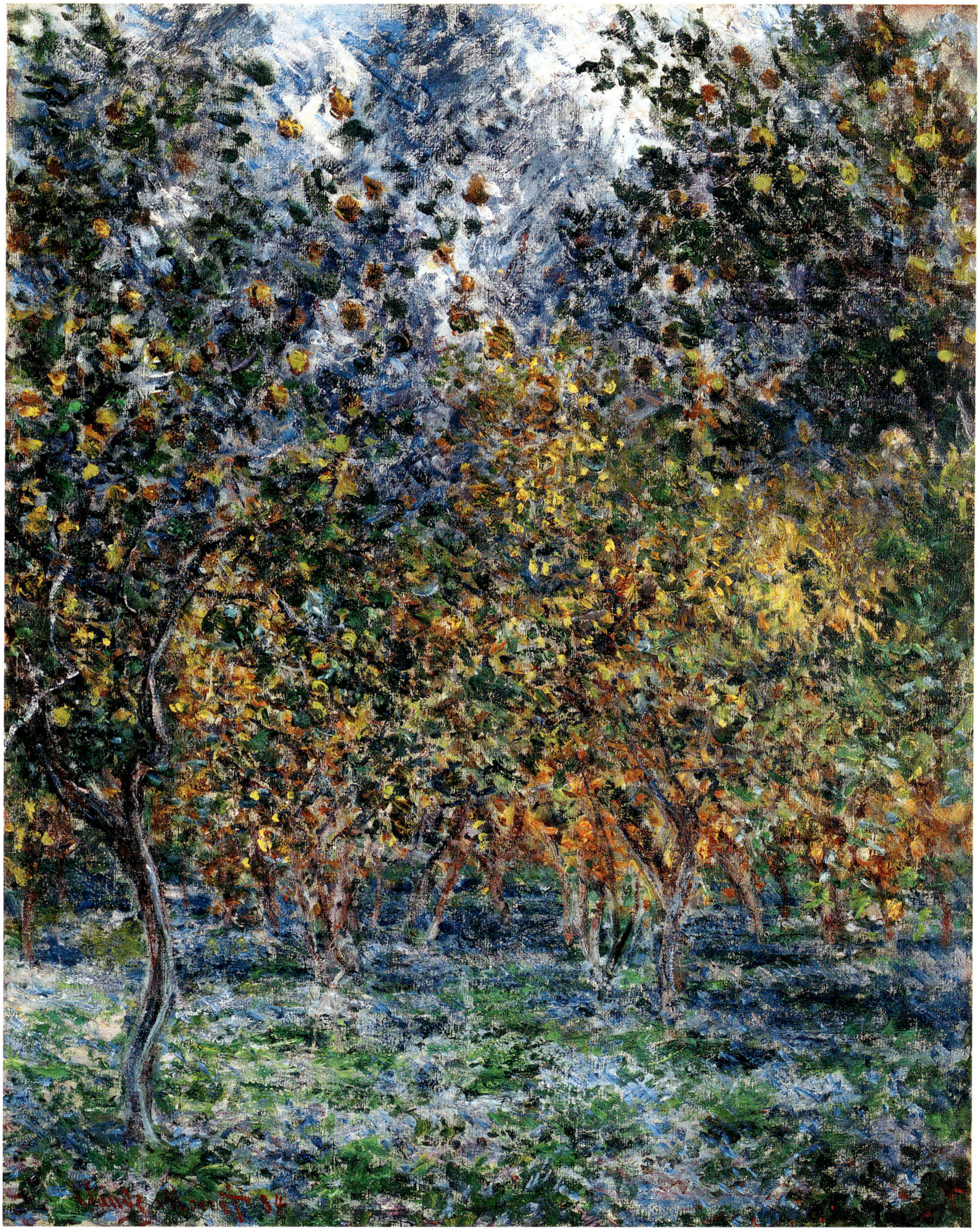

5| *A Field of Tulips in Holland*, 1886
Oil on canvas, 65 × 81,5 cm (25½ × 32 in.)
Musée d'Orsay, Paris

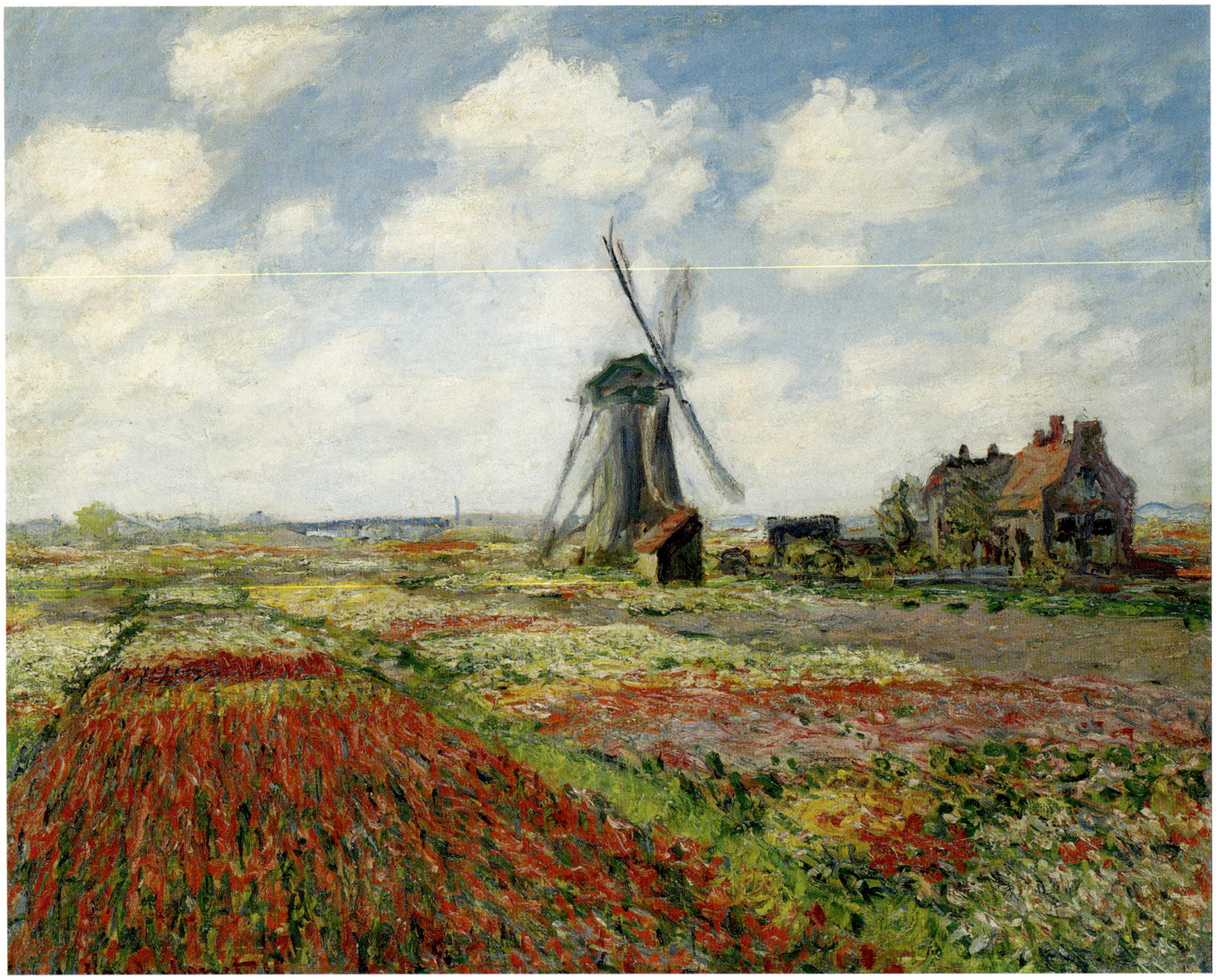

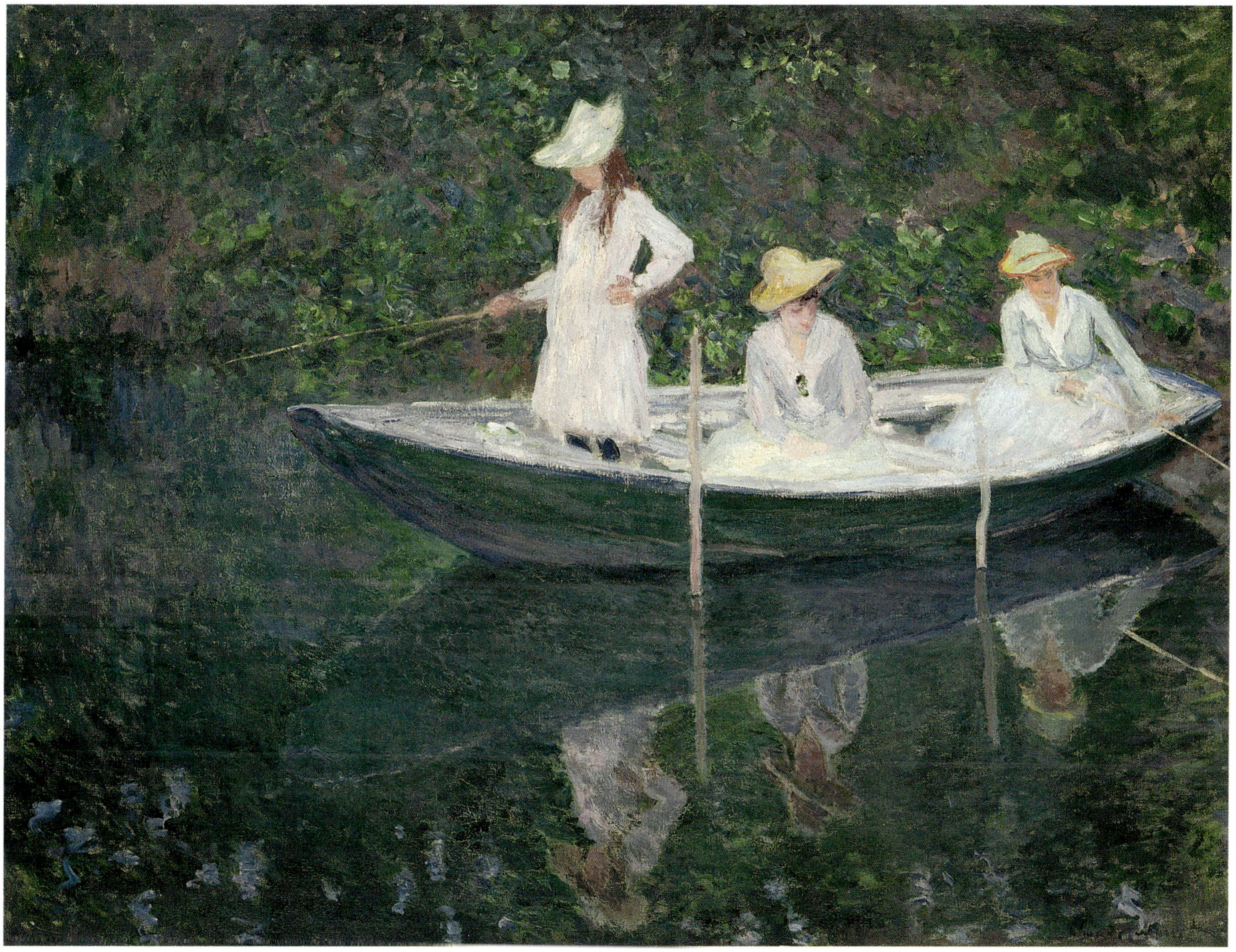

6| *In the 'Norvégienne'*,
or *The Boat at Giverny*, ca. 1887
Oil on canvas, 98 × 131 cm (38⅝ × 51$^{9}/_{16}$ in.)
Musée d'Orsay, Paris

7 | *Poplars on the Banks of the River Epte*, 1891
Oil on canvas, 81 × 92 cm (31 7/8 × 36 1/4 in.)
Private collection. Courtesy Galerie Bernheim-Jeune, Paris

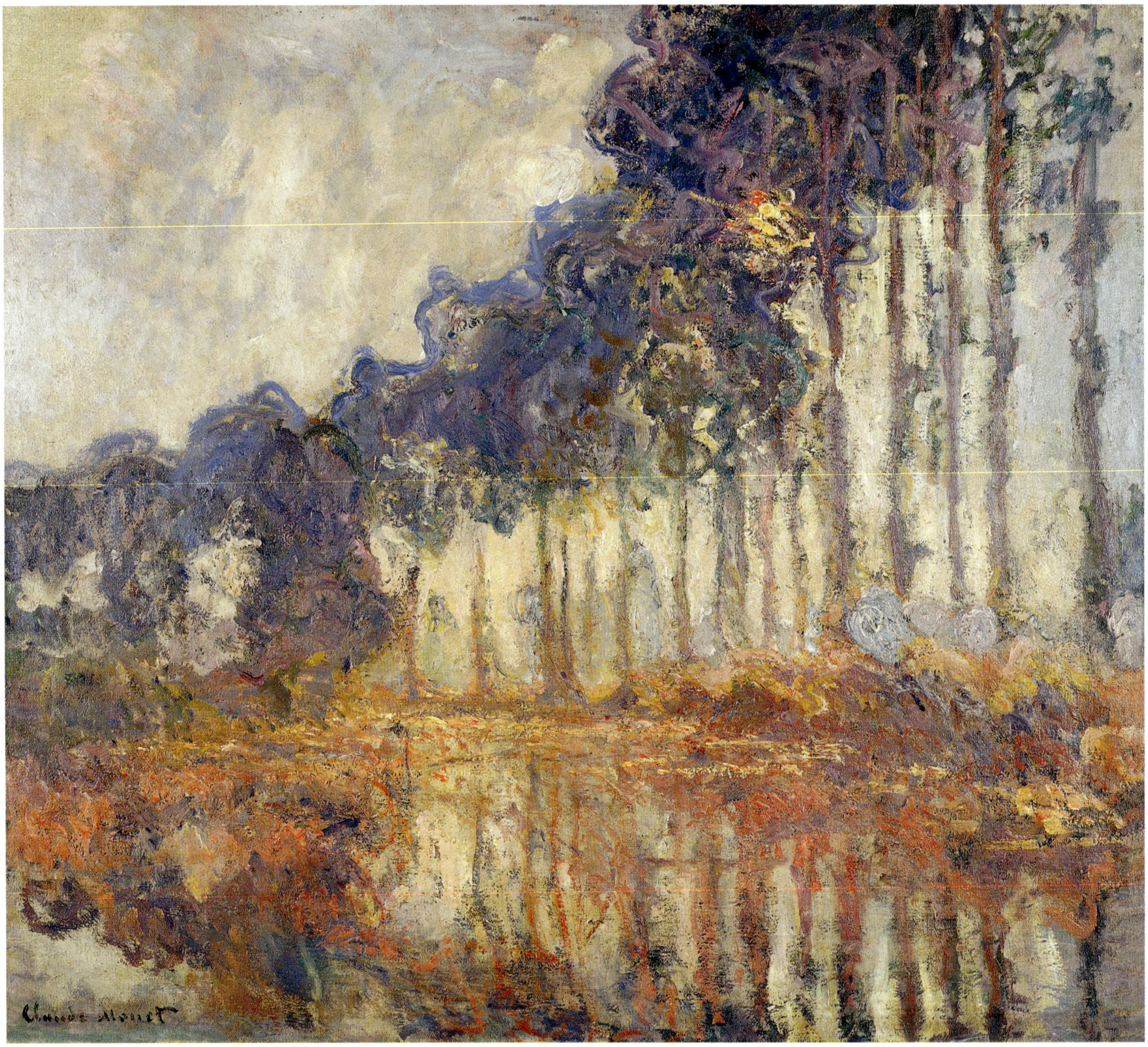

8 | *Morning on the Seine, near Giverny*, 1896
Oil on canvas, 89.3 × 91.8 cm
(35⅛ × 36⅛ in.)
Private collection, United Kingdom

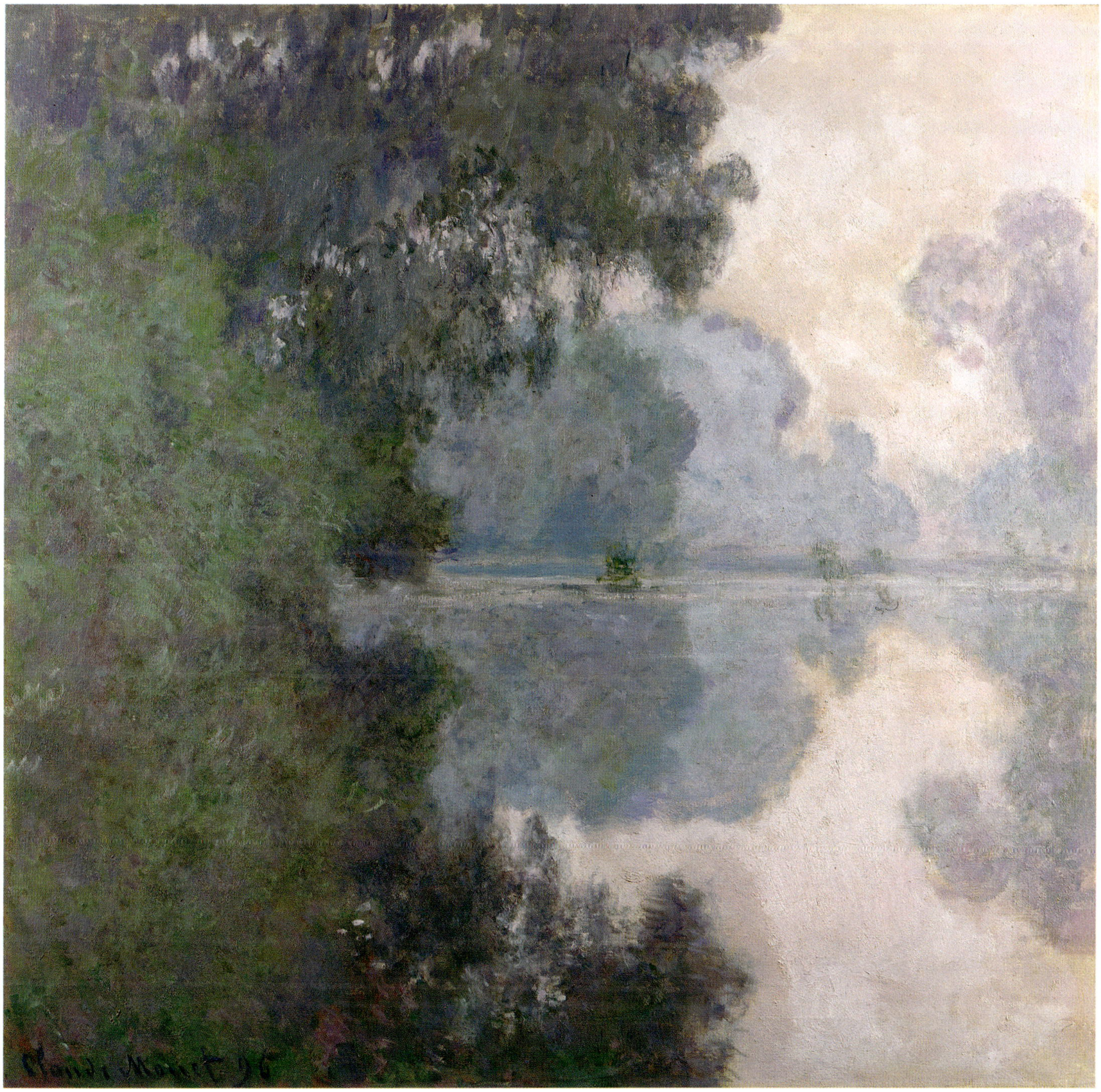

9 | *Peonies*, 1887
Oil on canvas, 73 × 100 cm
(28 3/4 × 39 3/8 in.)
Musées d'Art et d'Histoire, Geneva, long term loan from the Fondation Jean-Louis Prevost (1985-29)

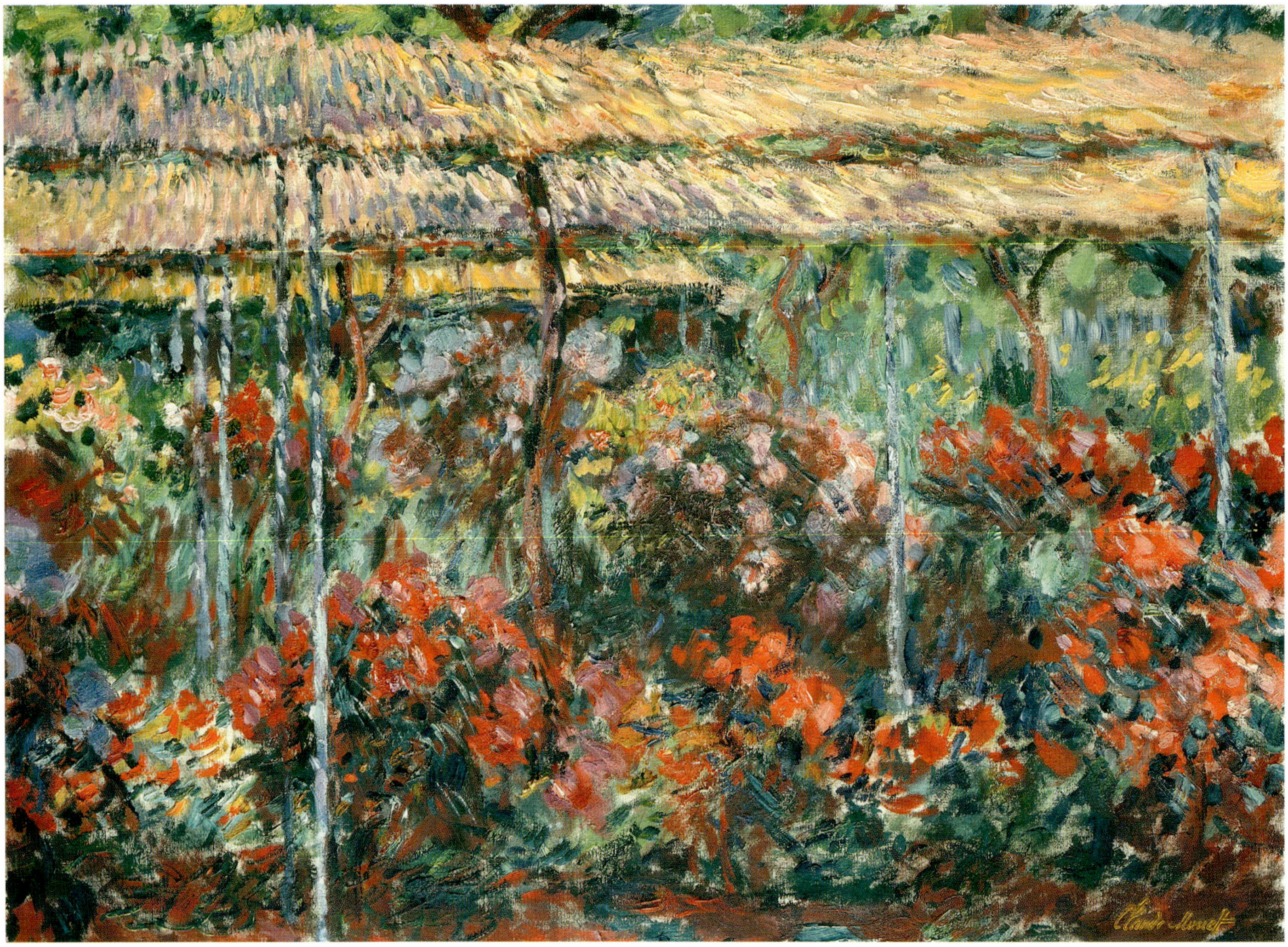

10 | *Monet's Garden at Giverny*, 1895
Oil on canvas, 81.5 × 92 cm (32 1/8 × 36 1/4 in.)
Fondation E. G. Bührle, Zurich

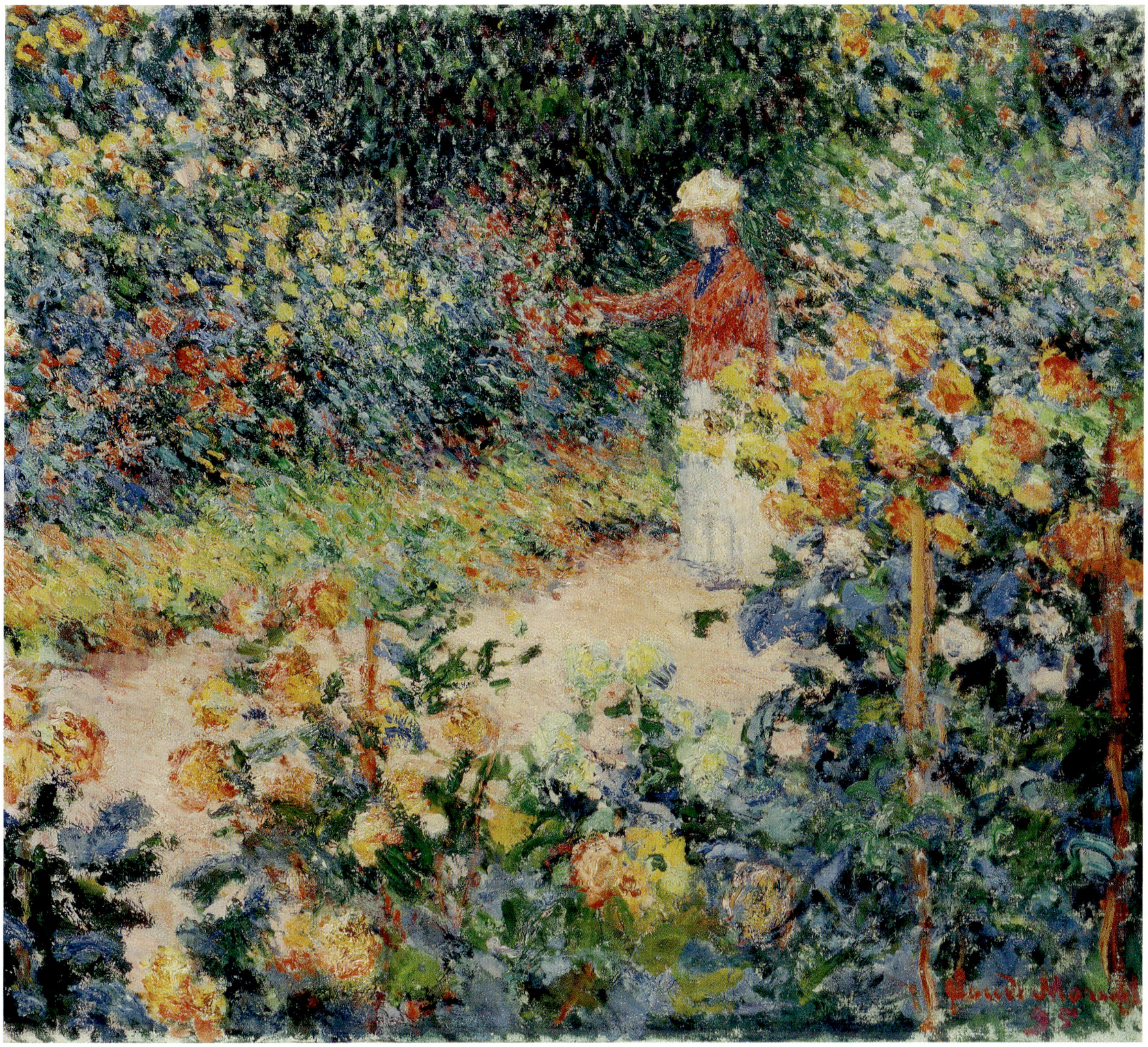

11 | *Pink Water Lilies*, 1897–99
Oil on canvas, 81 × 100 cm (31 7/8 × 39 3/8 in.)
Galleria Nazionale d'Arte Moderna, Rome

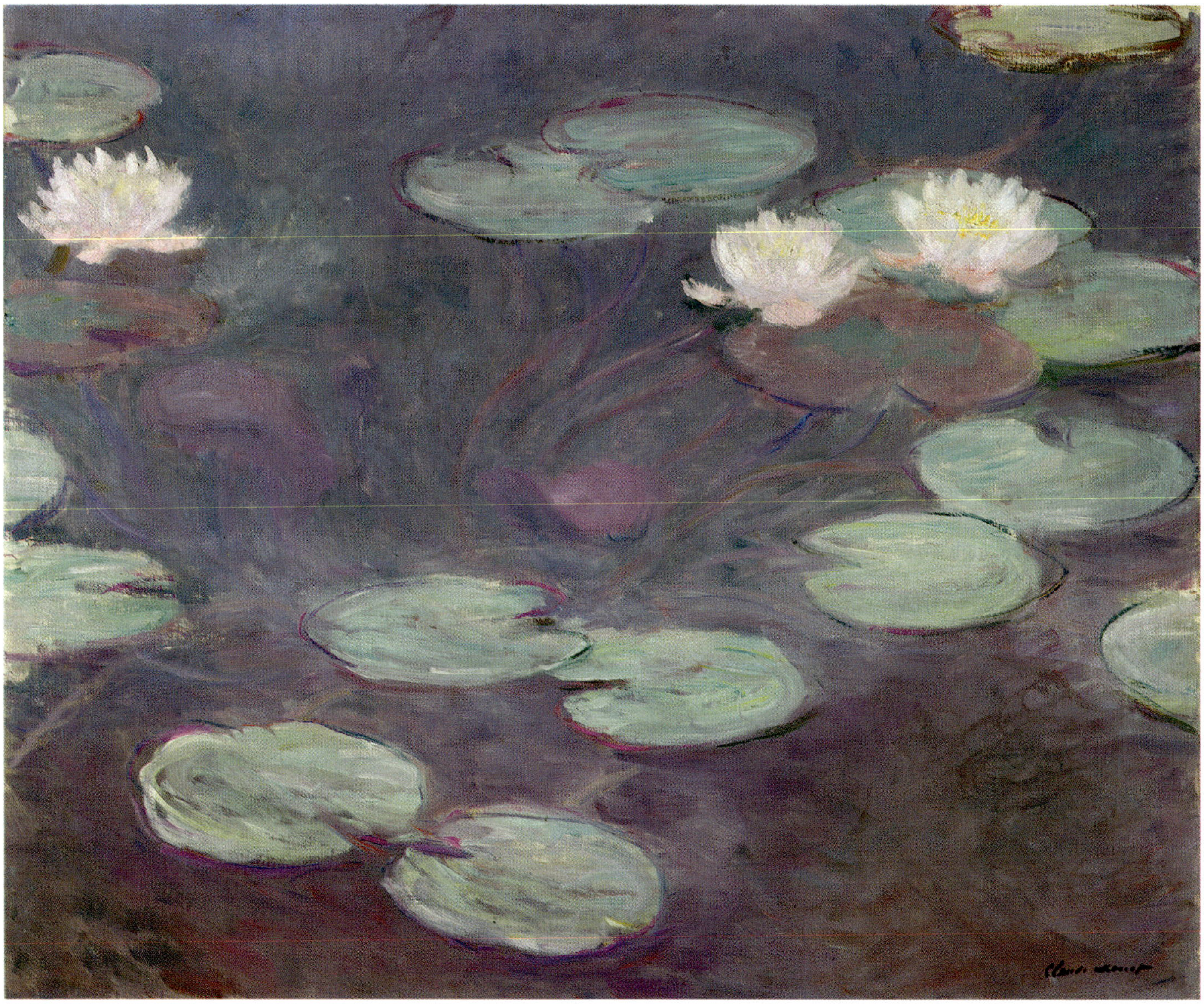

12 | *Water Lily Pond, Symphony in Green*, 1899
Oil on canvas, 89 × 93.5 cm
(35 × 36 13/16 in.)
Musée d'Orsay, Paris

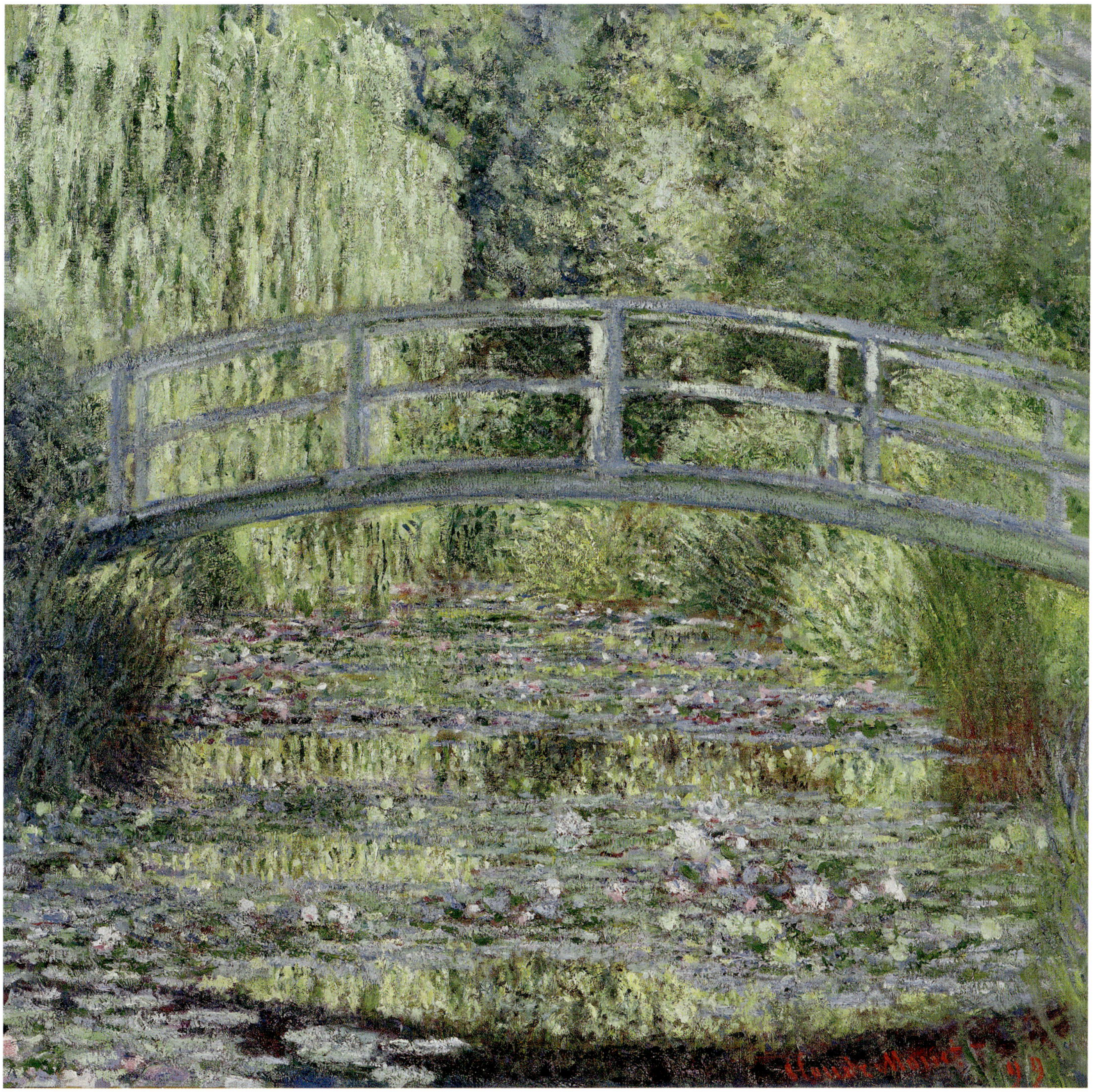

13 | *The Artist's Garden at Giverny*,
or *Irises in Monet's Garden*, 1900
Oil on canvas, 81 × 92 cm (31⅞ × 36¼ in.)
Musée d'Orsay, Paris

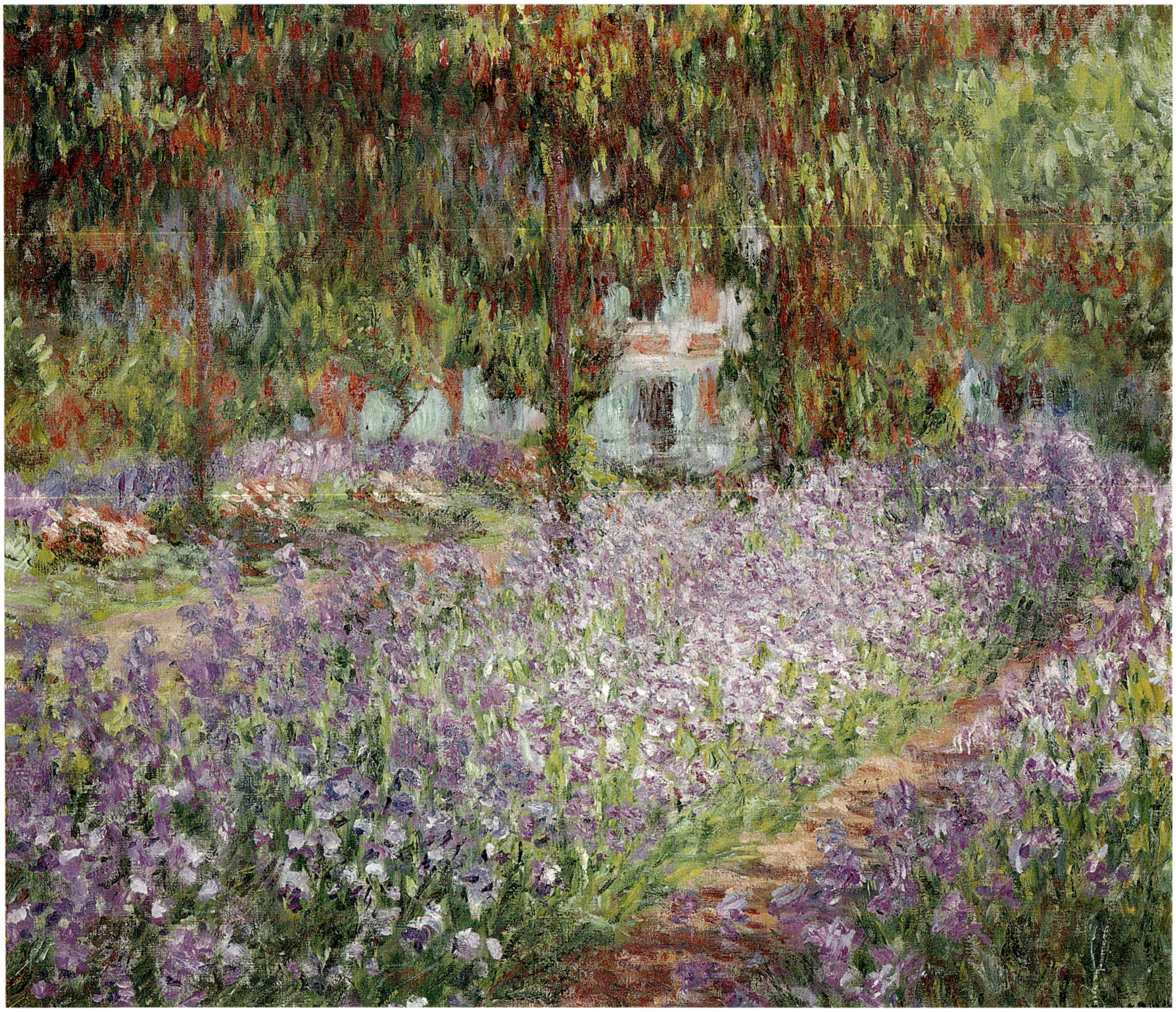

14 | *Water Lily Pond, Simphony in Rose*, 1900
Oil on canvas, 89.5 × 100 cm (35¼ × 39⅜ in.)
Musée d'Orsay, Paris

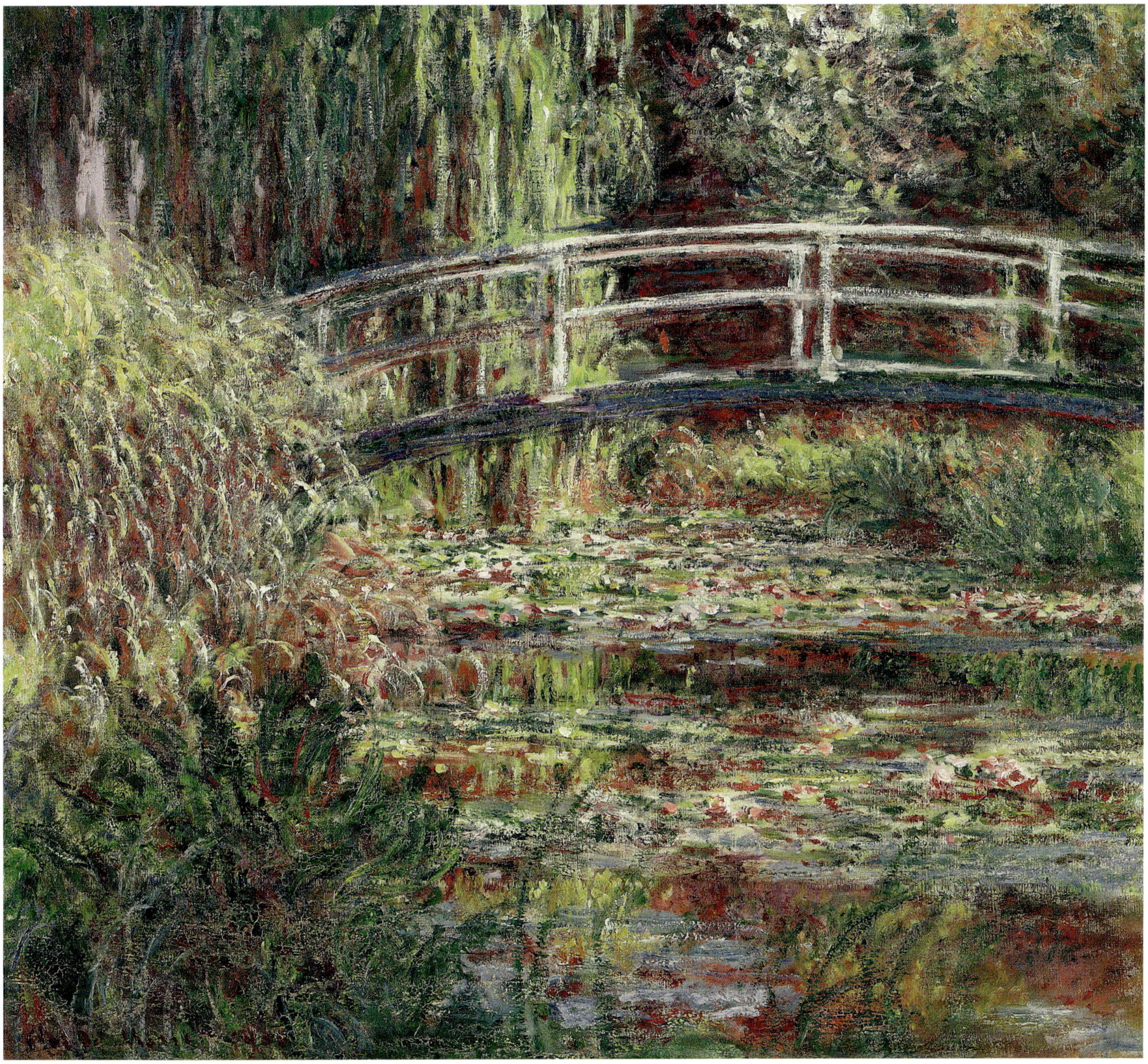

15 | *Water Lilies*, 1904
Oil on canvas, 87 × 93 cm (34¼ × 36⅝ in.)
Musée Malraux, Ville du Havre

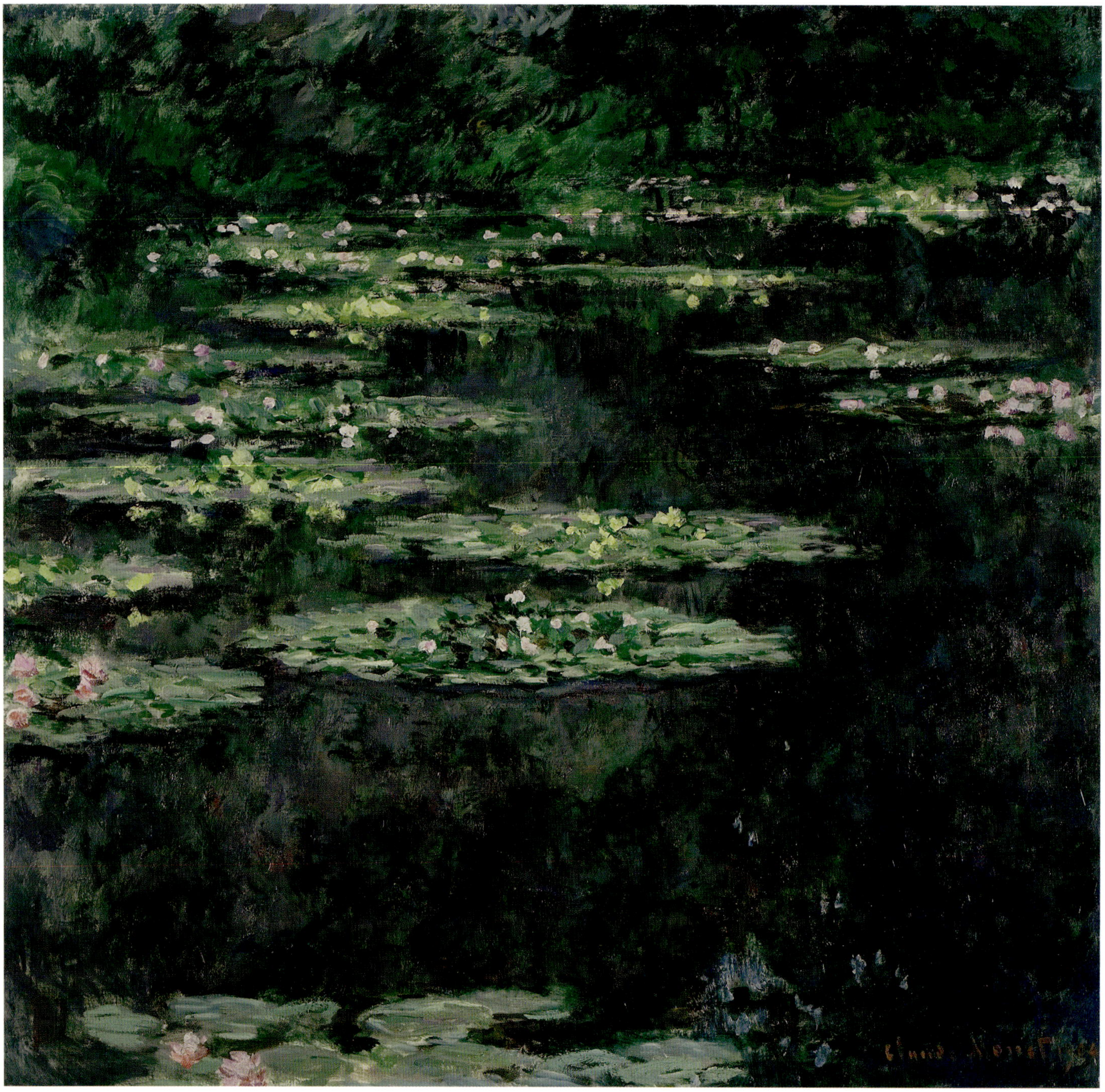

16 | *Water Lilies*, 1908
Oil on canvas, diam.: 81 cm ($31\frac{7}{8}$ in.)
Musée Municipal A.-G. Poulain, Vernon

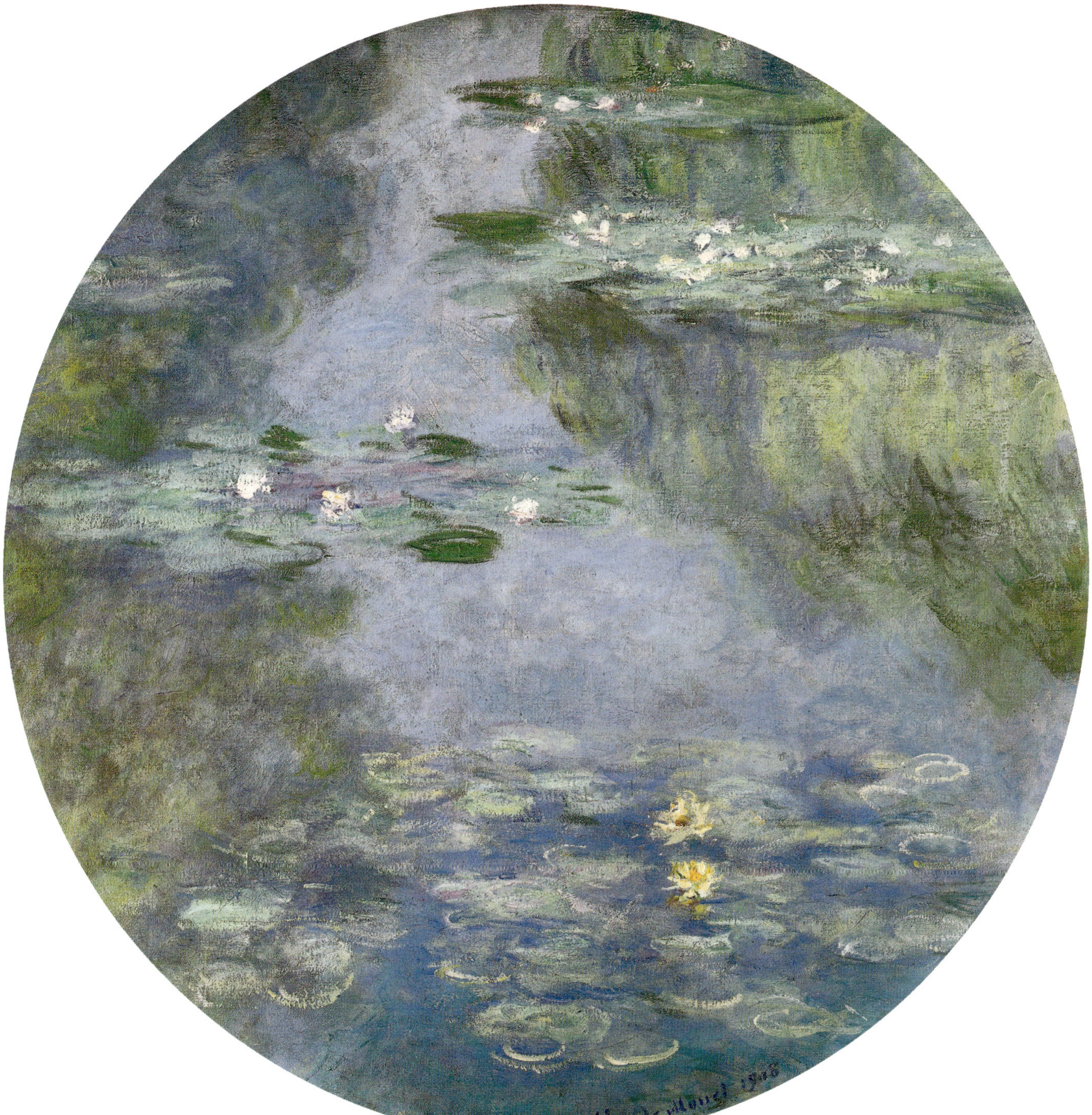

17 | *Water Lilies*, 1914–17
Oil on canvas, 150 × 200 cm
($59^{1}/_{16} \times 78^{3}/_{4}$ in.)
Galerie Beyeler, Basel

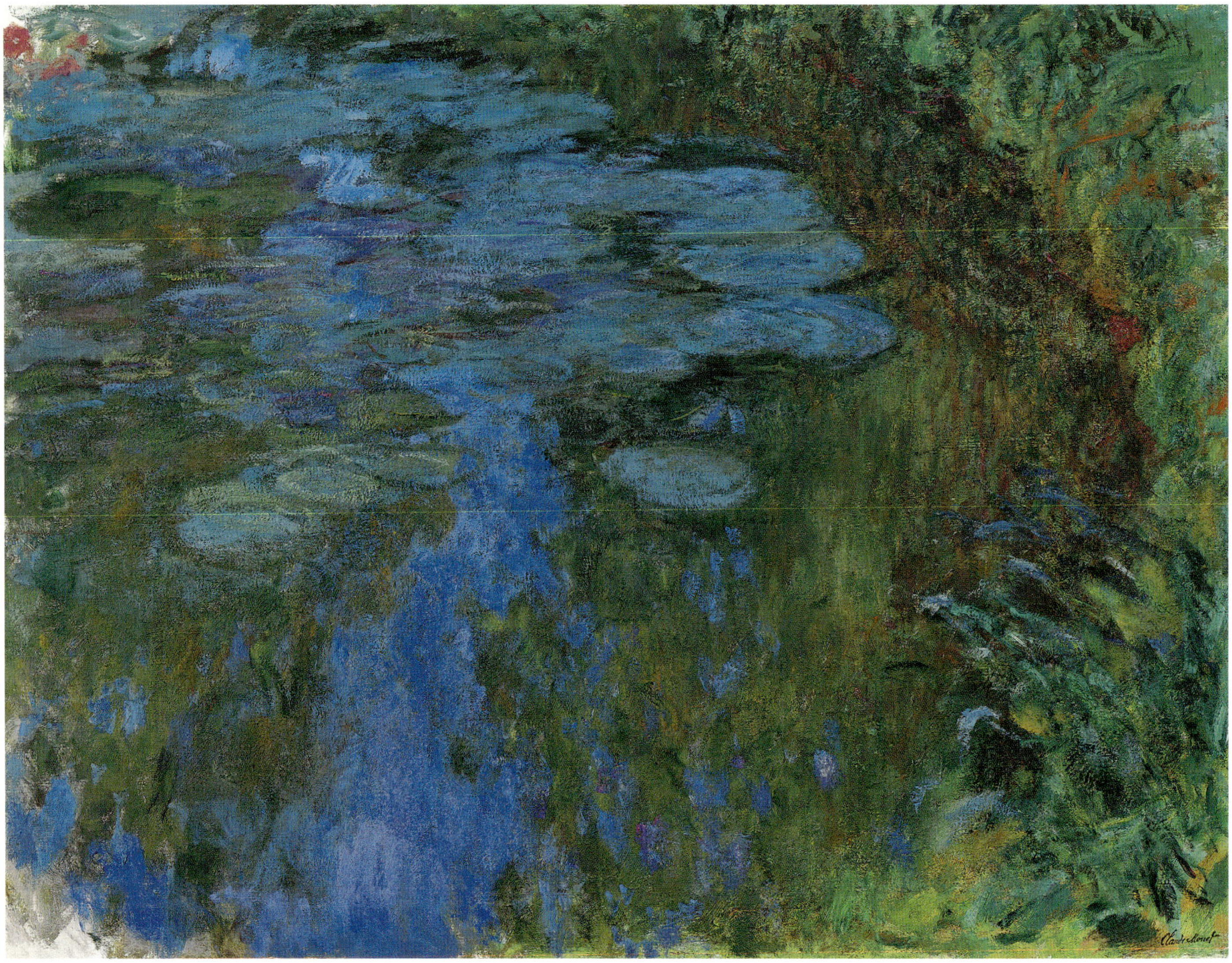

18 | *Water Lilies*, ca. 1914–17
Oil on canvas, 135 × 145 cm
(53 3/16 × 57 1/8 in.)
Private collection

→
19 | *Water Lilies and Agapanthus*, ca. 1914–17
Oil on canvas, 140 × 120 cm (55 1/8 × 47 1/4 in.)
Musée Marmottan Monet, Paris

20 | *Hemerocallis*, ca. 1914–17
Oil on canvas, 150 × 140 cm (59 1/16 × 55 1/8 in.)
Musée Marmottan Monet, Paris

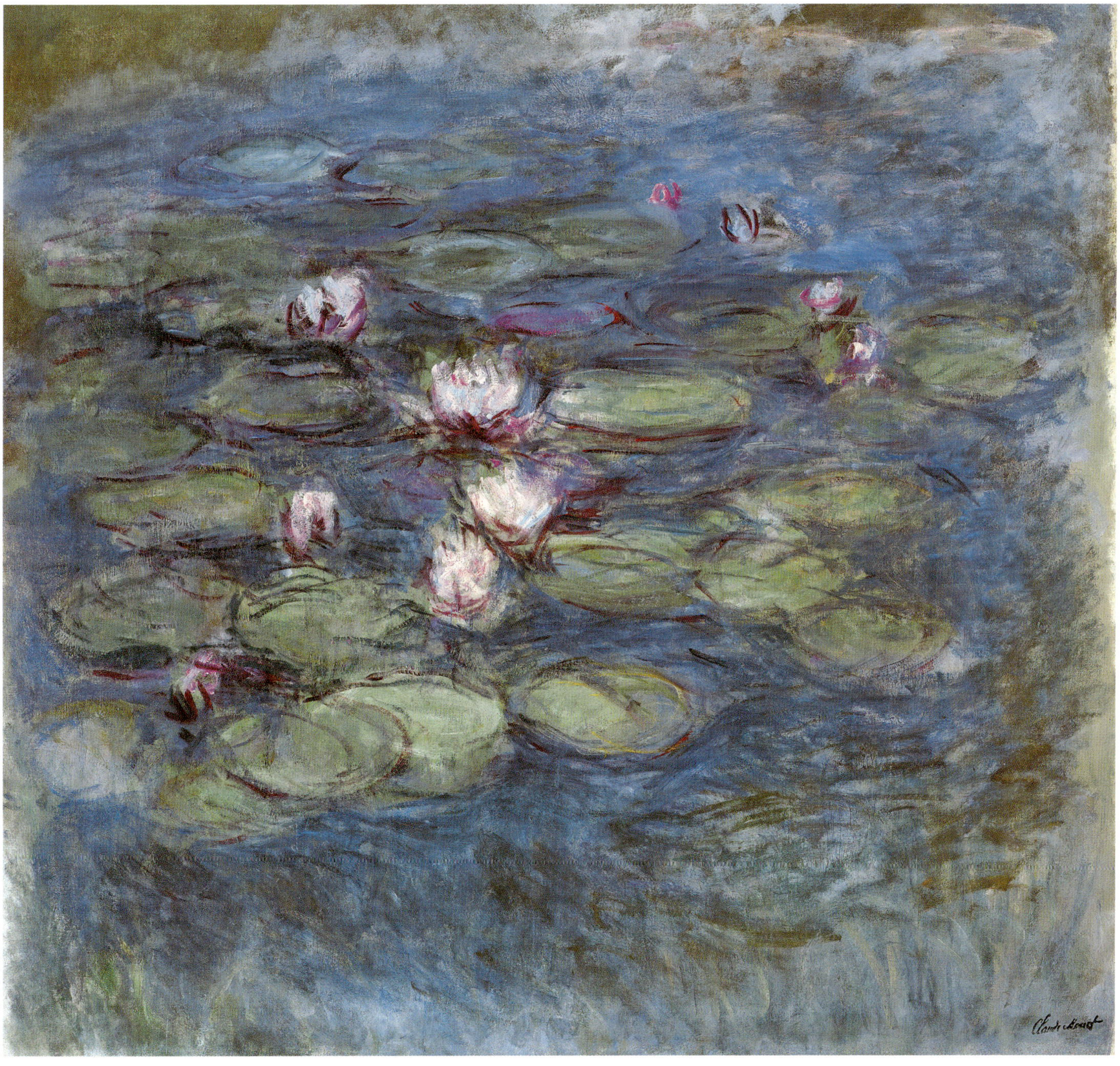

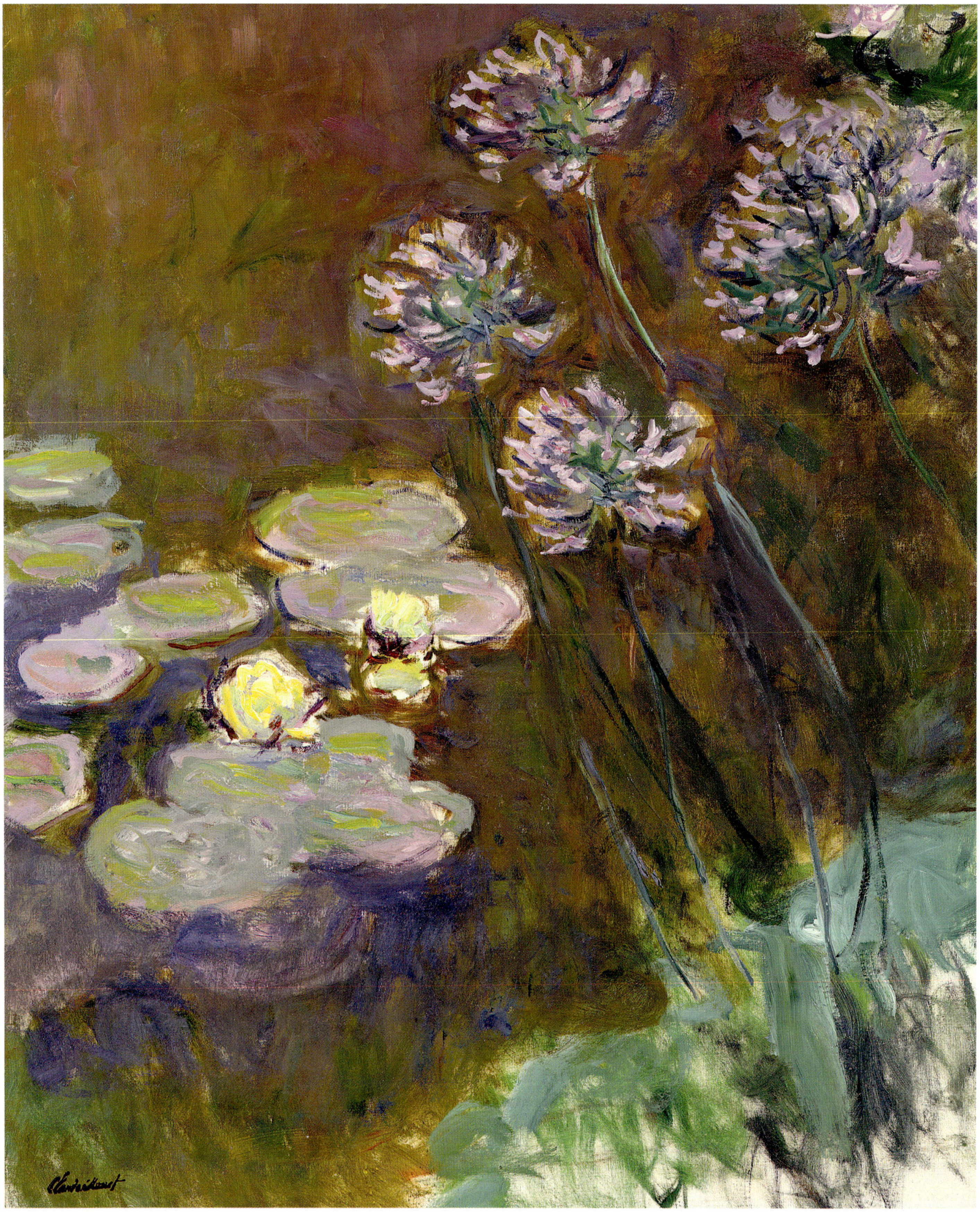

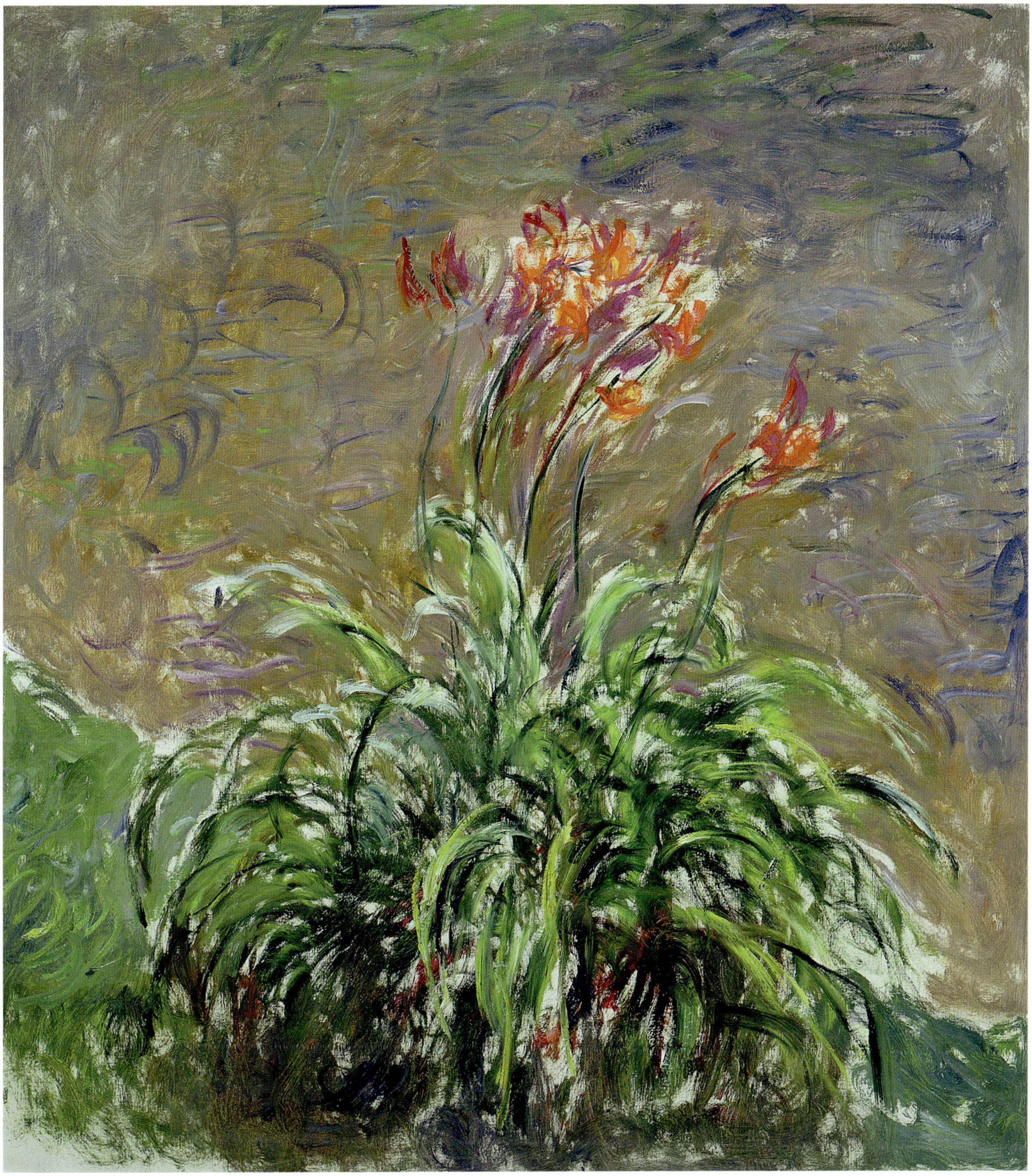

21 | *Water Lilies with Weeping Willow Branches*, ca. 1916–19
Oil on canvas, 160 × 180 cm (63 × 70⅞ in.)
Lycée Claude Monet, Paris

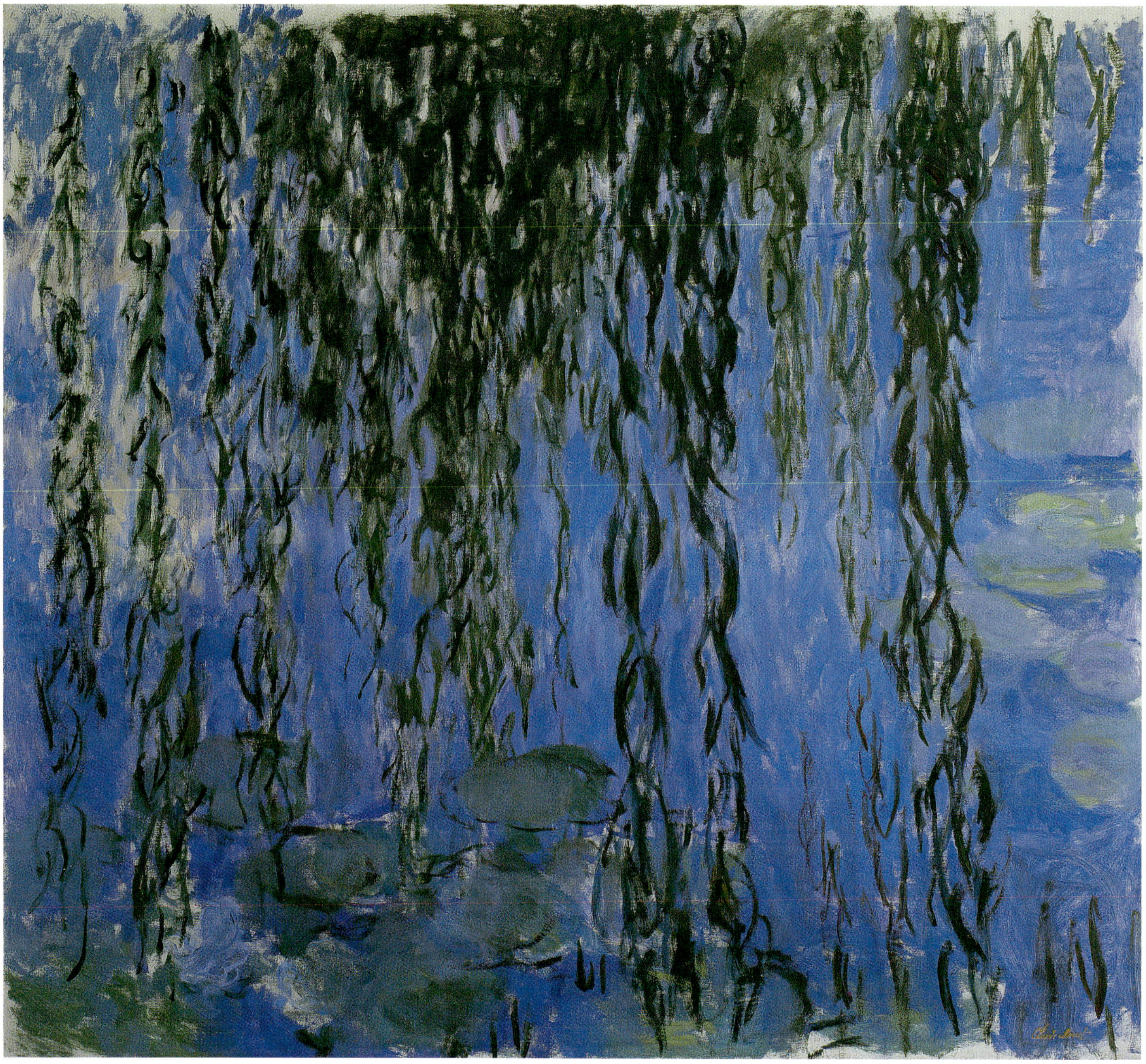

22 | *Blue Water Lilies*, ca. 1916–19
Oil on canvas, 200 × 200 cm (78 3/4 × 78 3/4 in.)
Musée d'Orsay, Paris

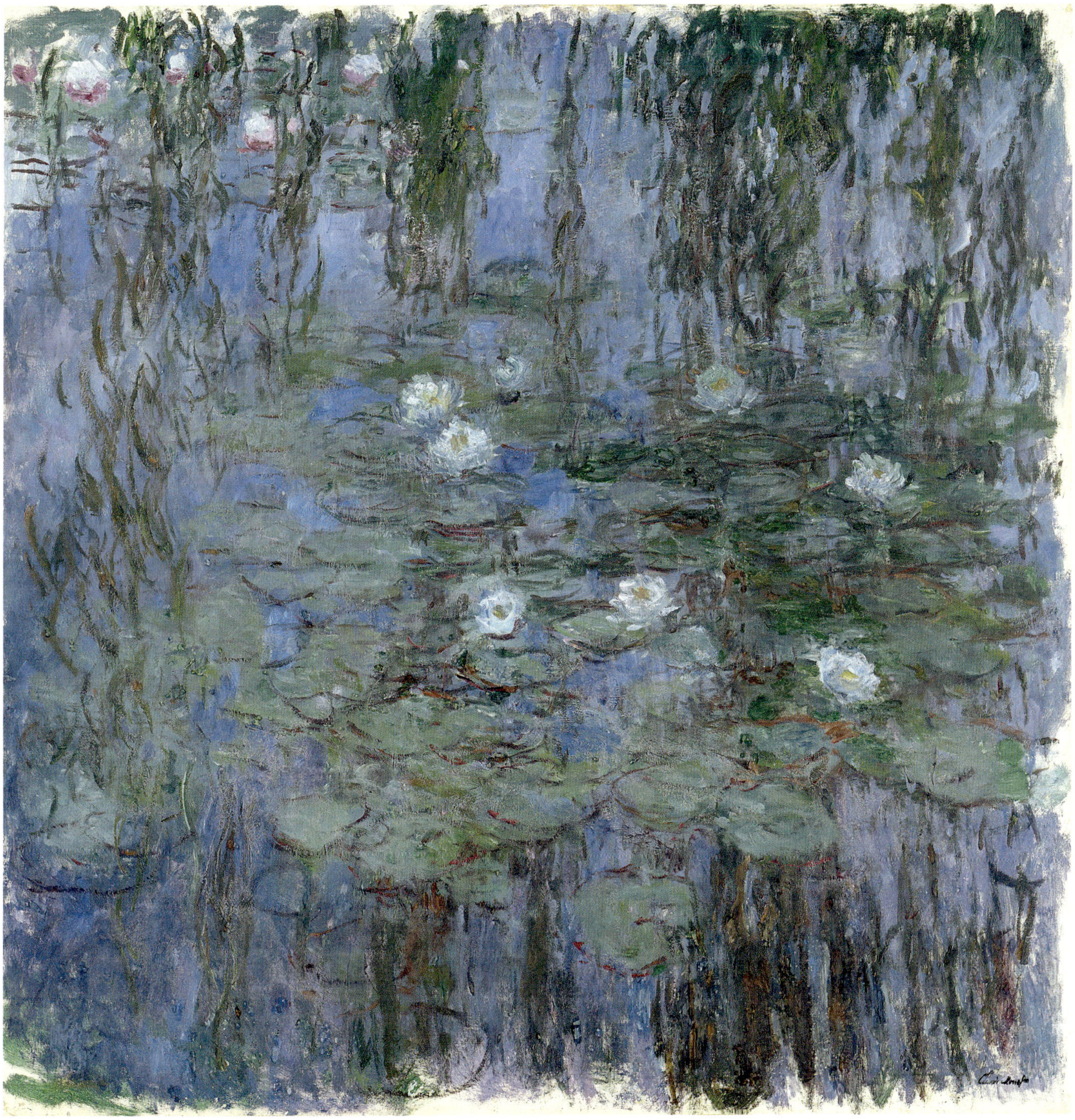

23 | *Wisteria*, 1919–20
Oil on canvas, 100 × 200 cm (39 3/8 × 78 3/4 in.)
Musée d'Art et d'Histoire Marcel Dessal, Dreux

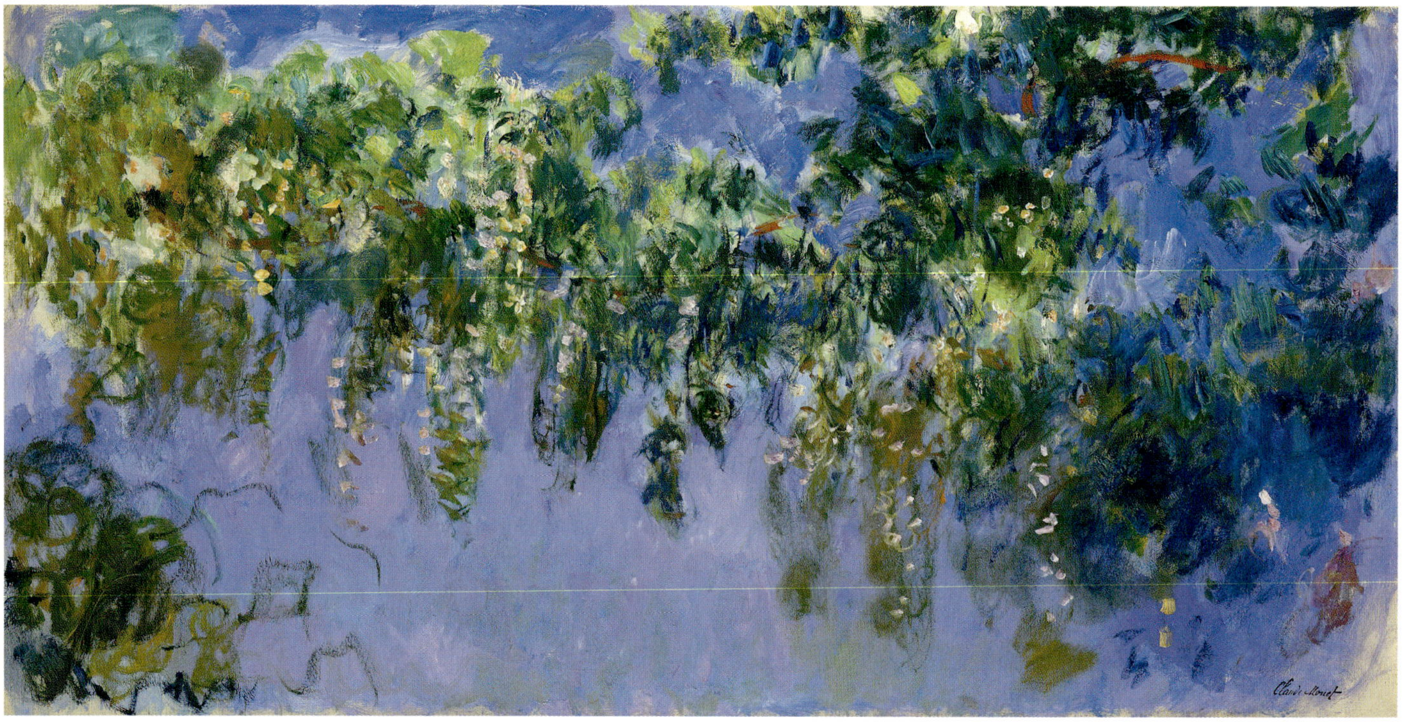

24 | *The Japanese Bridge*, ca. 1918–24
Oil on canvas, 89 × 115.5 cm
(35 1/16 × 45 7/16 in.)
Fondation Beyeler, Basel

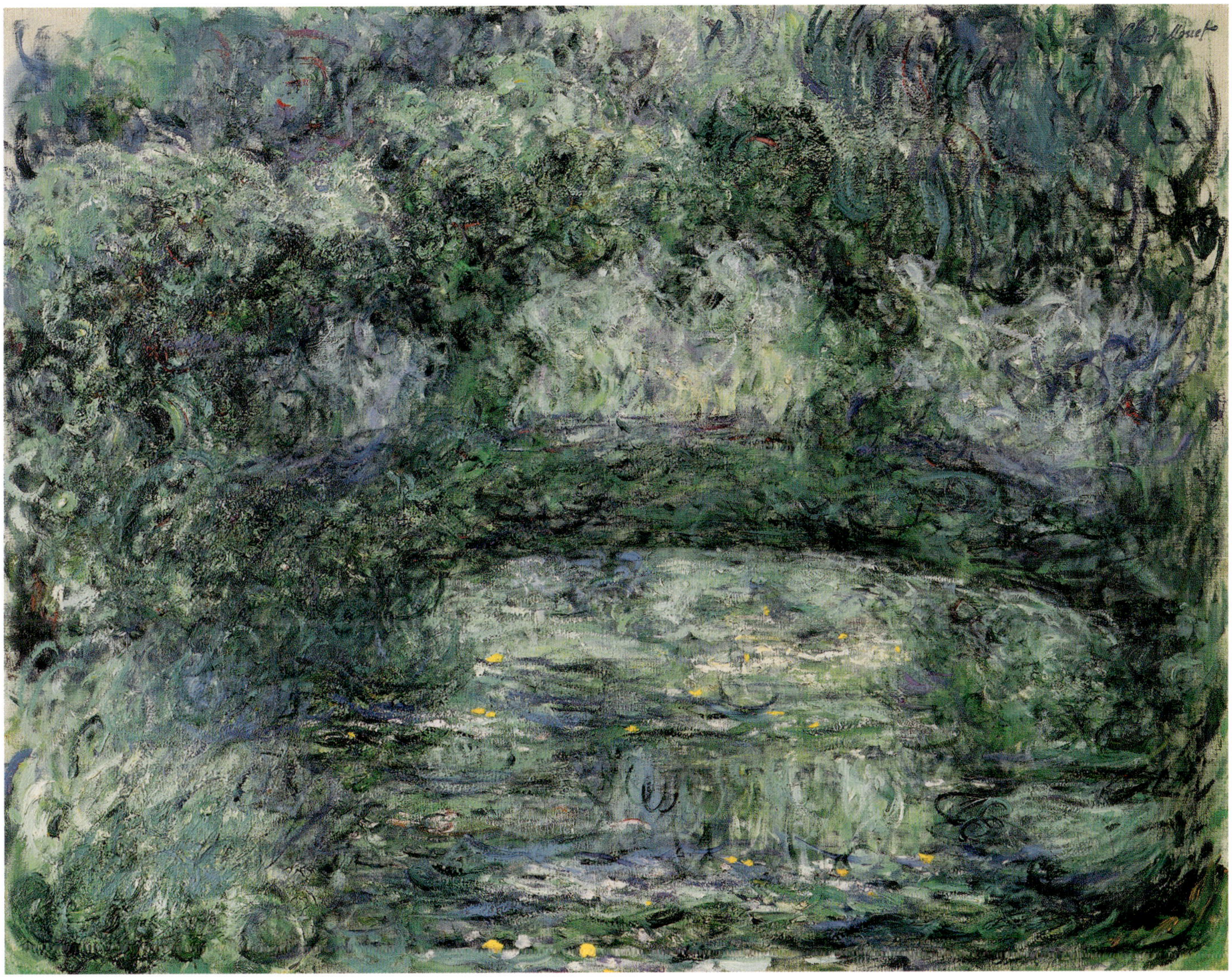

25 | *The Japanese Bridge*, ca. 1918–24
Oil on canvas, 89.5 × 116.3 cm
(35¼ × 45¾ in.)
Private collection

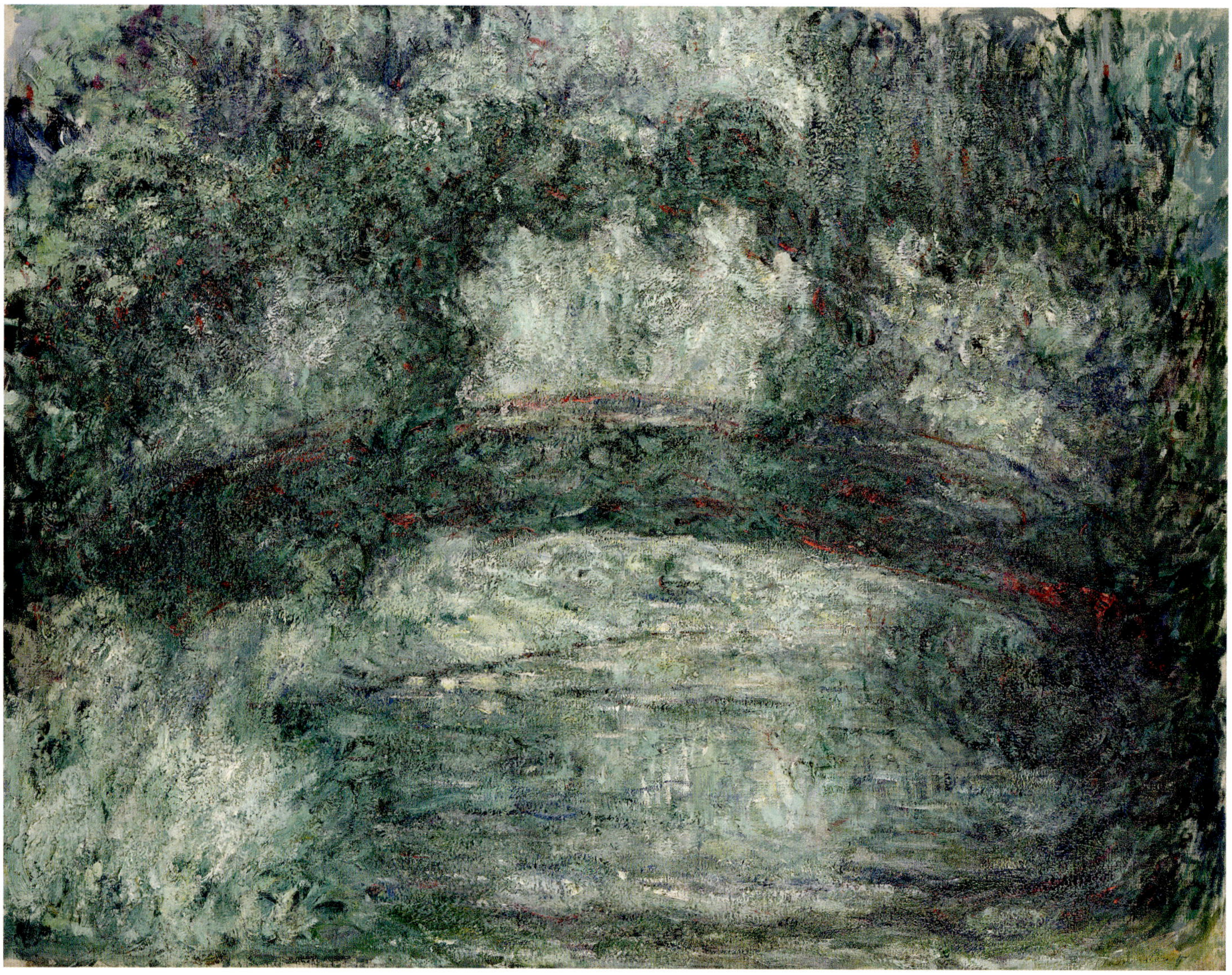

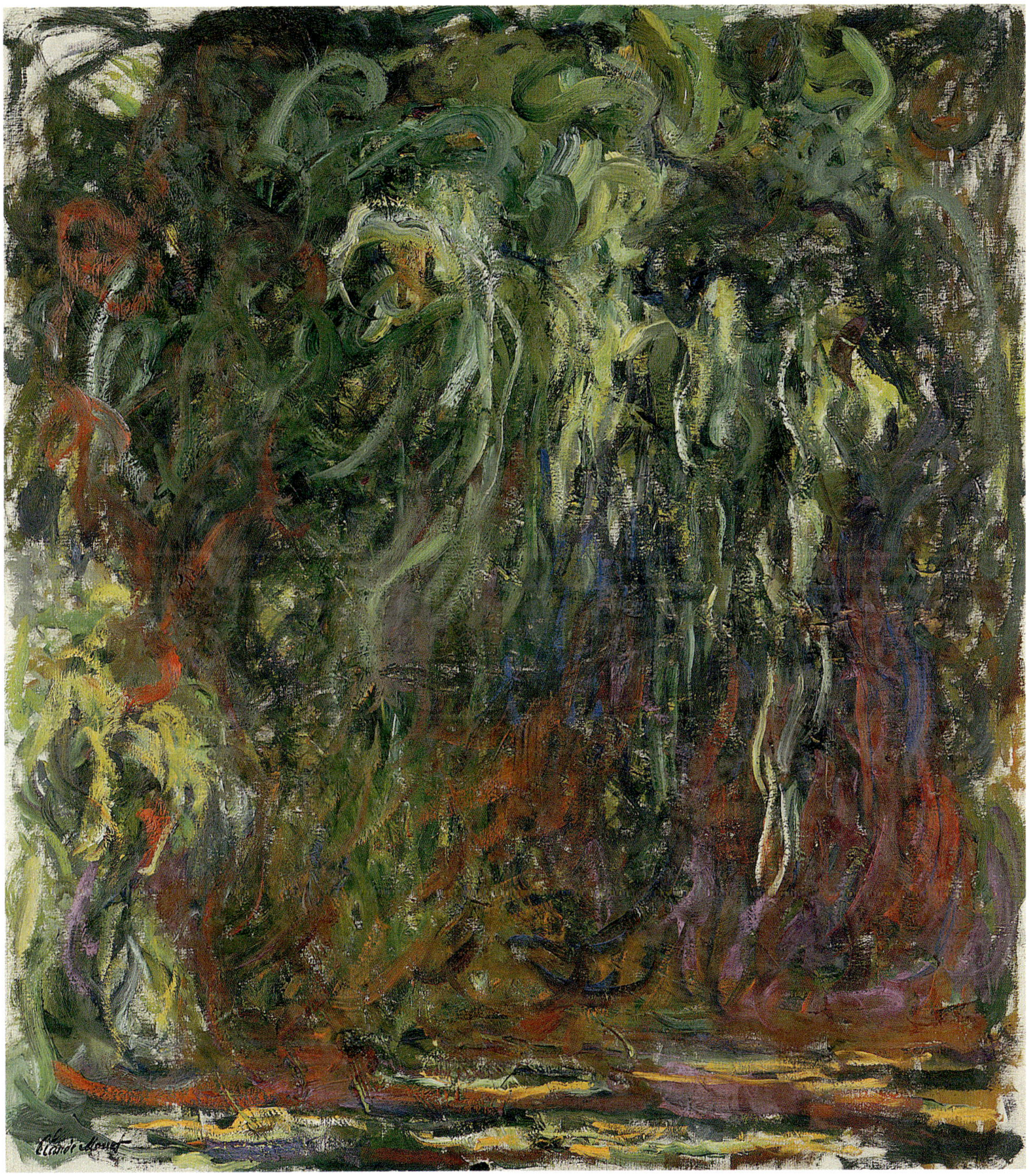

26 | *Weeping Willow*, 1920–22
Oil on canvas, 110 × 100 cm
(43 5/16 × 39 3/8 in.)
Musée d'Orsay, Paris

27 | *The House among Roses*, 1925
Oil on canvas, 89 × 100 cm (35 × 39 3/8 in.)
Private collection

28 | *The House among Roses*, 1925
Oil on canvas, 92.3 × 73.3 cm
(38 3/8 × 28 7/8 in.)
Collection Carmen Thyssen-Bornemisza,
long term loan at the Museo
Thyssen-Bornemisza, Madrid

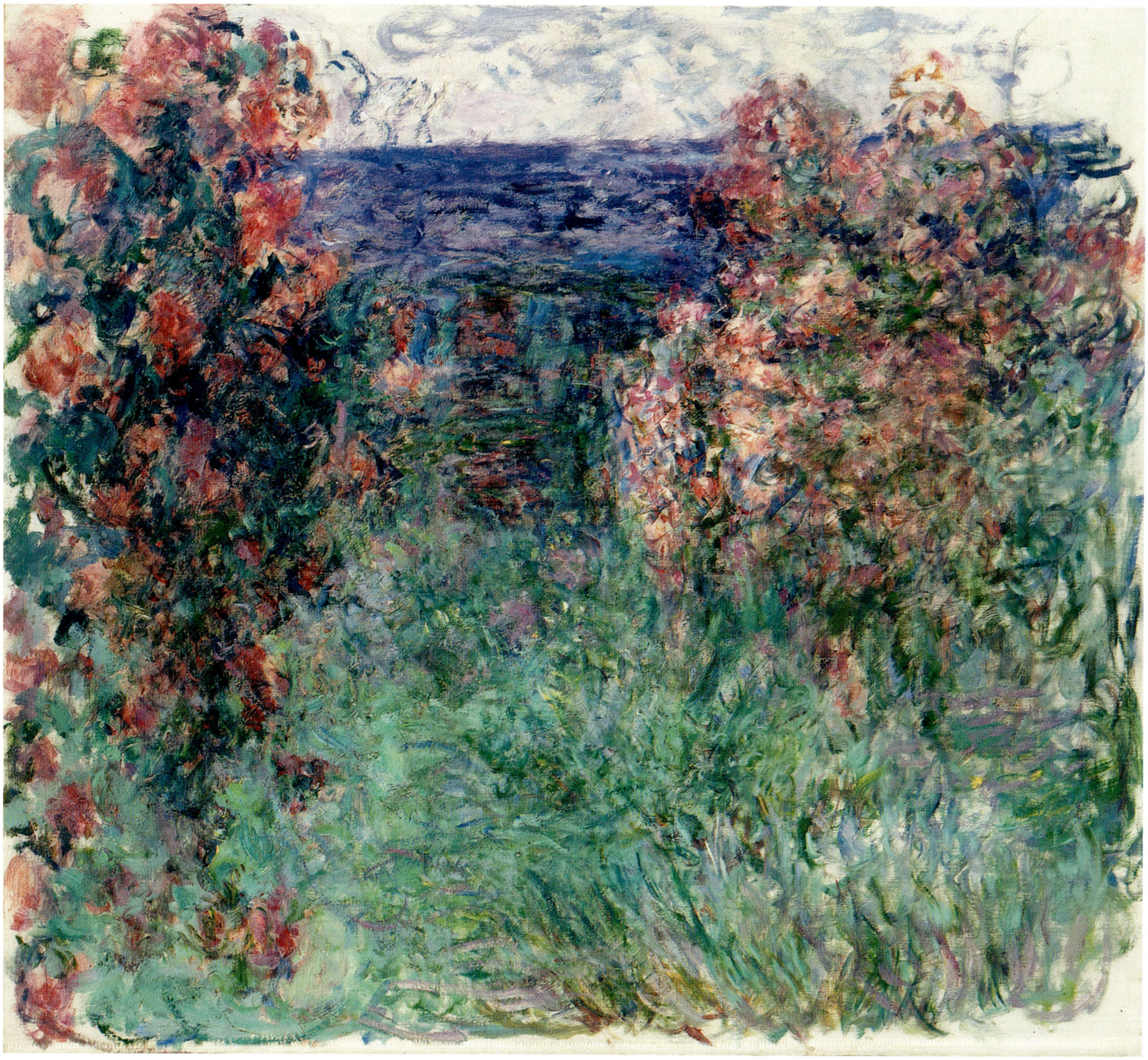

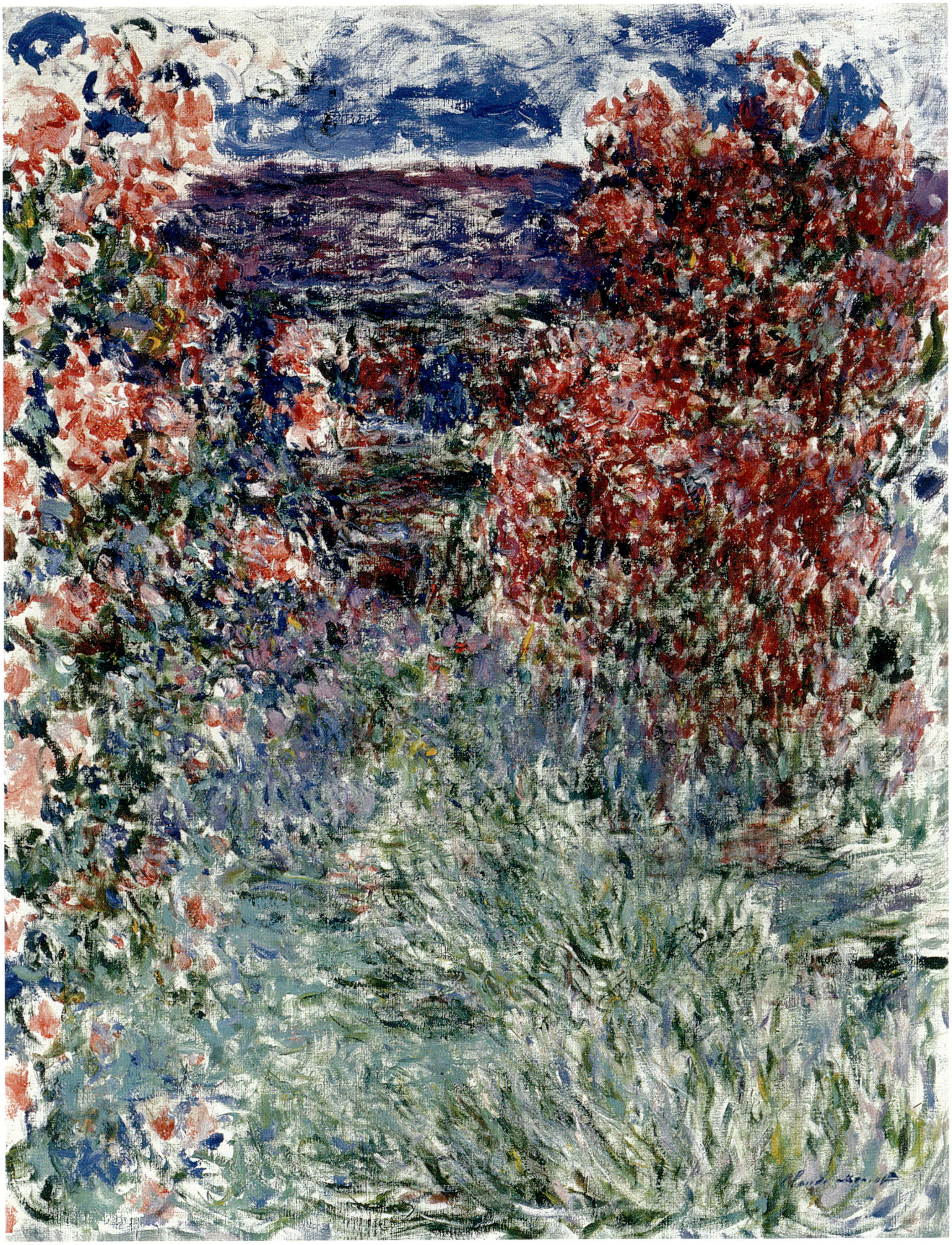

29 | John Leslie Breck,
Garden at Giverny (In Monet's Garden),
between 1887 and 1891
Oil on canvas, 46 × 55.6 cm (18 1/8 × 21 7/8 in.)
Terra Foundation for American Art, Chicago

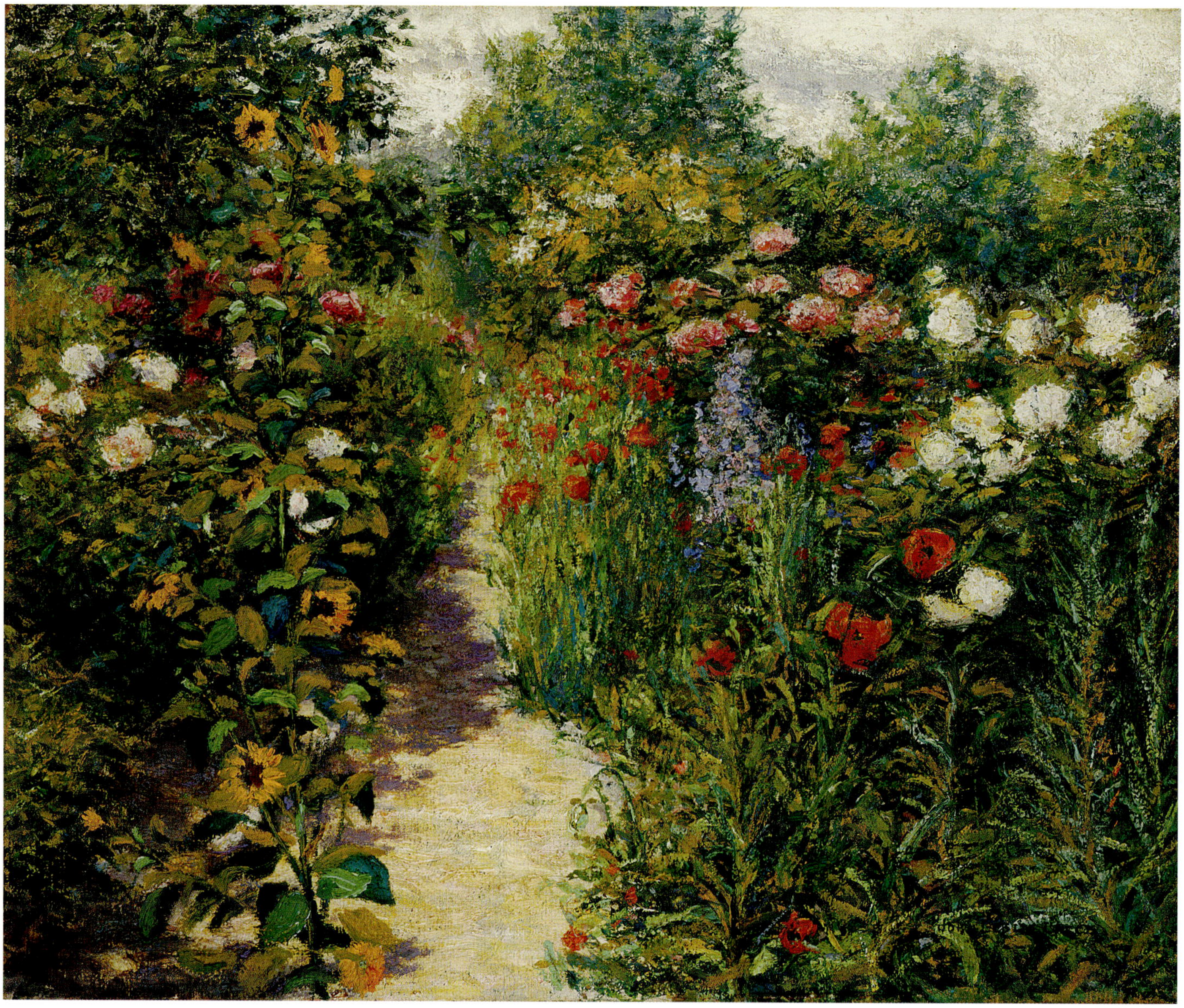

30 | Blanche Hoschedé-Monet,
Garden at Giverny (The Rose Path), after 1926
Oil on canvas, 73 × 74.5 cm (28 3/4 × 29 5/16 in.)
Musée Clemenceau, Paris

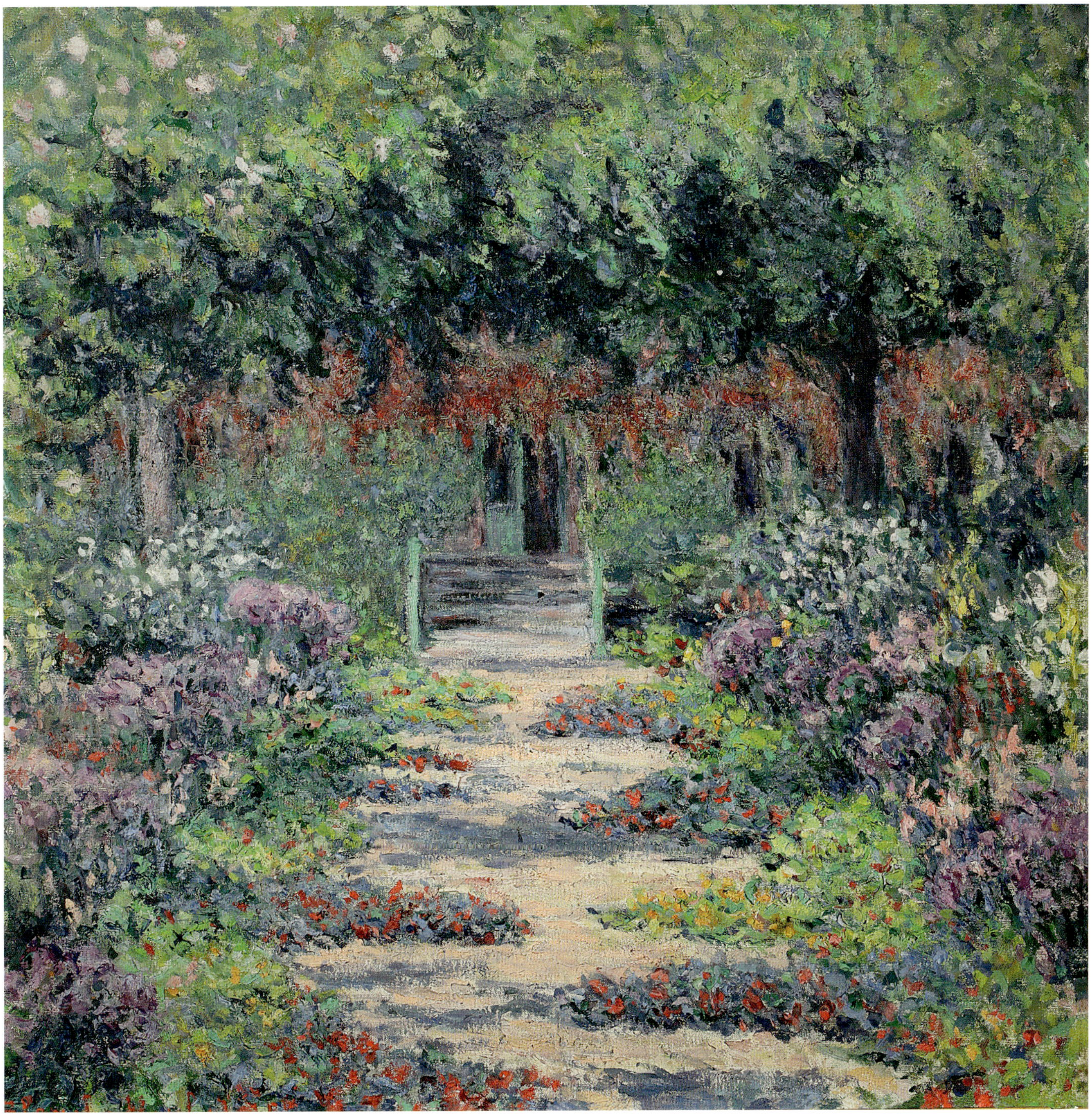

31 | Schaarwachter,
Monet, painter, ca. 1880
Modern duplicate from original silver print glued on board, 7.4 × 4.2 cm ($2^{15}/_{16}$ × $1^{5}/_{8}$ in.)
Musée d'Orsay, Paris

32 | Theodore Robinson
Portrait of Claude Monet, ca. 1888–90
Cyanotype, 24 × 16,8 cm ($9^{1}/_{2}$ × $6^{1}/_{2}$ in.)
Terra Foundation for American Art, Chicago

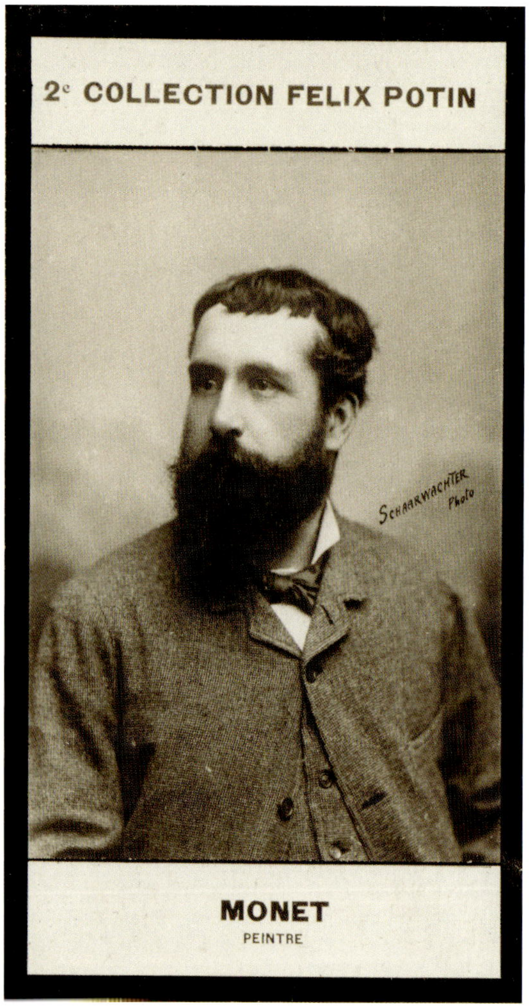

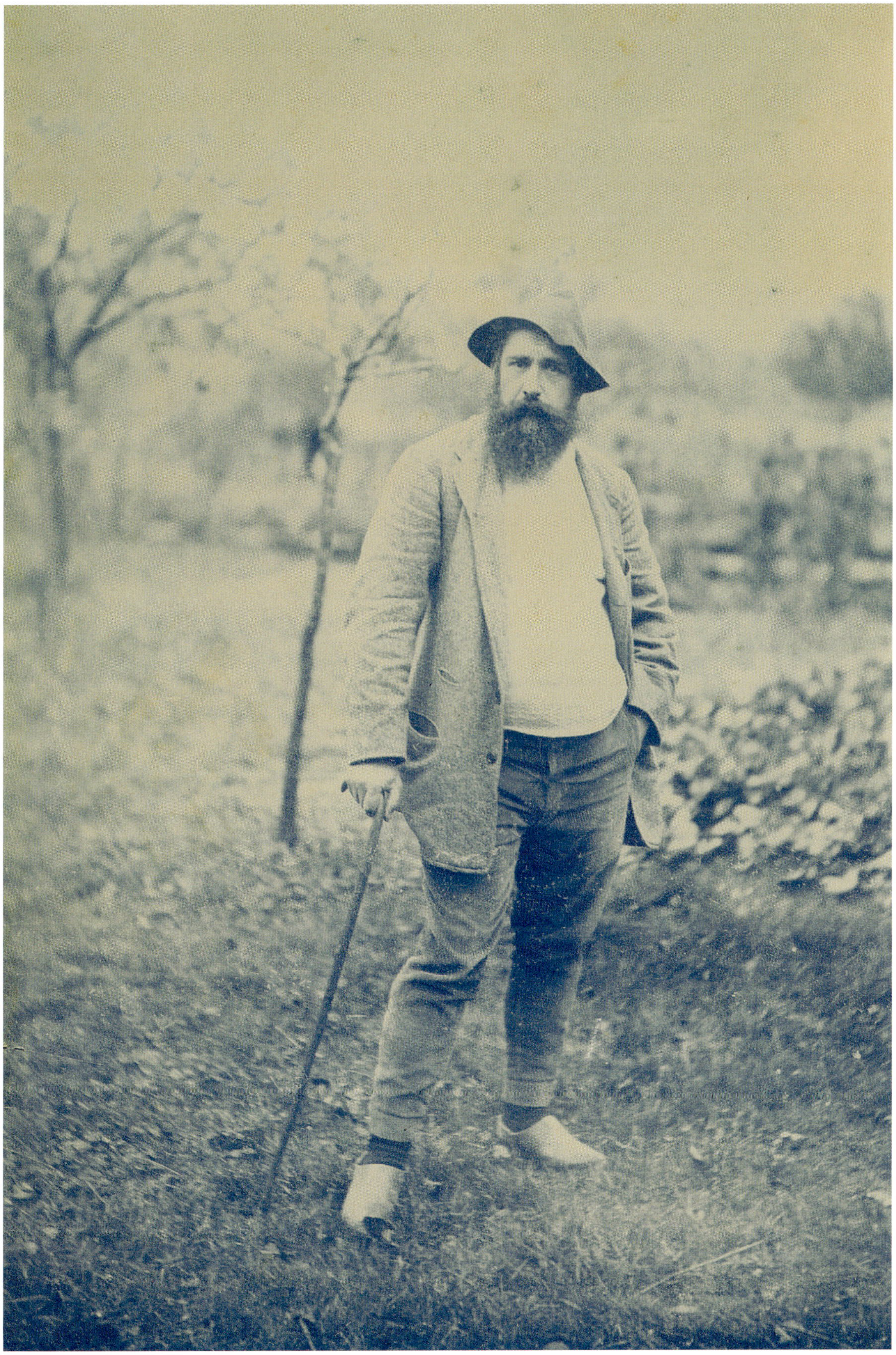

33 | Anonymous, *Michel and Claude Monet photographing the Pond, Giverny,* ca. 1895–1900
Original silver print,
5.8 × 8.4 cm (2¼ × 3⁵⁄₁₆ in.)
Philippe Piguet Collection

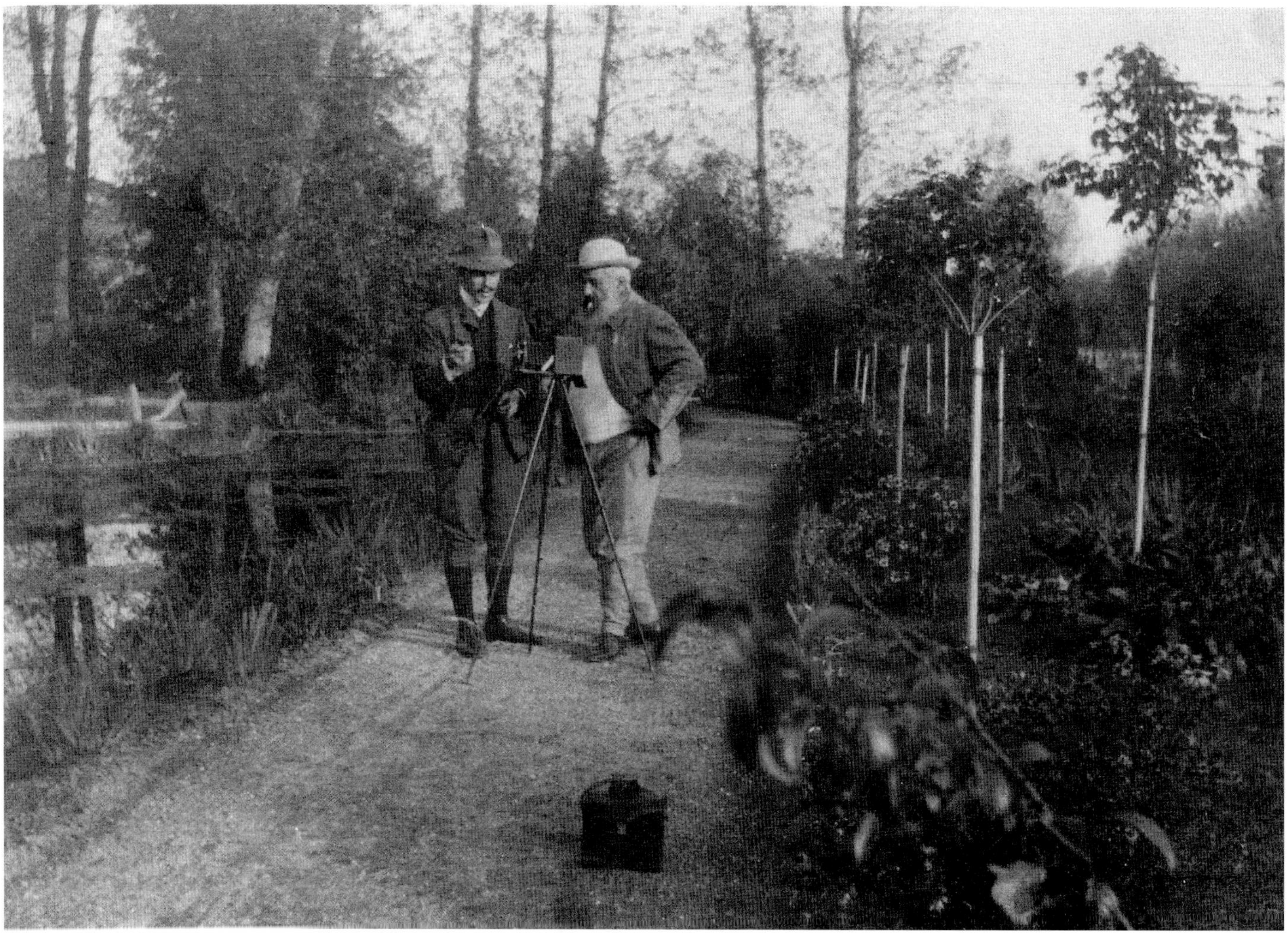

34 | *Self-Portrait on the Surface of the Water Lily Pond in Giverny*, ca. 1905
Citrate print from negative, 4.3 × 5.7 cm
(1 11/16 × 2 1/4 in.)
Philippe Piguet Collection

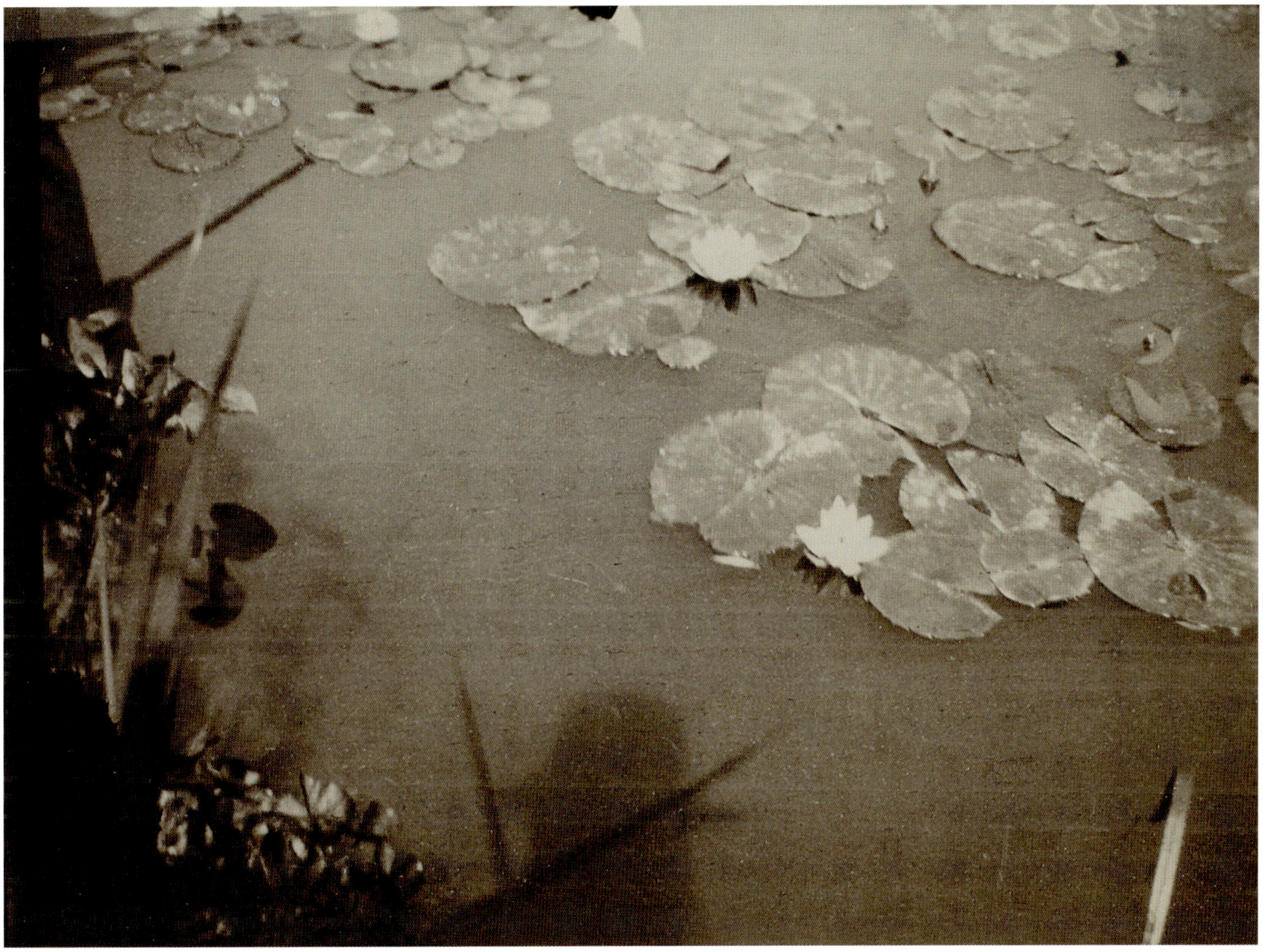

35 | Pierre Choumoff, *Monet before the Japanese Bridge, Giverny*, 1920
Silver print, 16.2 × 21.9 cm ($6\frac{3}{8} \times 8\frac{5}{8}$ in.)
Musée Clemenceau, Paris

36 | Jacques-Ernest Bulloz, *Claude Monet beside the Water Lily Pond*, summer 1905
Modern print, 29 × 20 cm ($11\frac{7}{16} \times 7\frac{7}{8}$ in.)
Musée Municipal A.-G. Poulain, Vernon

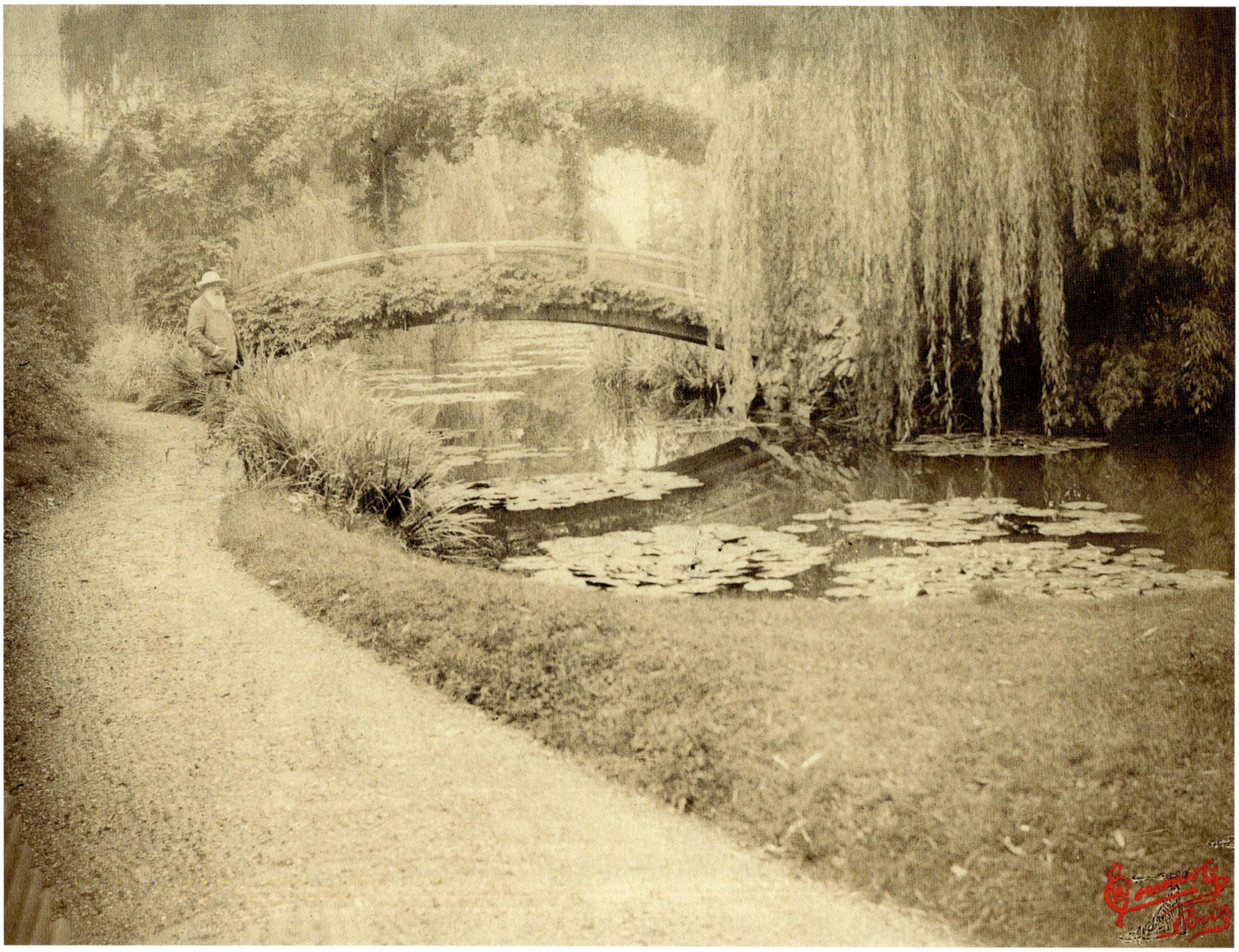

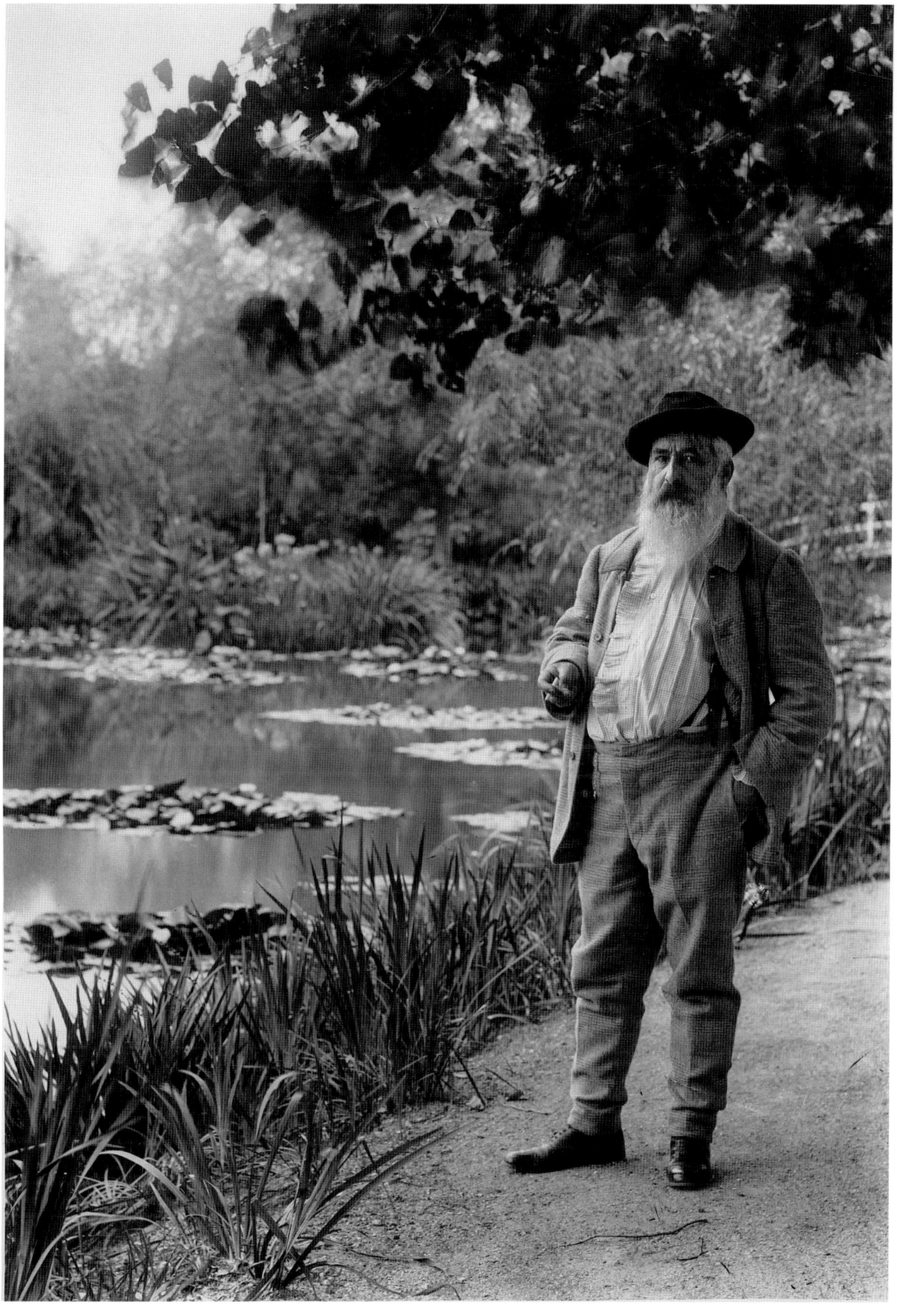

37 | Baron Adolf de Meyer,
Claude Monet in Profile Looking at his Garden, Giverny, 27 October 1905
Platinum print on Japan paper,
21 × 16.5 cm (8 1/4 × 6 1/2 in.)
Philippe Piguet Collection

38 | Baron Adolf de Meyer, *Claude Monet Entering the Second Studio, Giverny*,
27 October 1905
Platinum print on Japan paper,
22.8 × 11.6 cm (9 × 4 9/16 in.)
Philippe Piguet Collection

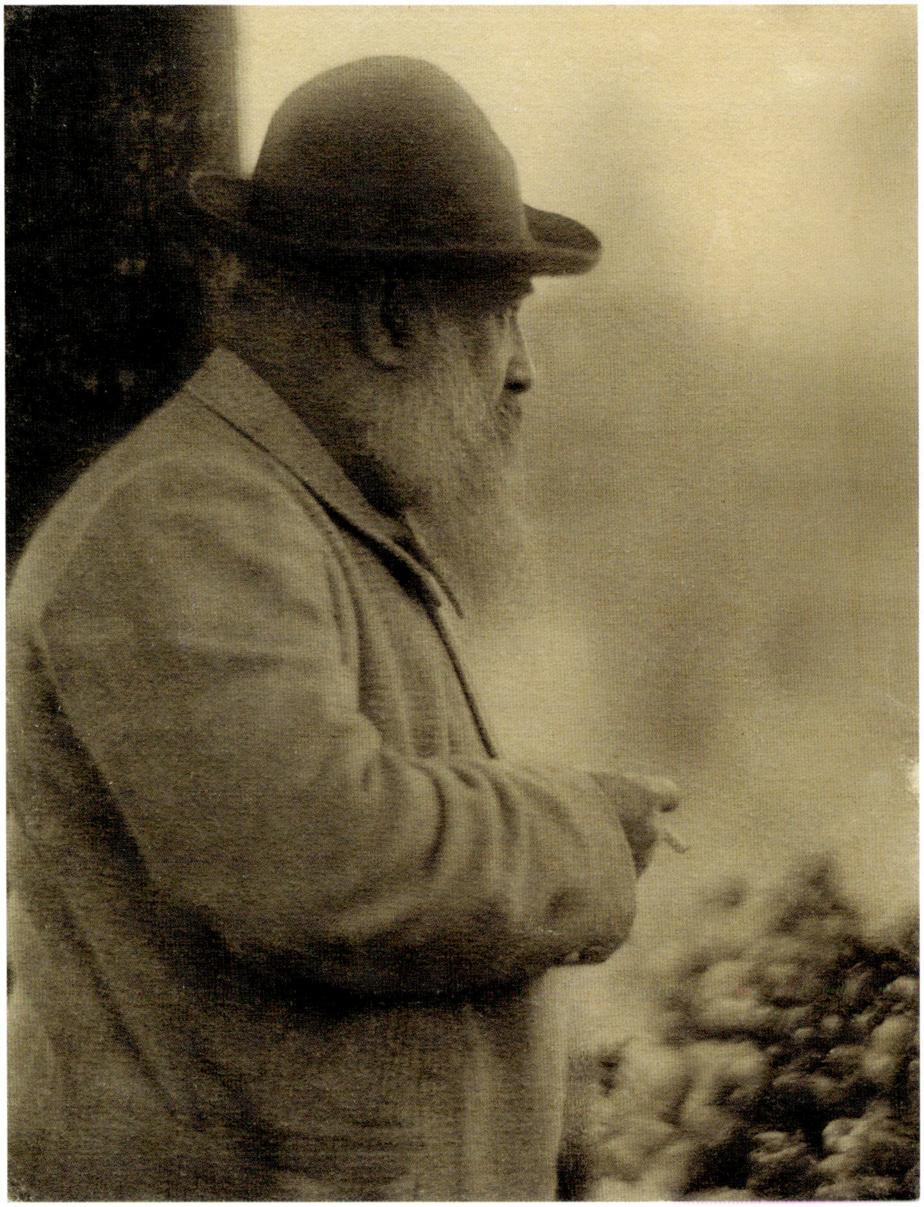

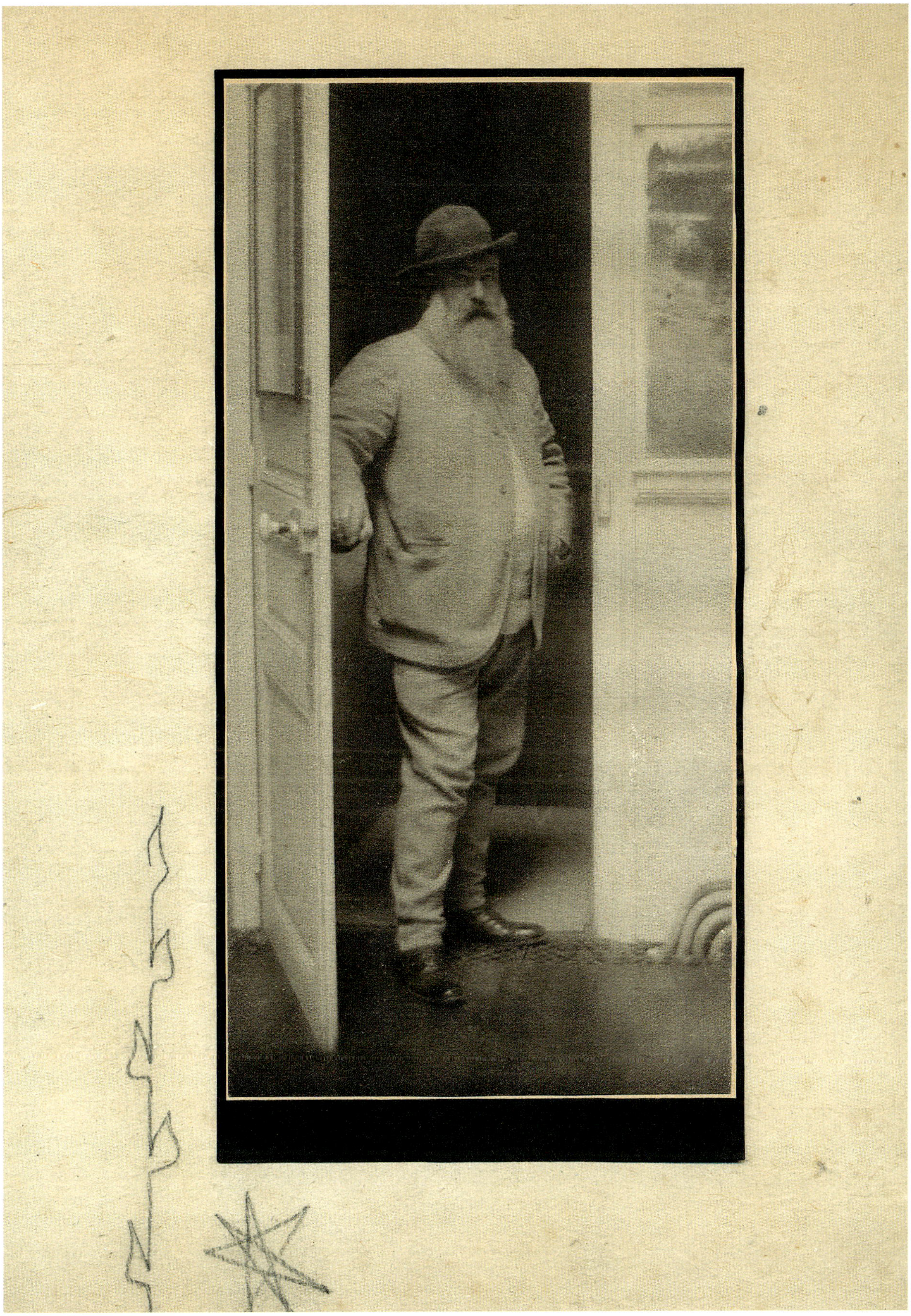

39 | Sacha Guitry, *Claude Monet in his Garden, Giverny*, ca. 1915
Enlarged silver print, 30 × 40 cm
($11^{13}/_{16}$ × $15^{3}/_{4}$ in.)
Musée Clemenceau, Paris

40 | [Sacha Guitry], *Claude Monet and Gustave Geffroy*, ca. 1920
Modern duplicate
Unknown location

41 | Sacha Guitry, *Claude Monet in the Giverny Garden*, ca. 1915
Enlarged palladium print, 38.4 × 29.5 cm
($15^{1}/_{8}$ × $11^{5}/_{8}$ in.)
Musée d'Orsay, Paris

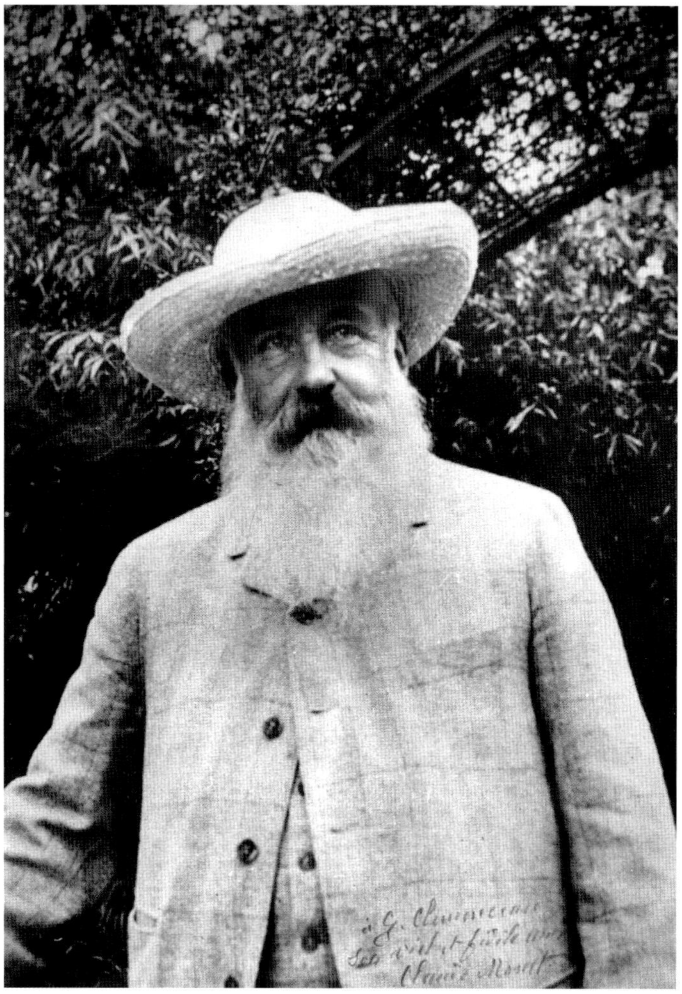

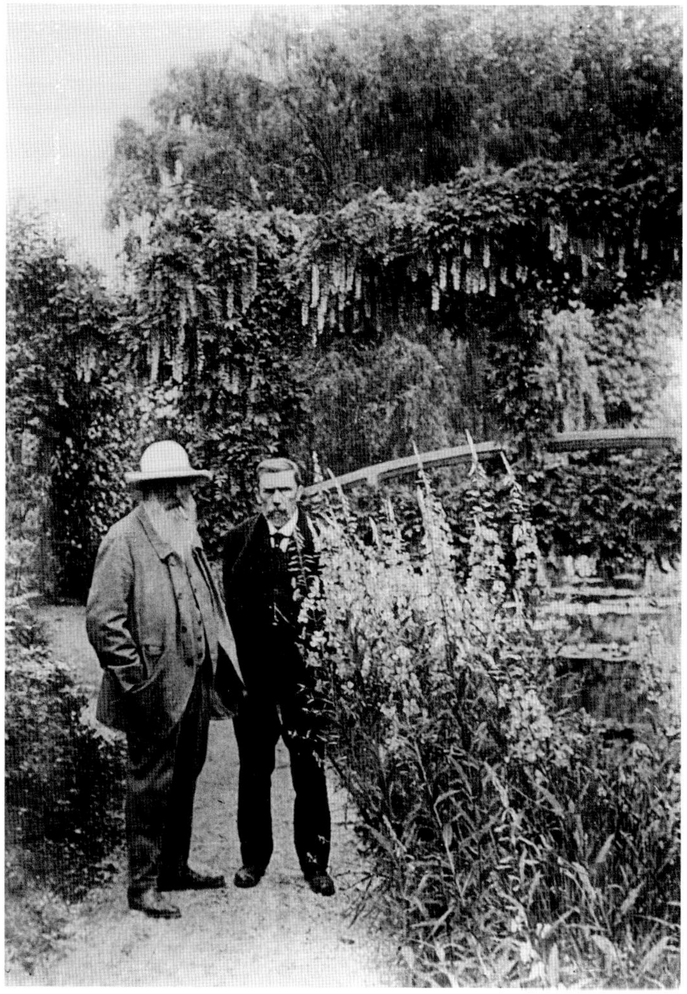

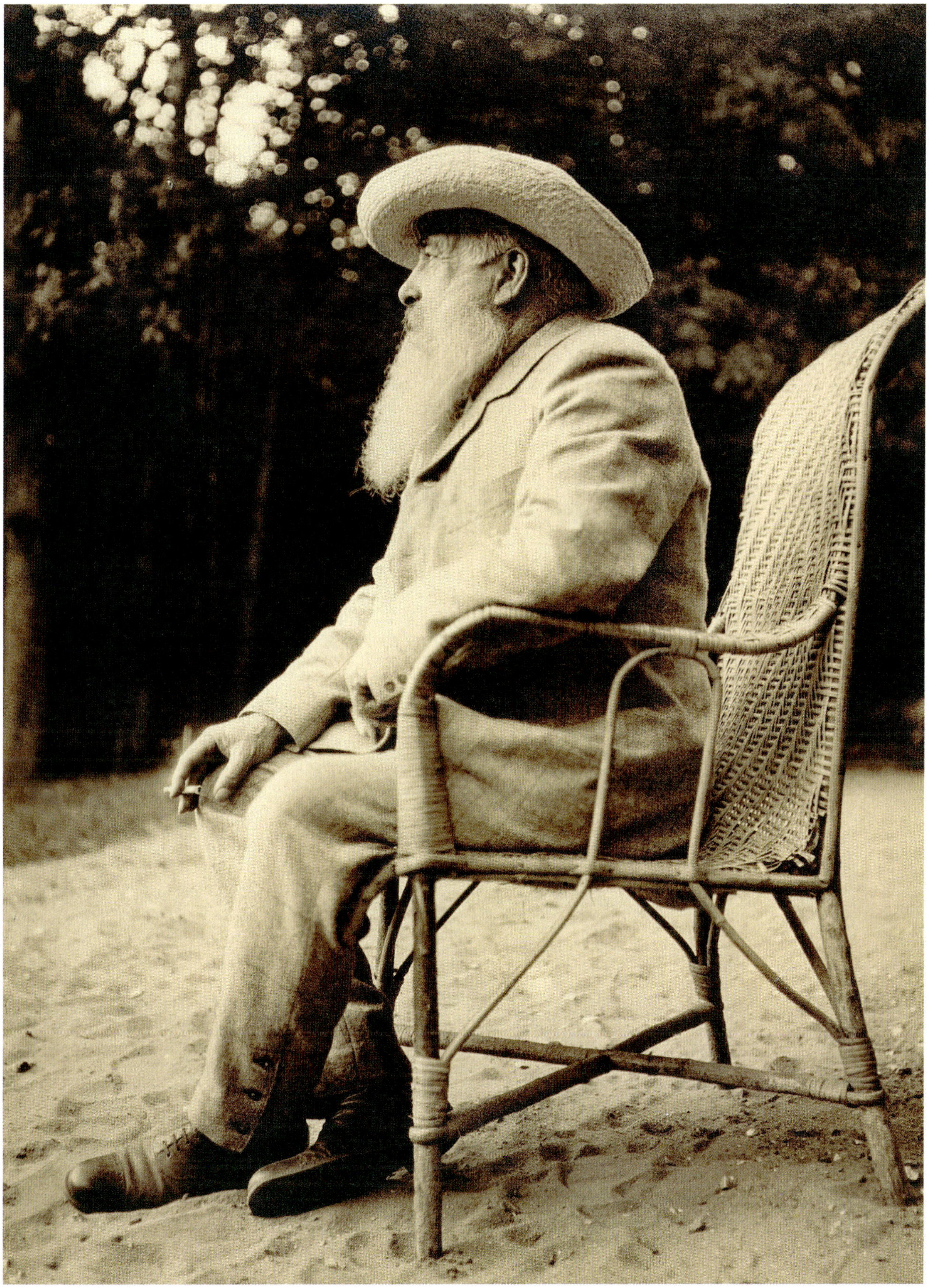

42 | Étienne Clémentel, *Claude Monet Standing before the Water Lilies, in the Giverny Garden*, ca. 1920
Ektachrome by Patrice Schmidt from the stereoscopic autochrome, 4.5 × 10.5 cm (1 3/4 × 4 1/8 in.)
Musée d'Orsay, Paris

43 | Étienne Clémentel, *Claude Monet Standing by the Bridge in Giverny*, ca. 1920
Ektachrome by Patrice Schmidt from the stereoscopic autochrome, 4.5 × 10.5 cm (1 3/4 × 4 1/8 in.)
Musée d'Orsay, Paris

44 | Anonymous for *L'Illustration*, *The Water Lily Pond in Giverny*, spring 1921
Ektachrome by Patrice Schmidt from the autochrome made for *L'Illustration*, 18 × 24 cm (7 1/8 × 9 7/16 in.)
Musée d'Orsay, Paris

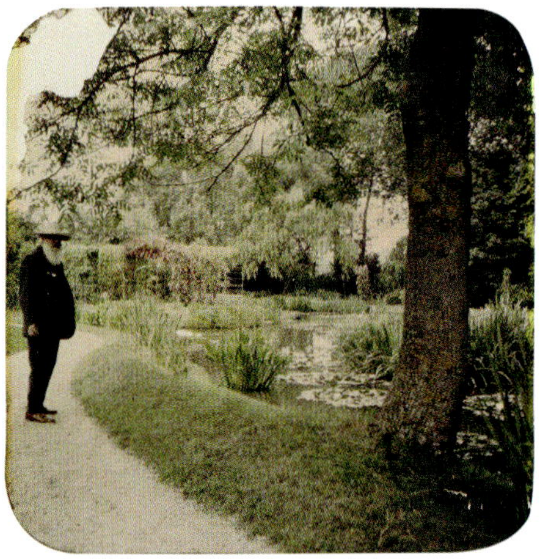

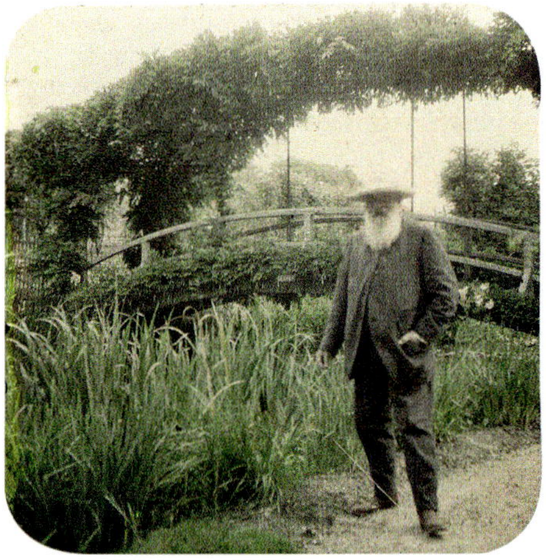

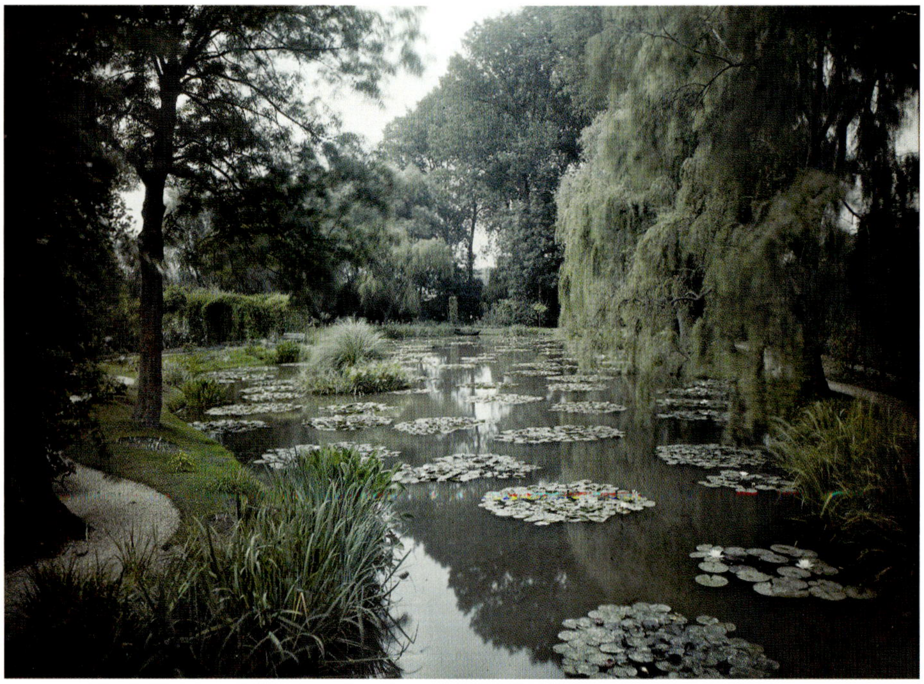

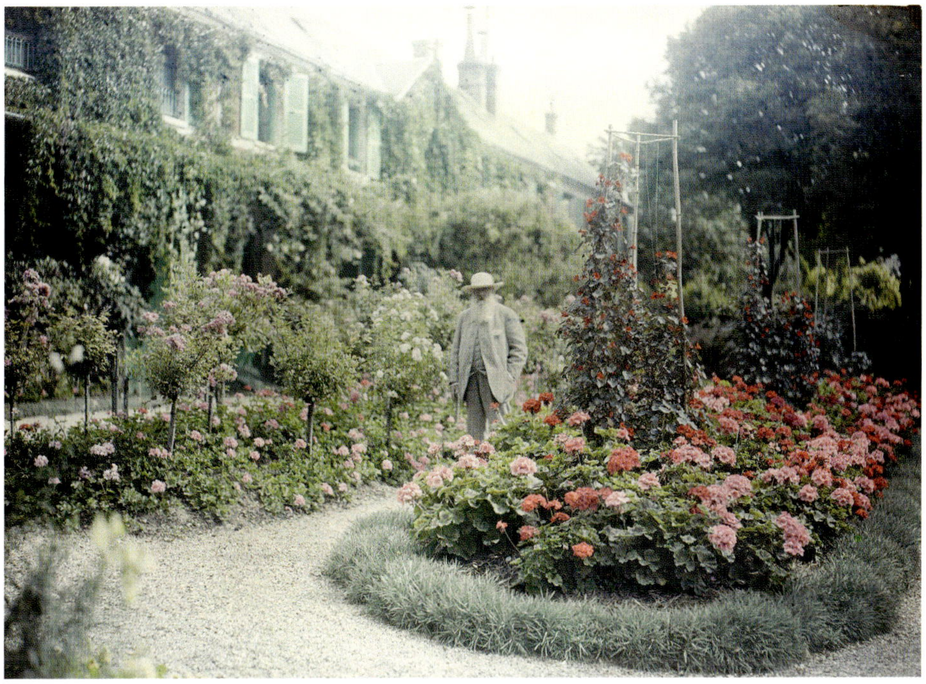

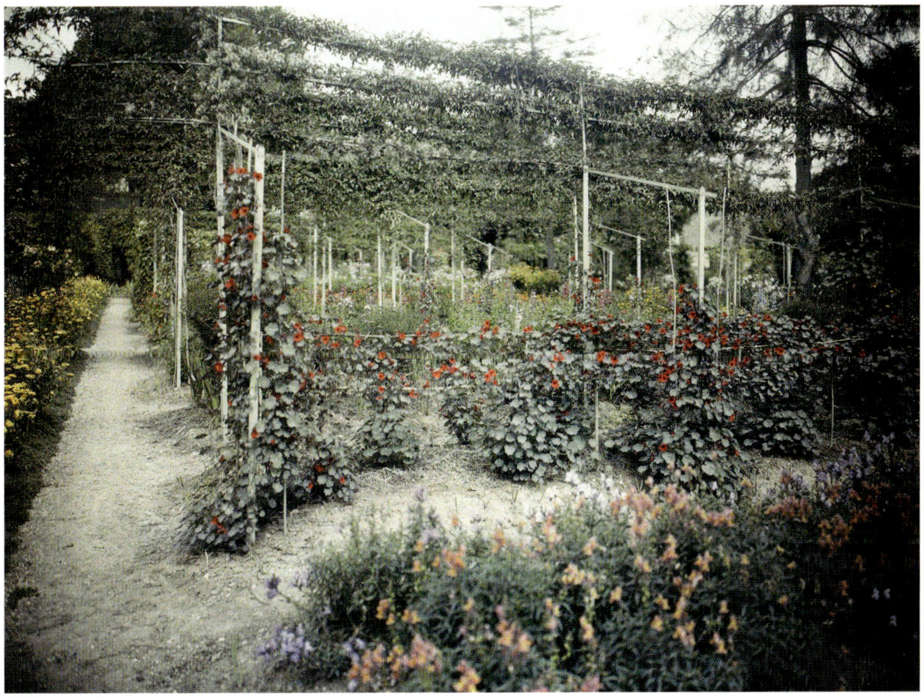

45 | Anonymous for *L'Illustration*, *Claude Monet before his House in Giverny*, spring 1921
Ektachrome by Patrice Schmidt from the stereoscopic autochrome made for *L'Illustration*, 18 × 24 cm ($7\,^{1}/_{8} \times 9\,^{7}/_{16}$ in.)
Musée d'Orsay, Paris

46 | Anonymous for *L'Illustration*, *The Rose Garden in Giverny*, spring 1921
Ektachrome by Patrice Schmidt from the autochrome made for *L'Illustration*, 18 × 24 cm ($7\,^{1}/_{8} \times 9\,^{7}/_{16}$ in.)
Musée d'Orsay, Paris

47 | Henri Martinie, *Mme Kuroki, Claude Monet, Lili Butler, Blanche Hoschedé-Monet, and Georges Clemenceau in the Giverny Garden*, June 1921
Silver print, 17.5 × 23.6 cm (6$^{7}/_{8}$ × 9$^{1}/_{4}$ in.)
Musée Clemenceau, Paris

48 | Henri Martinie, *Georges Clemenceau, Claude Monet, and Alice Butler on the Japanese Bridge, Giverny*, June 1921
Sepia silver print, 19.8 × 24.5 cm
(7$^{13}/_{16}$ × 9$^{5}/_{8}$ in.)
Musée Clemenceau, Paris

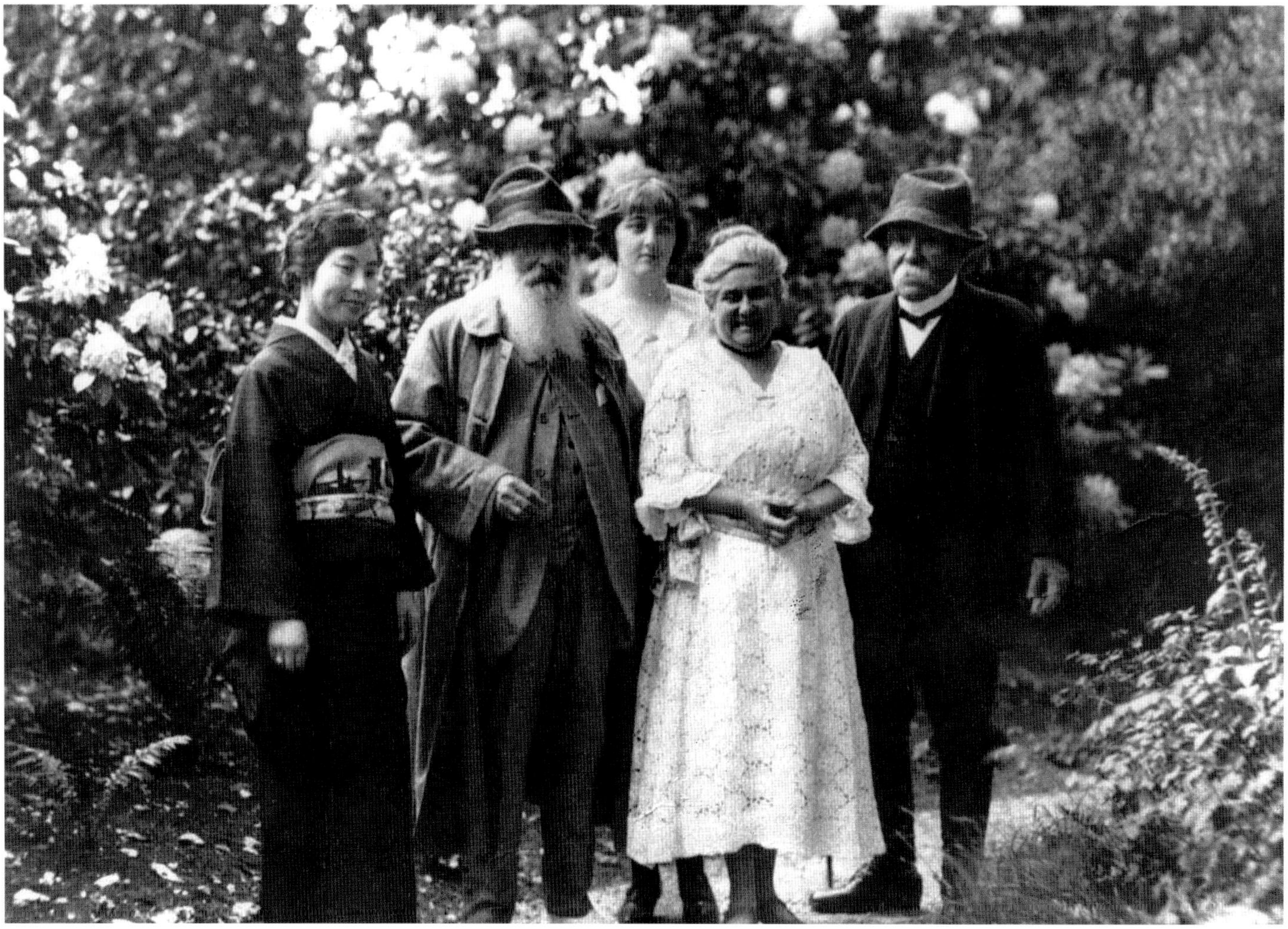

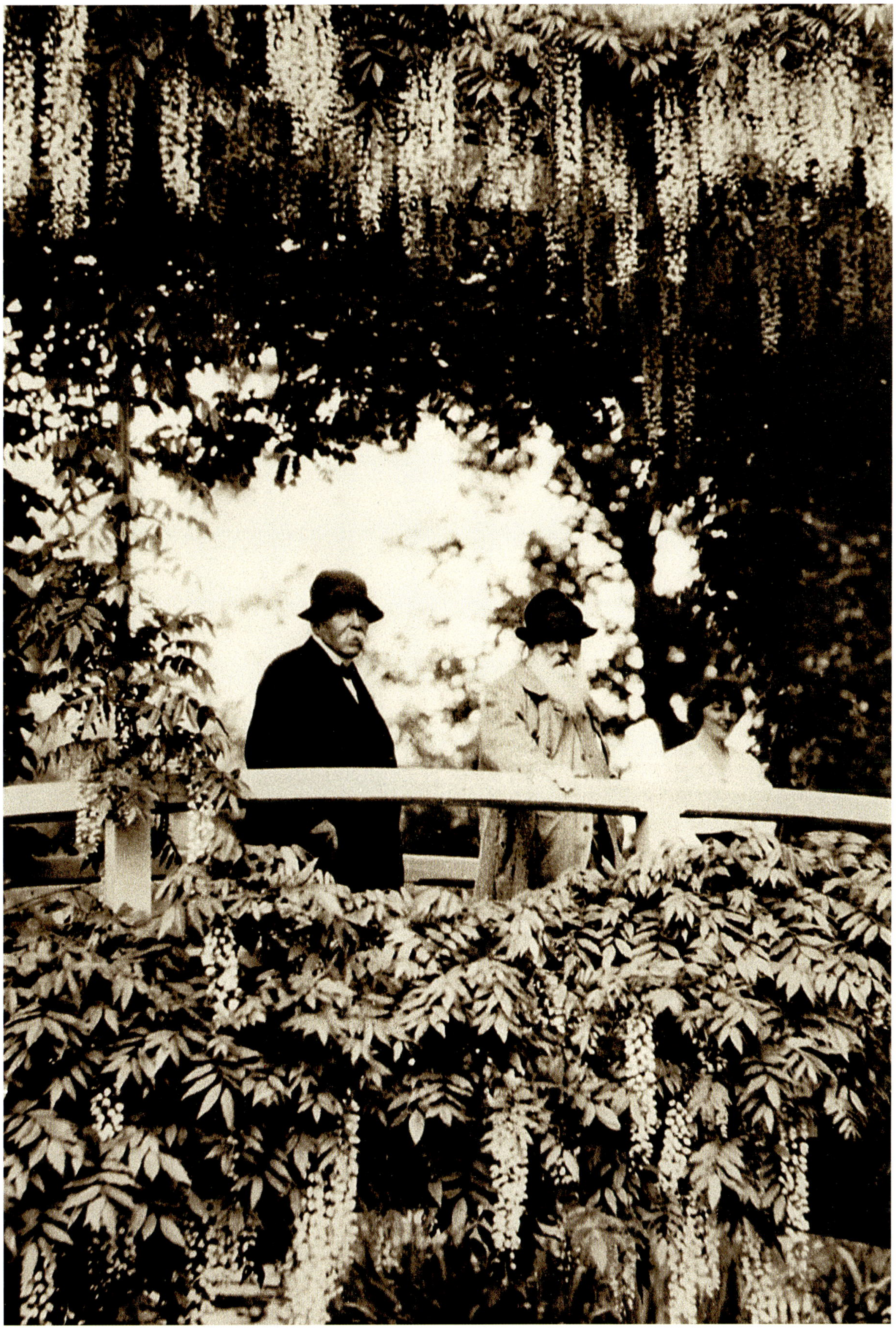

49 | Sacha Guitry, *Claude Monet and the American Singer Marguerite Namara at the Pond, Giverny*, 1922
Modern silver print, 12.5 × 9.7 cm
($4^{15}/_{16} \times 3^{13}/_{16}$ in.)
Philippe Piguet Collection

50 | Anonymous, *Claude Monet and Georges Clemenceau on a Path in the Giverny Garden (facing)*, 1921
Silver print, 17.8 × 12.7 cm (7 × 5 in.)
Musée Clemenceau, Paris

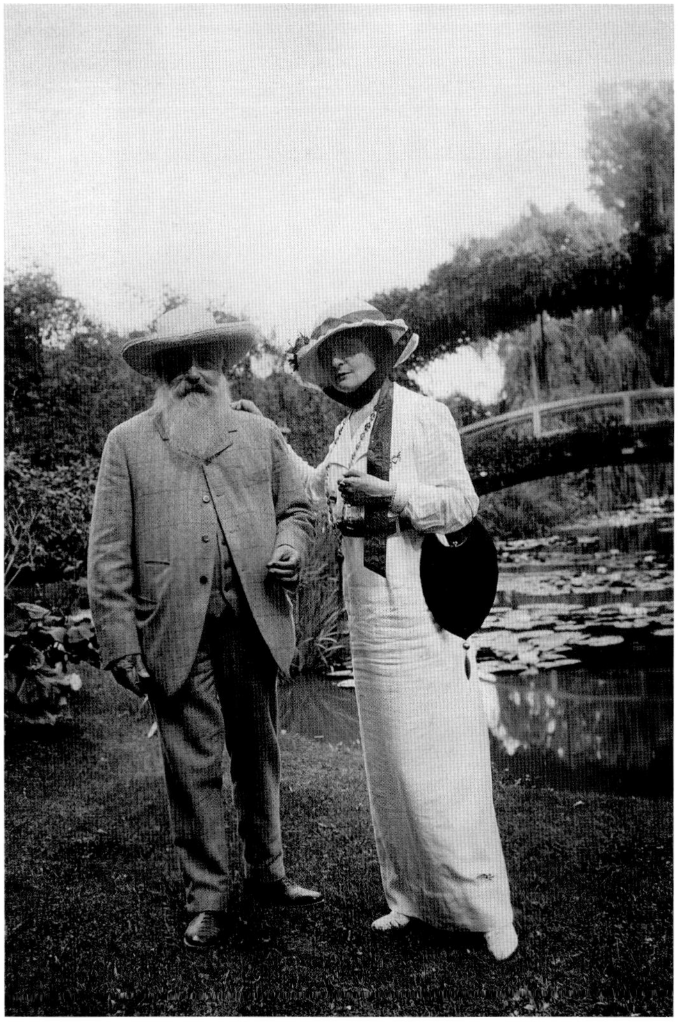

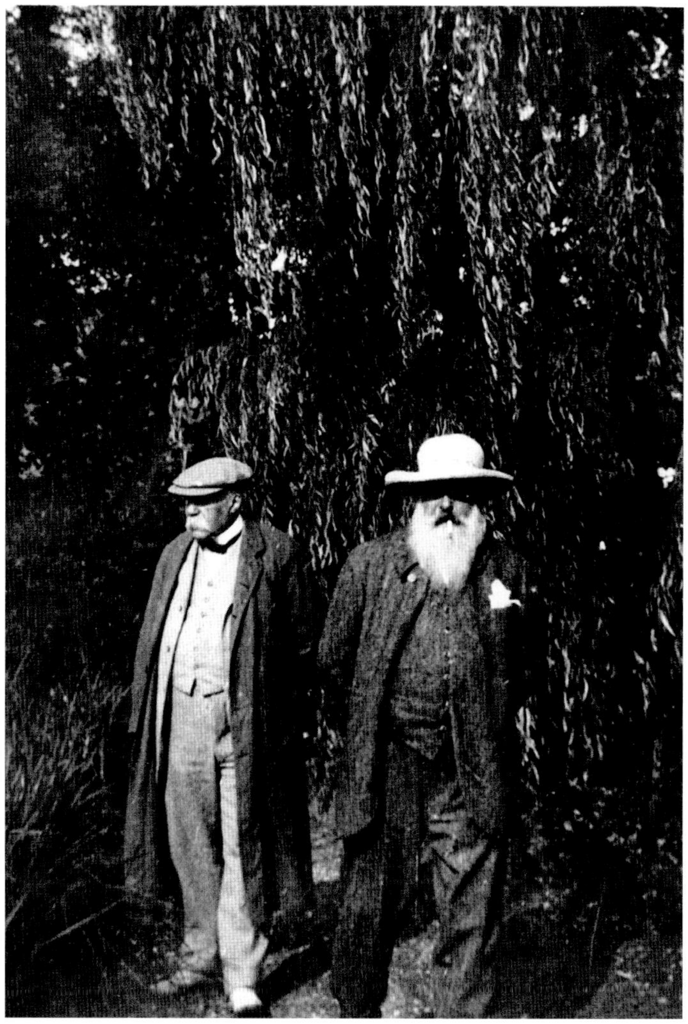

51 | Henri Martinie, *Claude Monet and Georges Clemenceau in a Path in the Giverny Garden (from behind)*, 1921
Silver print, 12.7 × 17.8 cm (5 × 7 in.)
Musée Clemenceau, Paris

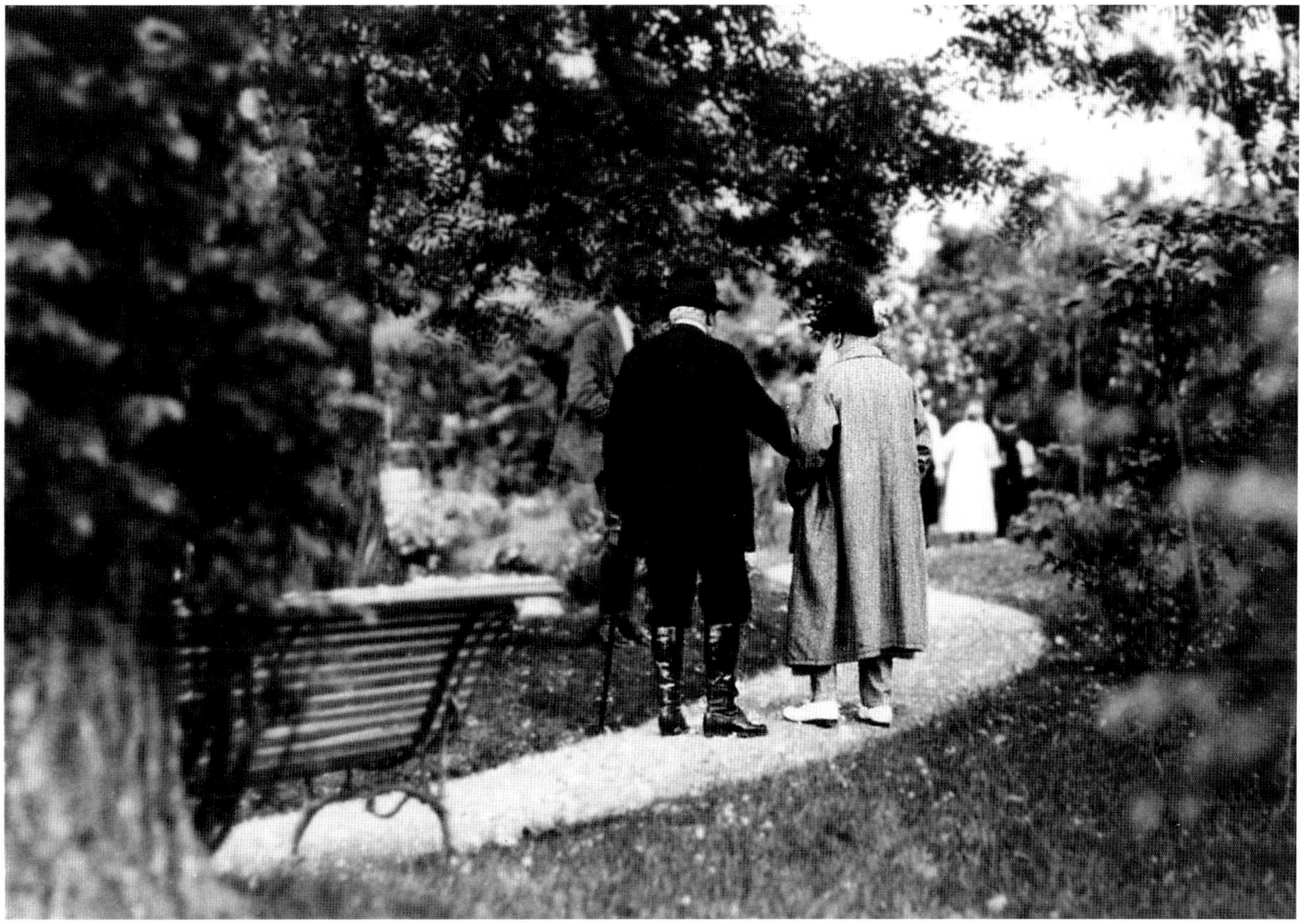

52 | Anonymous, *Claude Monet in the Great Rose Path, Giverny*, ca. 1923
Silver print, 29 × 39.1 cm (11 7/16 × 15 3/8 in.)
Philippe Piguet Collection

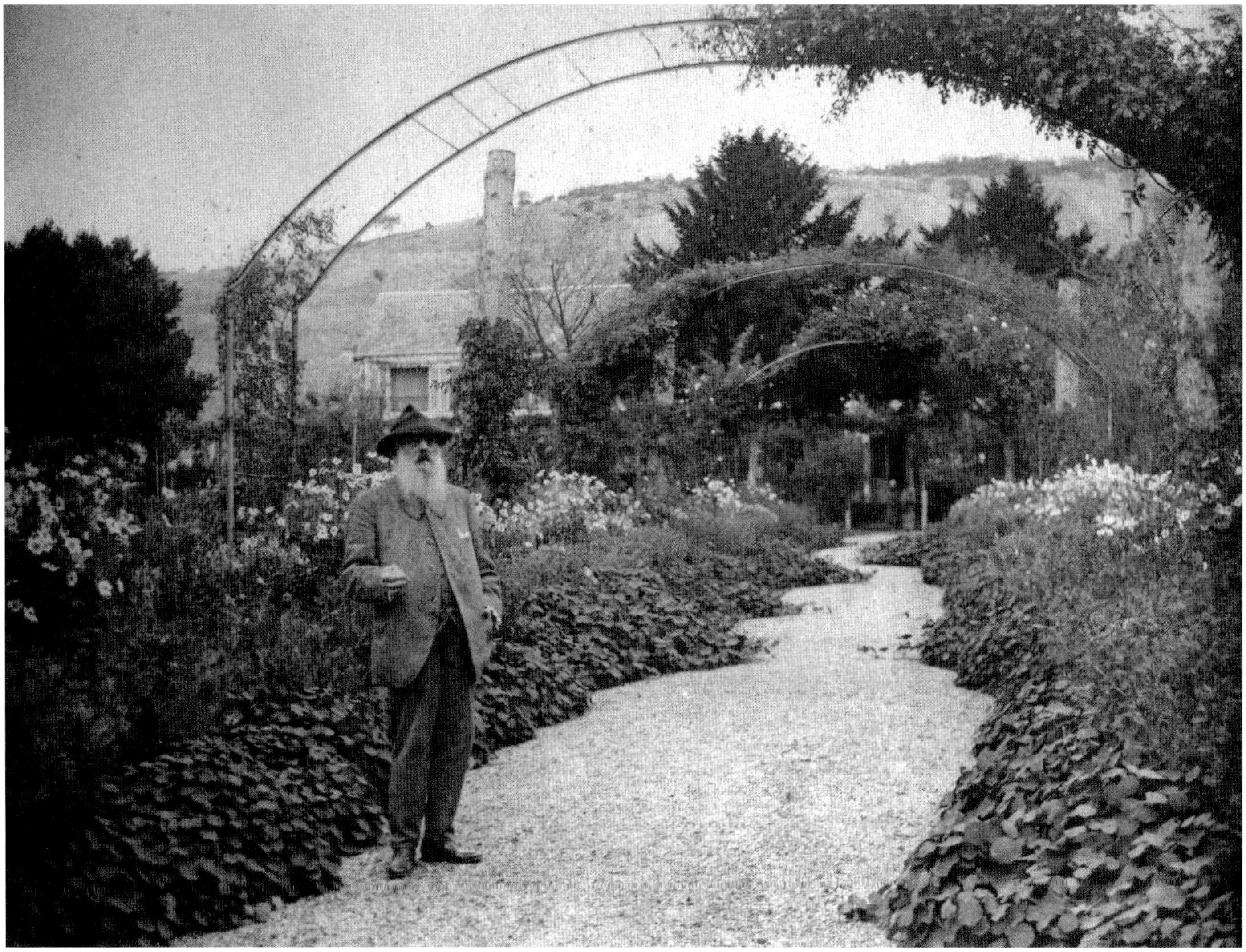

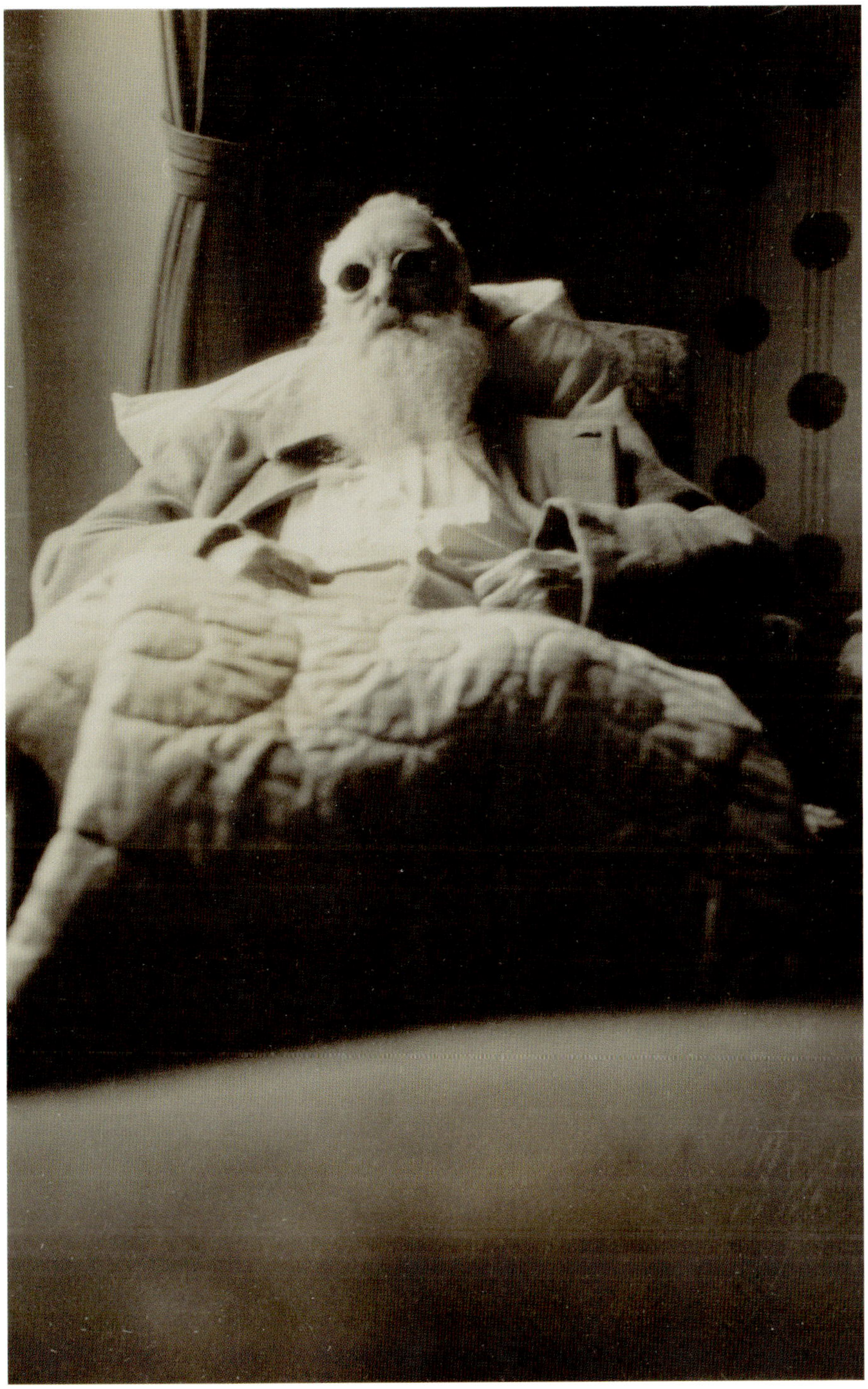

53 | [Michel Monet], *Claude Monet during his Cataract Operation at the Neuilly Clinic*, 1923
Modern silver print, 7.1 × 4.8 cm (2¾ × 2 in.)
Philippe Piguet Collection

54 | Thérèse Bonney, *Claude Monet near the Water Garden*, 1925
Original silver print, 17.4 × 22.8 cm
(6⅞ × 9 in.)
Musée Clemenceau, Paris

55 | Thérèse Bonney, *Claude Monet on the Japanese Bridge in his Giverny Garden*, 1925
Original silver print, 22.5 × 17.4 cm
(8⅞ × 6⅞ in.)
Musée Clemenceau, Paris

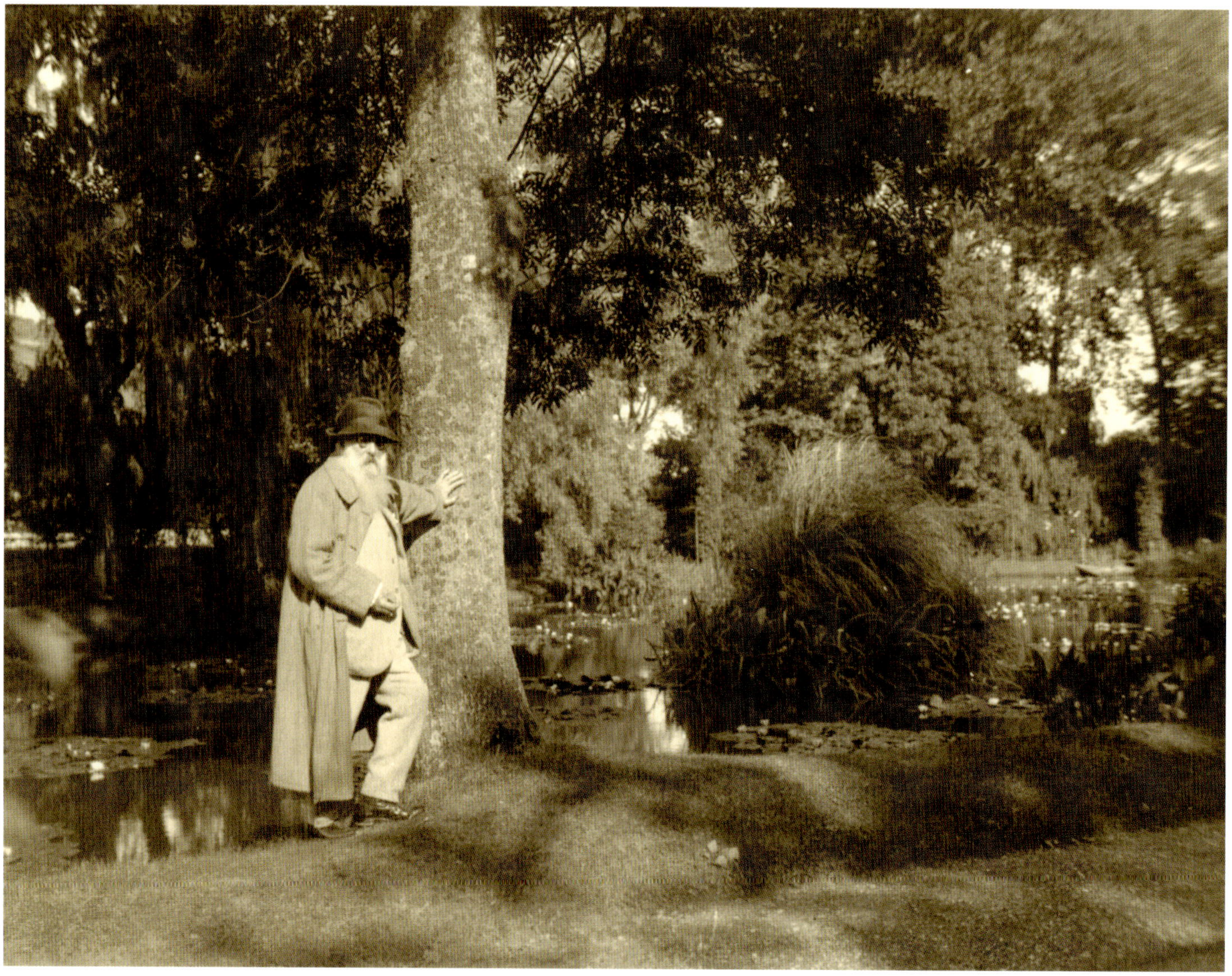

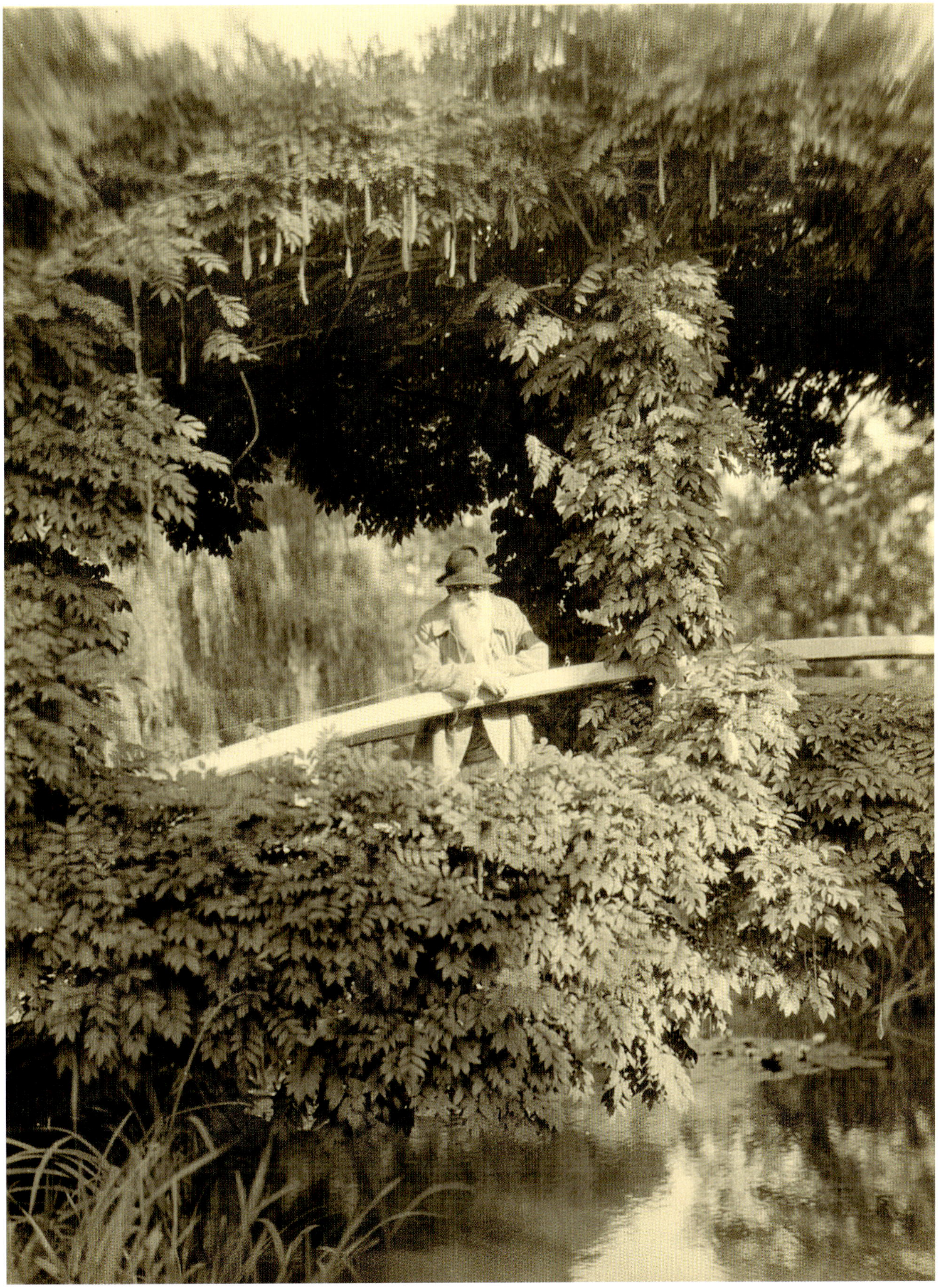

56 | Reine Natanson, *Pierre Bonnard with Claude Monet in Giverny*, 1926
Enlarged silver print, 11.2 × 16 cm
(4 3/8 × 6 5/16 in.)
Private collection

57 | Jacques Salomon, *Édouard Vuillard, Ker Xavier Roussel, Claude Monet, Blanche Hoschedé-Monet and Mme Salomon in Giverny*, 1926
Enlarged and tinted silver print,
16 × 18.4 cm (6 5/16 × 7 1/4 in.)
Private collection

58 | Nickolas Muray, *Claude Monet Seated in his Garden in Giverny*, 1926
Original silver print, signed and dated,
19 × 23.50 cm (7 1/2 × 9 1/4 in.)
Musée Clemenceau, Paris

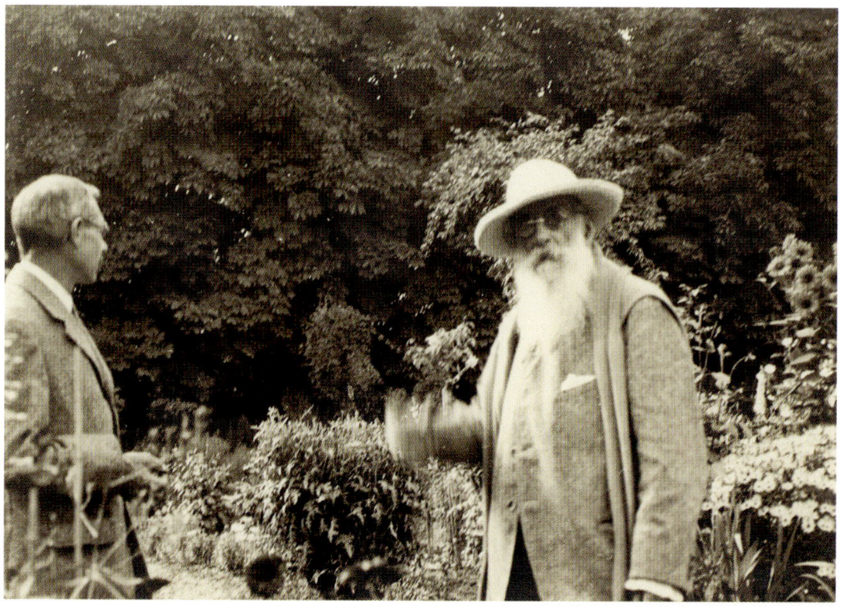

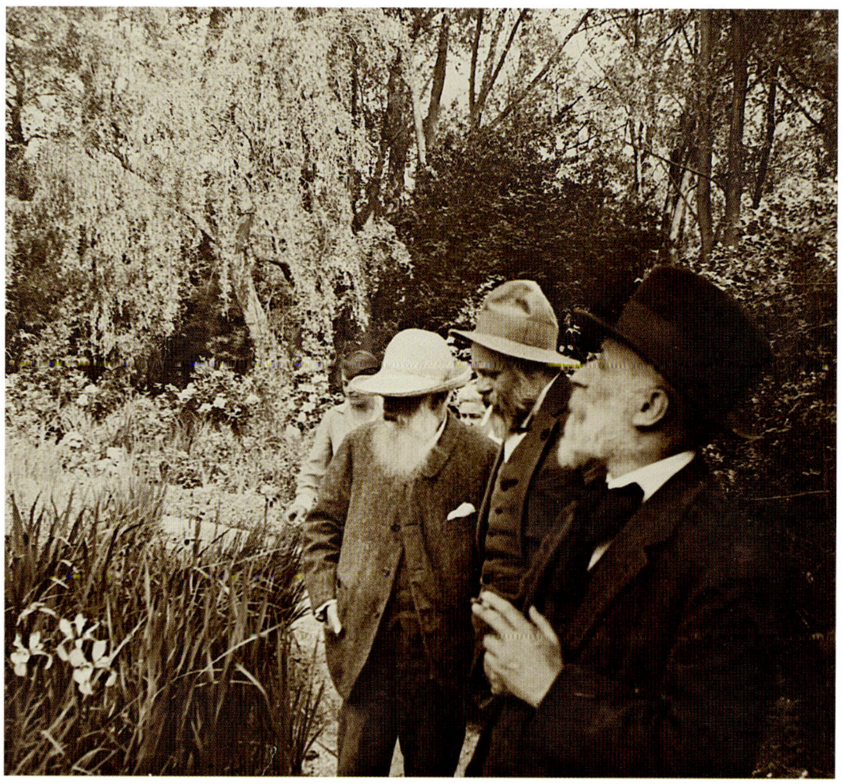

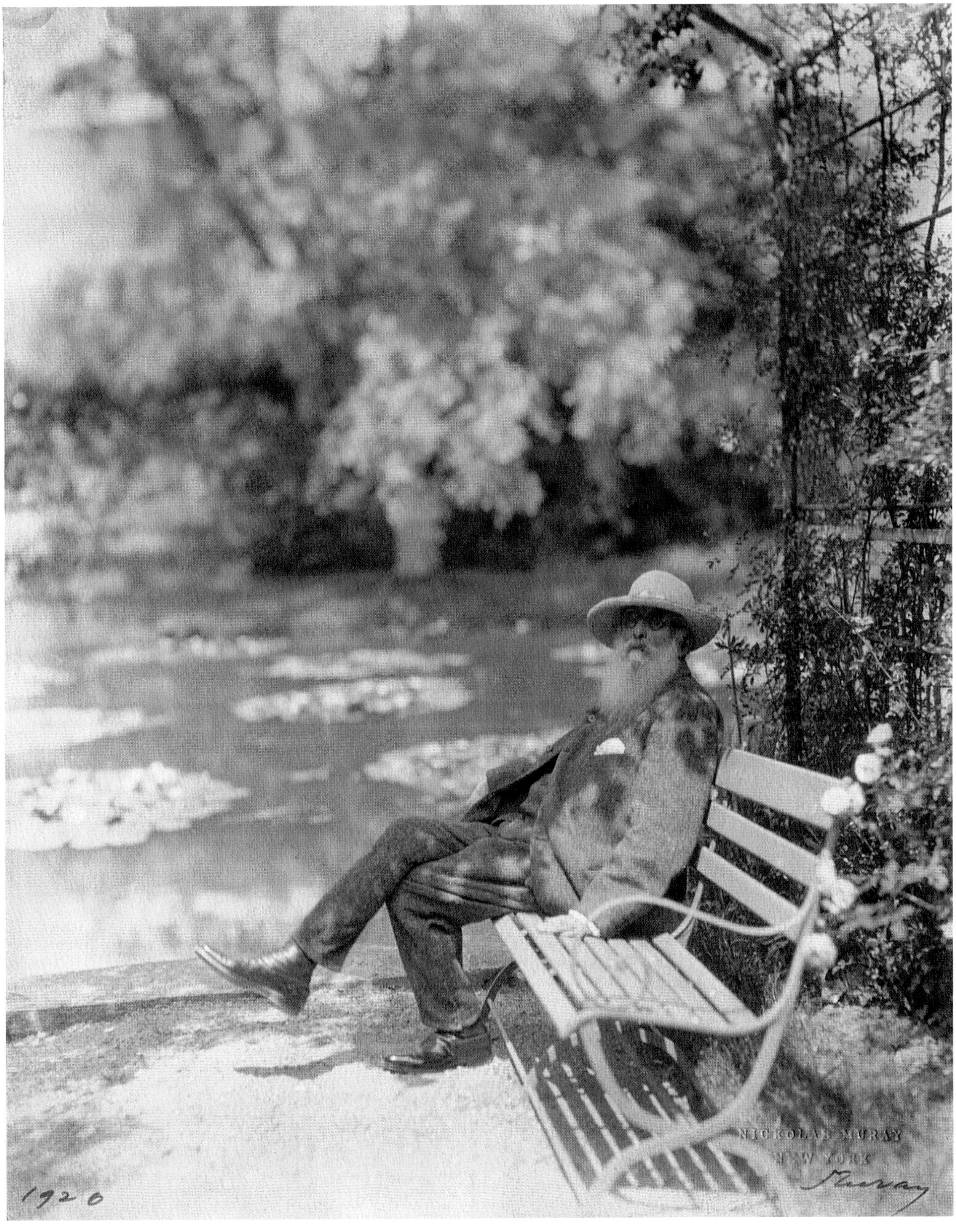
NICKOLAS MURAY
NEW YORK

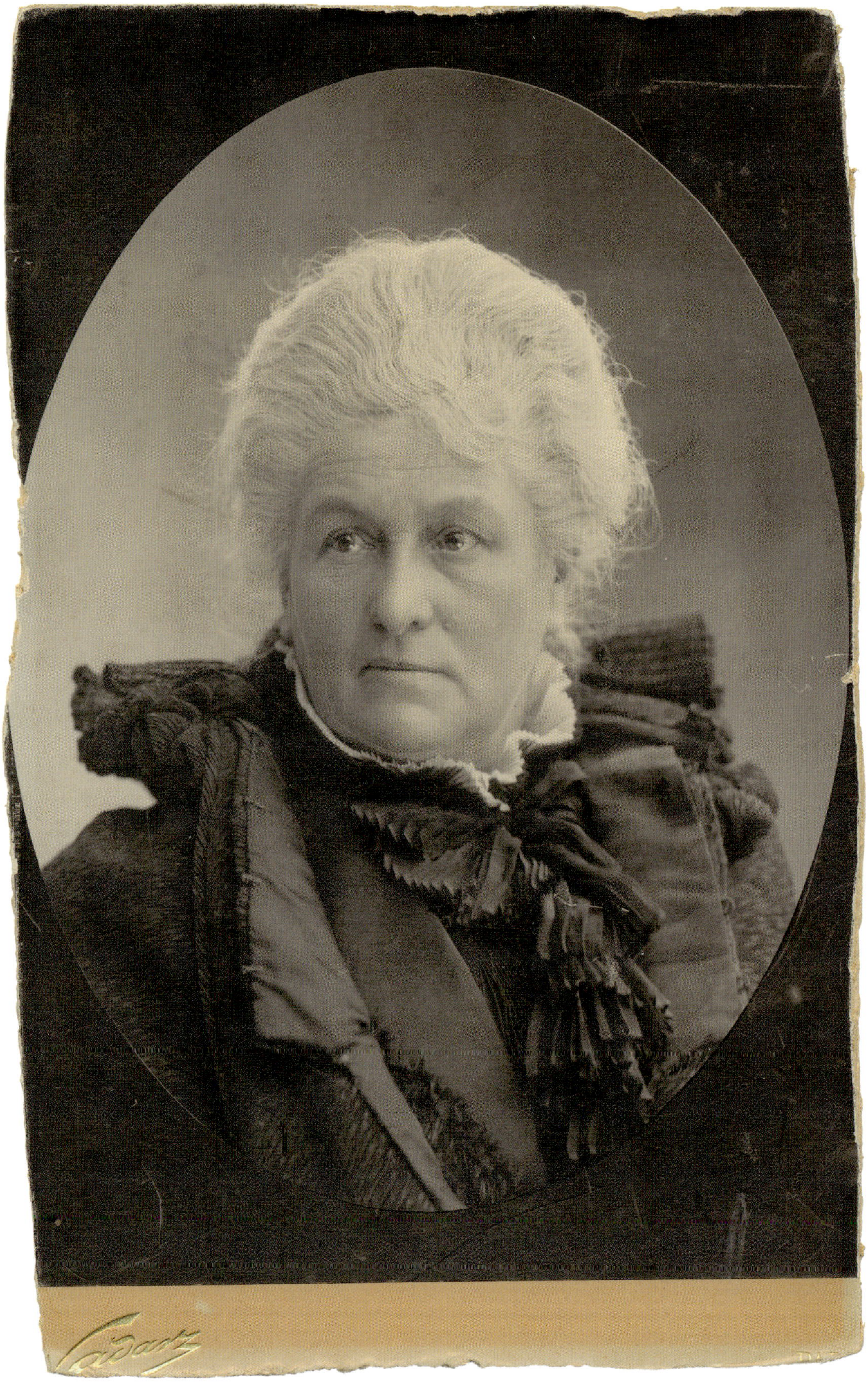

59 | Paul Nadar, *Portrait of Alice Monet*, 1899
Signed original silver print, 24.2 × 15.5 cm
($9^1/_2 \times 6^1/_8$ in.)
Philippe Piguet Collection

60 | Anonymous, *The Hoschedé-Monet Family by the House, Giverny*, ca. 1886
Silver print, 16.6 × 23 cm ($6^1/_2 \times 9^1/_{16}$ in.)
Philippe Piguet Collection

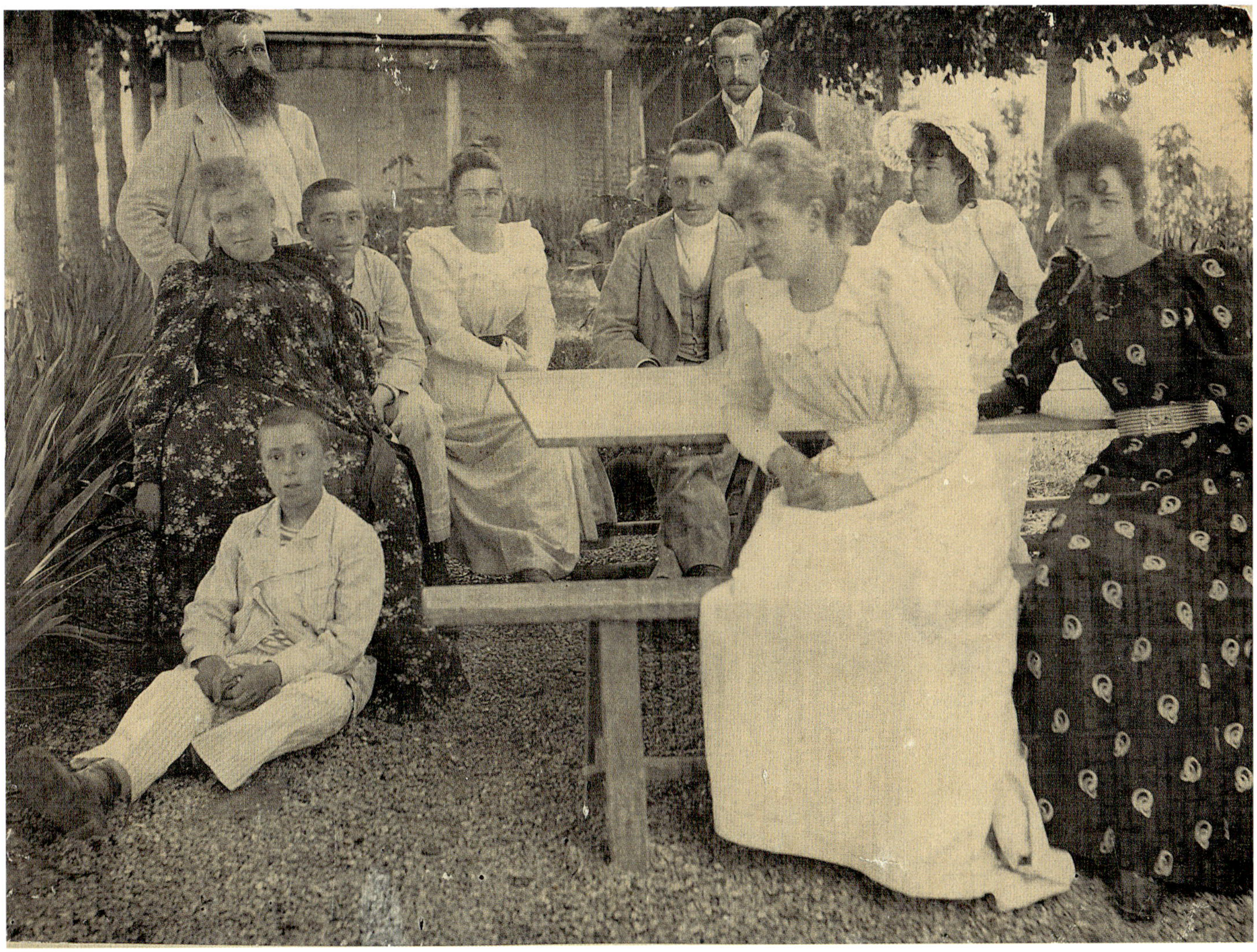

61-63 | Anonymous,
Hoschedé-Monet Family, n. d.
Silver print, 9 × 9.5 cm (3 9/16 × 3 3/4 in.)
Musée Municipal A.-G. Poulain, Vernon

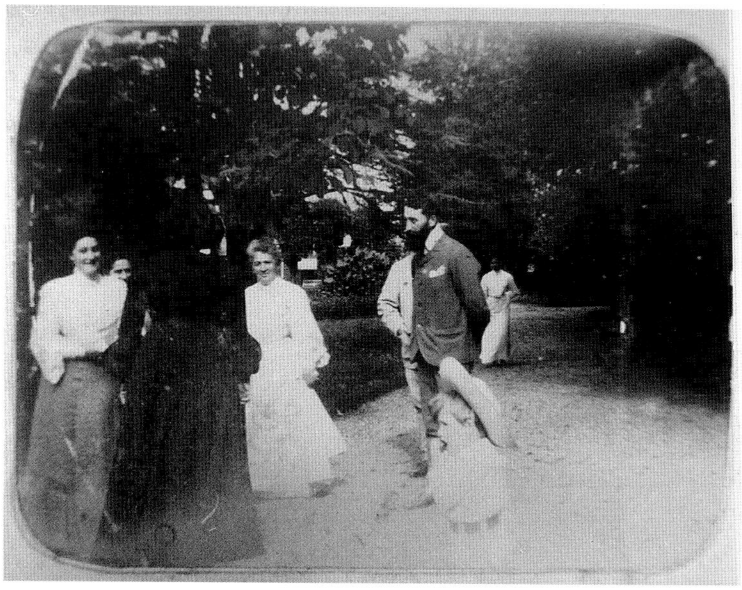

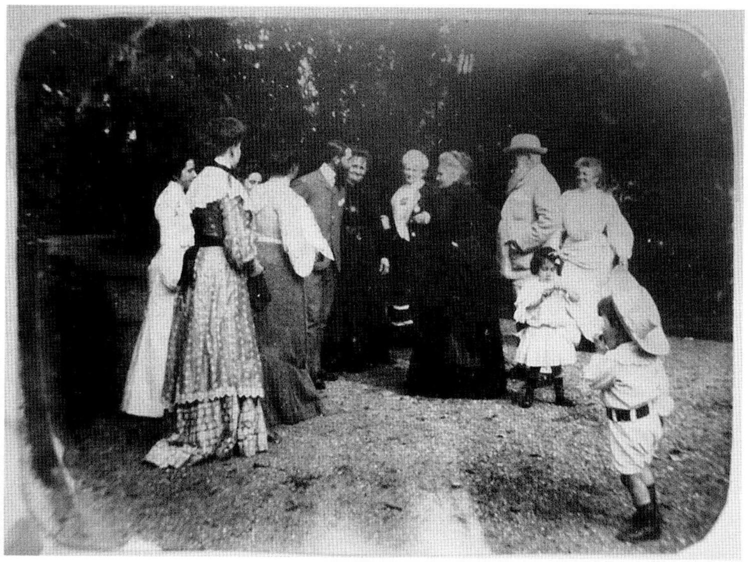

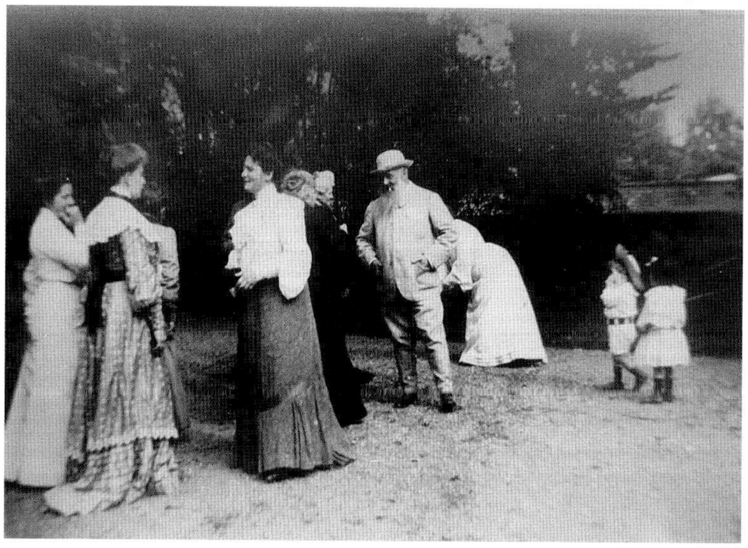

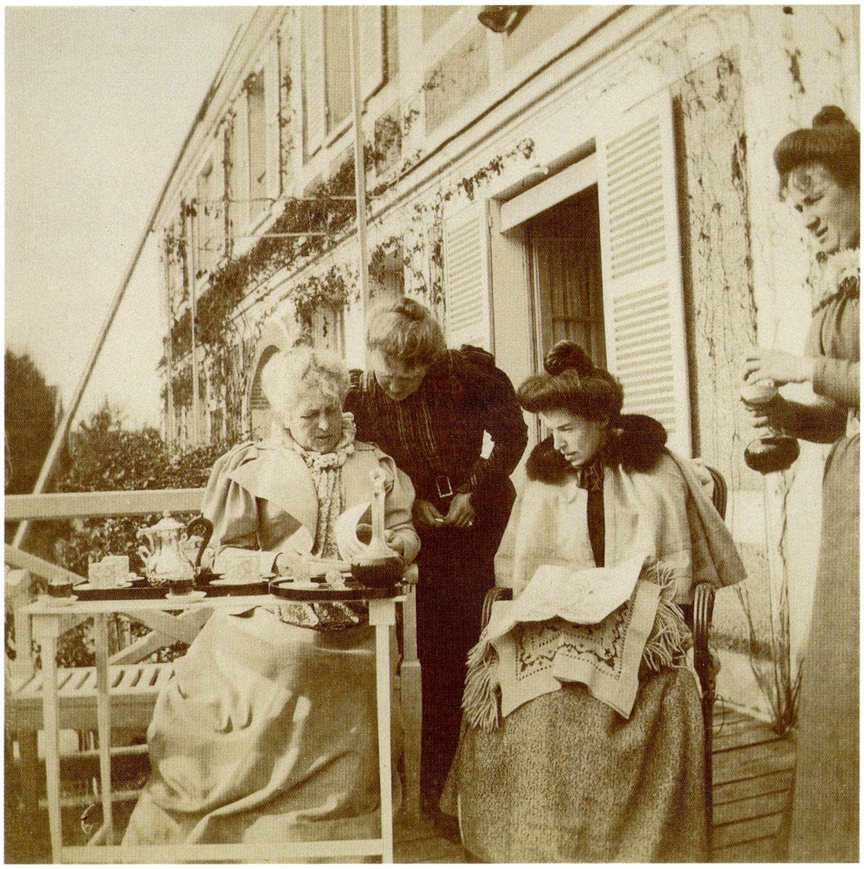

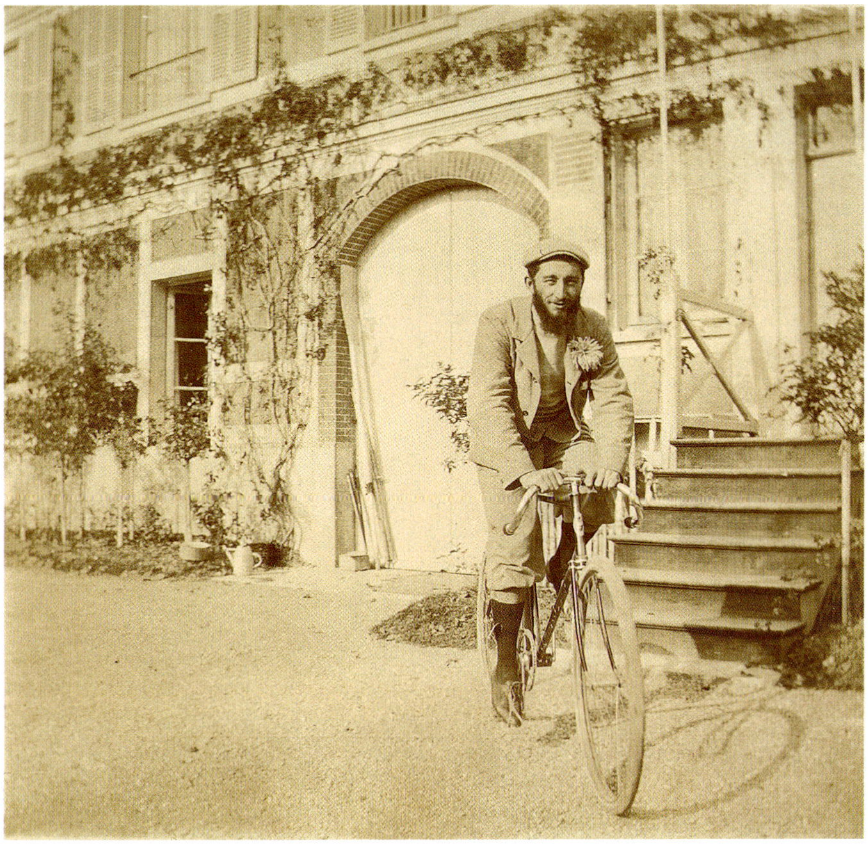

64 | Anonymous, *Alice Hoschedé-Monet and her Daughters Having Tea on the Terrace*, n. d.
Silver print, 9 × 9.5 cm (3 9/16 × 3 3/4 in.)
Véronique and Philippe Perdrix Collection

65 | Anonymous, *Michel Monet on his Bicycle in front of the Family Home*, n. d.
Silver print, 9 × 9.5 cm (7 1/8 × 9 7/16 in.)
Véronique and Philippe Perdrix Collection

66 | Joseph Durand-Ruel, *Germaine Hoschedé, Lili Butler, Mme Joseph Durand-Ruel, Georges Durand-Ruel and Claude Monet*, September 1900
Digital print, 12 × 15 cm (4¾ × 6 in.)
Archives Durand-Ruel, Paris

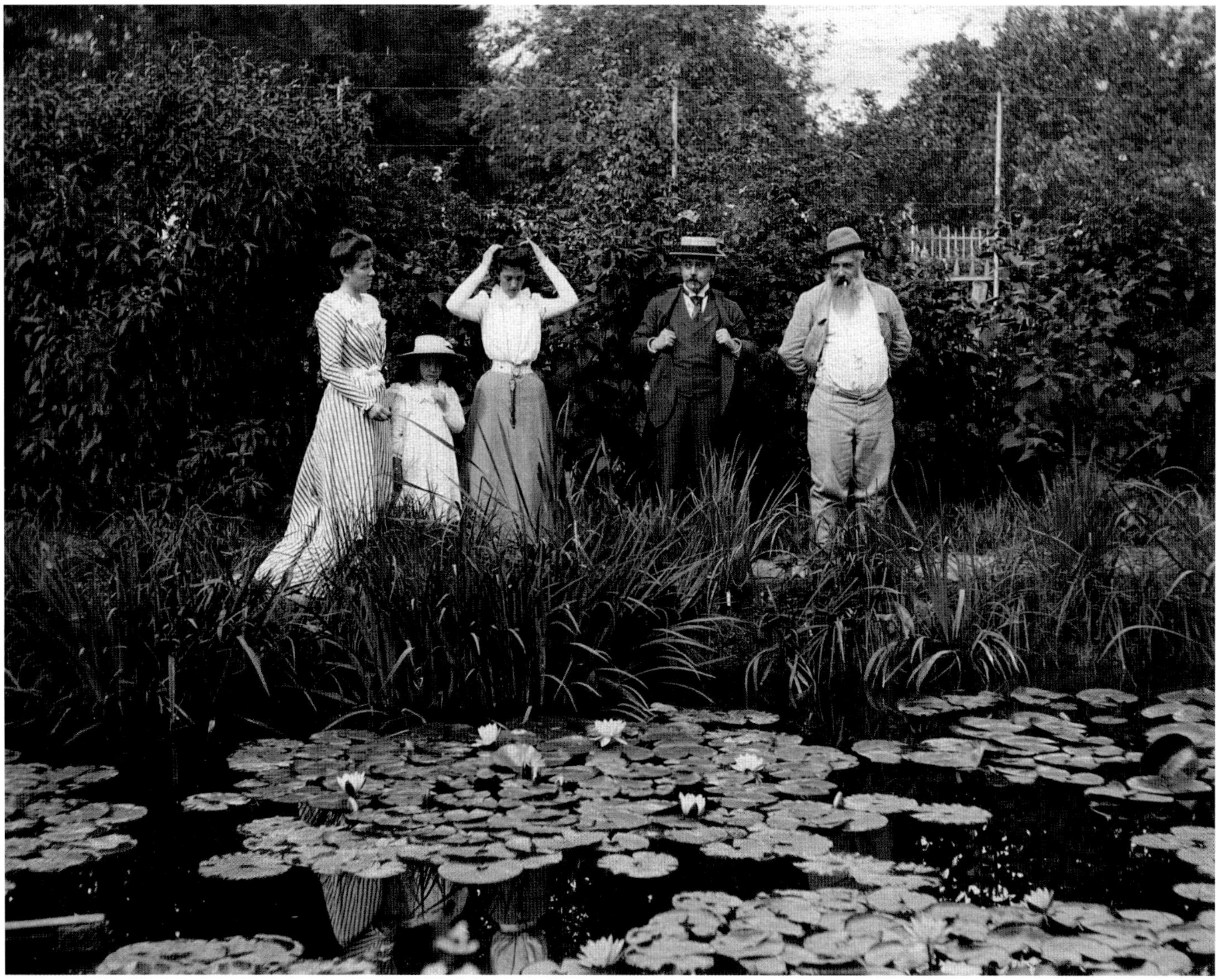

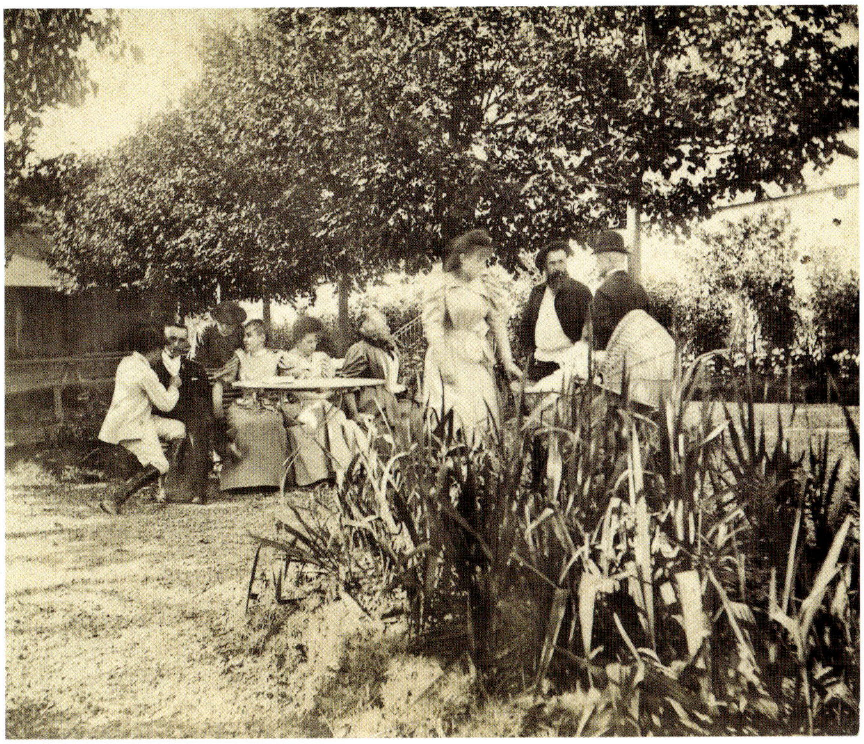

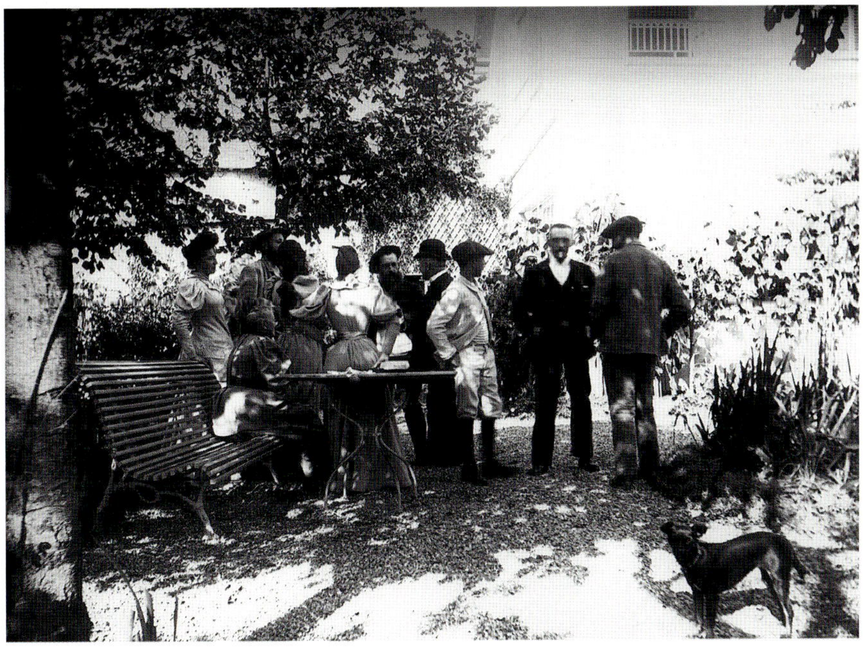

67 | Joseph Durand-Ruel, *Claude Monet, his Family and Paul Durand-Ruel in the Garden, Giverny*, June 1893
Silver print, 9.8 × 11.7 cm (3³/₄ × 4¹/₂ in.)
Philippe Piguet Collection

68 | Joseph Durand-Ruel, *The Durand-Ruel Family Visiting Giverny, the Hoschedé-Monet Family, Butler, Durand-Ruel with Paul in a Bowler Hat*, June 1893
Digital print, 12 × 15 cm (4³/₄ × 6 in.)
Archives Durand-Ruel, Paris

69 | Anonymous, *View of the Orchard with the House in the Background, Giverny*, 1890s
Silver print, 15.6 × 22.4 cm (6 1/8 × 8 13/16 in.)
Philippe Piguet Collection

70 | Anonymous, *Monet's Garden in Giverny, View of the Greenhouse*, 1897
Silver print, 3.8 × 5.5 cm (1 1/2 × 2 3/16 in.)
Philippe Piguet Collection

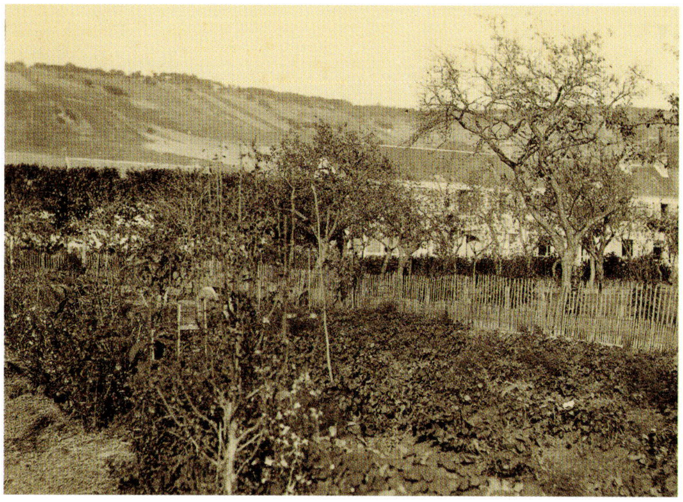

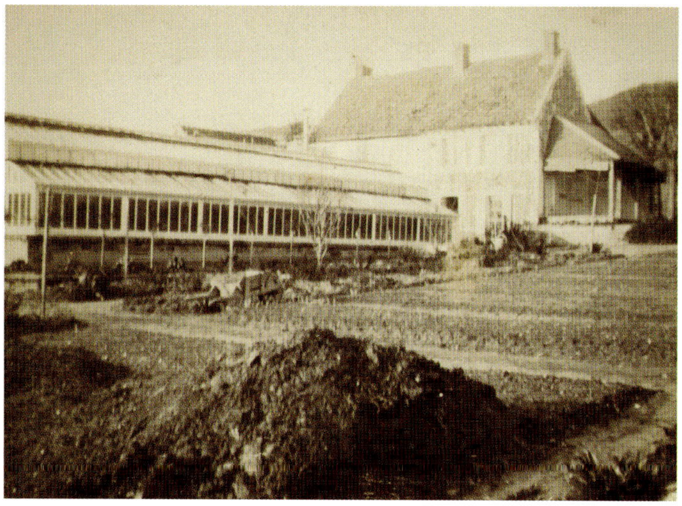

71 | Anonymous, *Monet's House in Giverny with a Flowerbed in the Foreground*, 1910
Silver print, 7.8 × 10.8 cm (3 1/16 × 4 1/4 in.)
Philippe Piguet Collection

72 | Anonymous, *Monet's Garden in Giverny, Flowerbeds and View of the Second Studio*, ca. 1910
Silver print, 5.5 × 8.2 cm (2 3/16 × 3 1/4 in.)
Philippe Piguet Collection

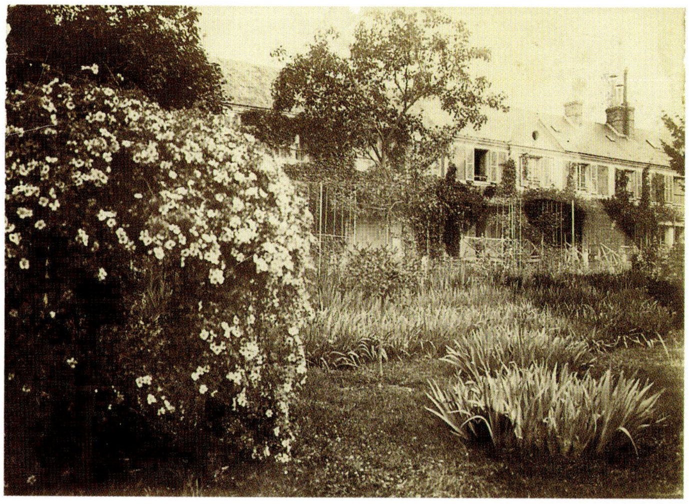

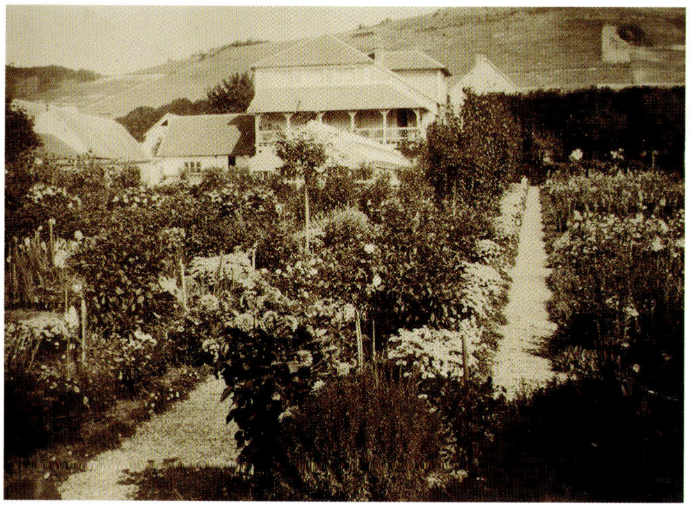

73 | Pogany, *Félix Breuil, the Head Gardener, at Work, Giverny*, ca. 1913
Modern silver print, 12.6 × 17.7 cm (5 × 7 in.)
Philippe Piguet Collection

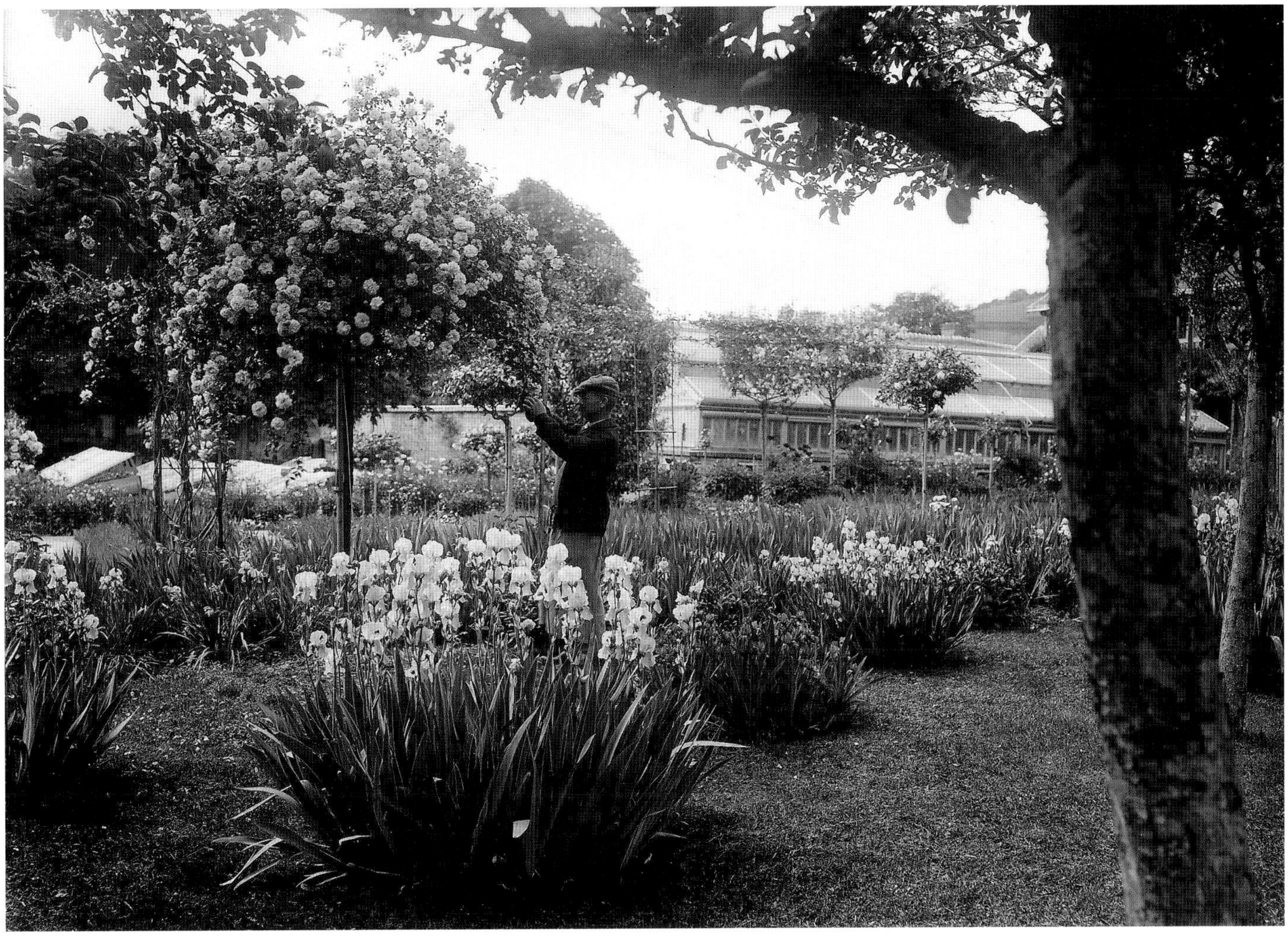

74 | Anonymous, *Giverny – Claude Monet's Garden – Central Path*, n. d.
Vintage postcard, 9 × 14 cm ($3\frac{9}{16} \times 5\frac{1}{2}$ in.)
Terra Foundation for American Art, Chicago

75 | [Ed. Lavergne, Vernon]
Giverny (Eure) – Property of the Painter Claude Monnet [sic], n. d.
Vintage postcard, 9 × 14 cm ($3\frac{9}{16} \times 5\frac{1}{2}$ in.)
Terra Foundation for American Art, Chicago

76 | Anonymous, *Giverny (Eure) – Property of Master Claude Monet – Central Path*, n. d.
Vintage postcard, 9 × 14 cm ($3\frac{9}{16} \times 5\frac{1}{2}$ in.)
Terra Foundation for American Art, Chicago

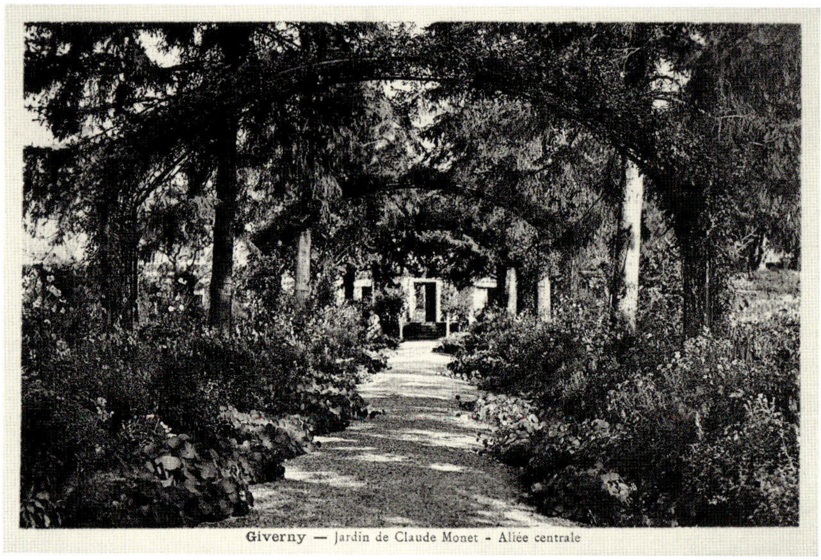

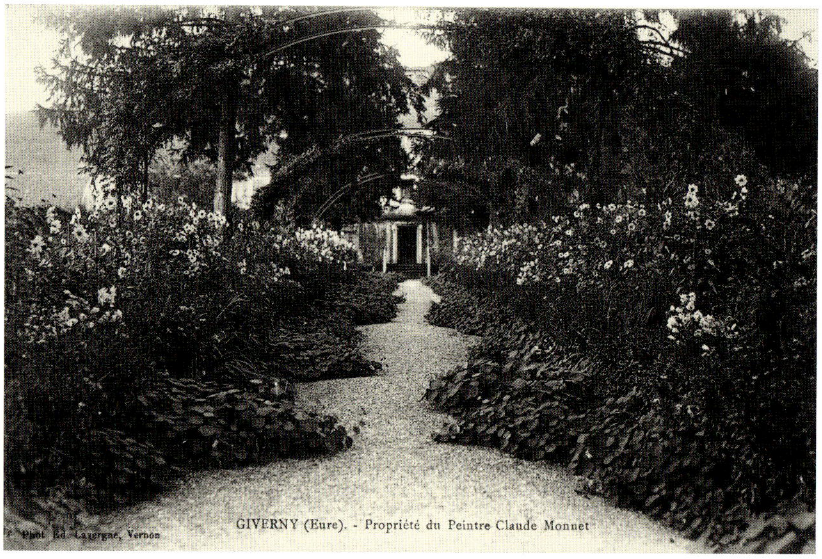

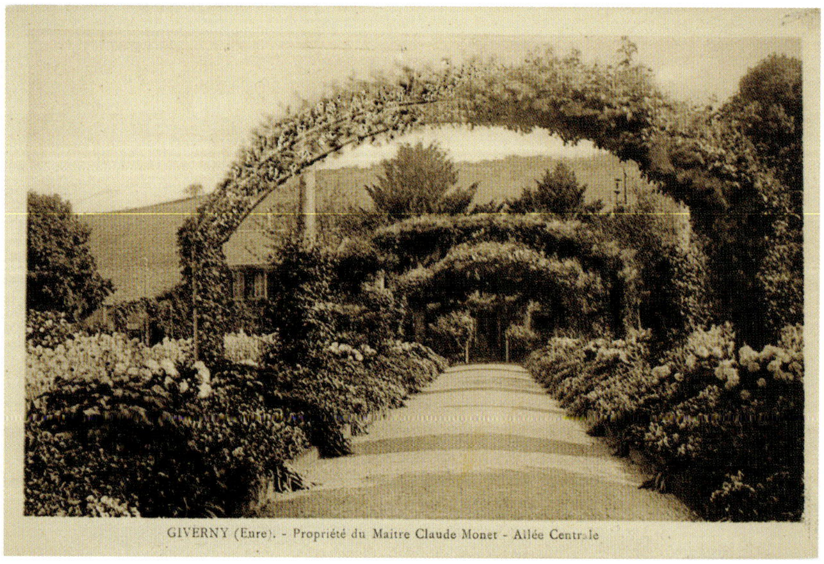

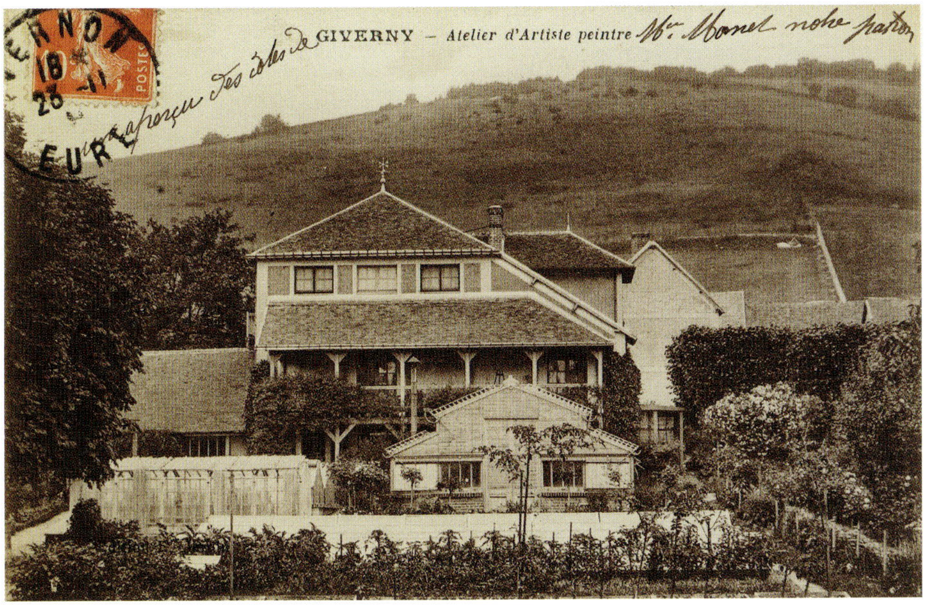

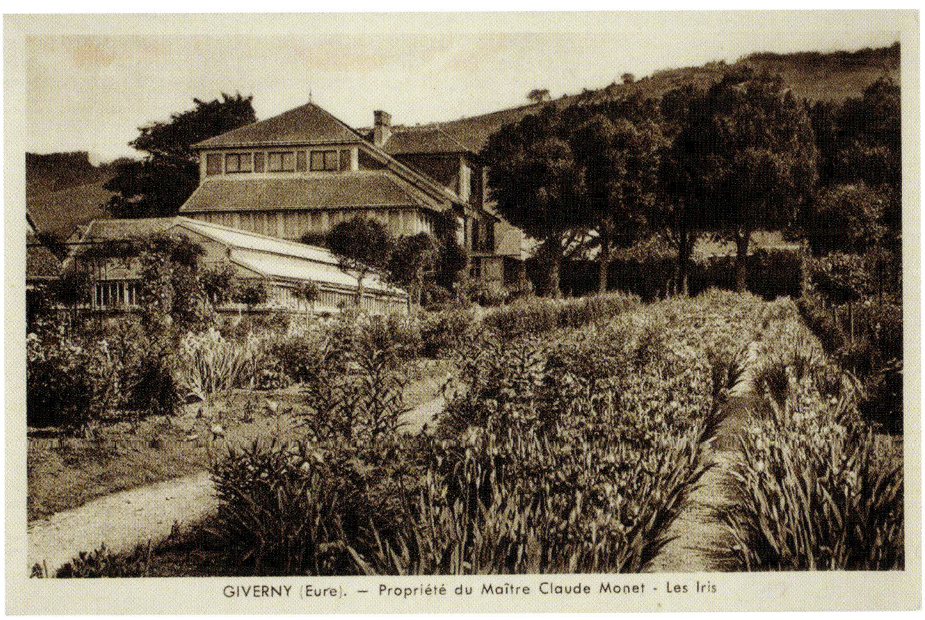

77 | Anonymous, *Giverny – Artist's studio*, n. d.
Vintage postcard, 9 × 14 cm ($3\frac{9}{16} \times 5\frac{1}{2}$ in.)
Terra Foundation for American Art, Chicago

78 | Anonymous, *Giverny (Eure) – Property of Master Claude Monet – Irises*, n. d.
Vintage postcard, 9 × 14 cm ($3\frac{9}{16} \times 5\frac{1}{2}$ in.)
Terra Foundation for American Art, Chicago

79 | Anonymous, *Giverny – Claude Monet's Garden – Water Lilies*, n. d.
Vintage postcard, 9 × 14 cm ($3\frac{9}{16} \times 5\frac{1}{2}$ in.)
Terra Foundation for American Art, Chicago

80 | Anonymous, *Giverny (Eure) – Property of Master Claude Monet – General View of the Water Garden*, n. d.
Vintage postcard, 9 × 14 cm ($3\frac{9}{16} \times 5\frac{1}{2}$ in.)
Terra Foundation for American Art, Chicago

81 | [Georges André Vernon], *Giverny (Eure) - Property of Master Claude Monet - Water Lilies*, n. d.
Vintage postcard, 9 × 14 cm ($3\frac{9}{16} \times 5\frac{1}{2}$ in.)
Terra Foundation for American Art, Chicago

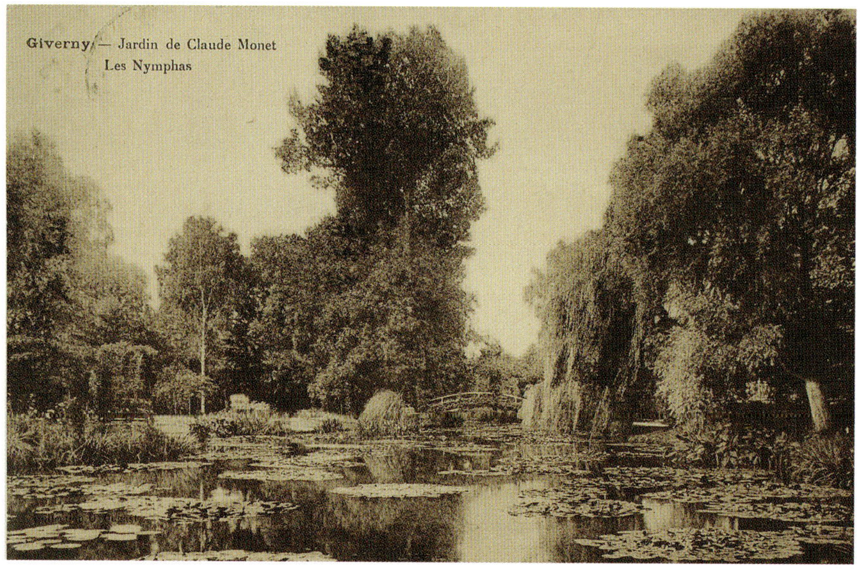

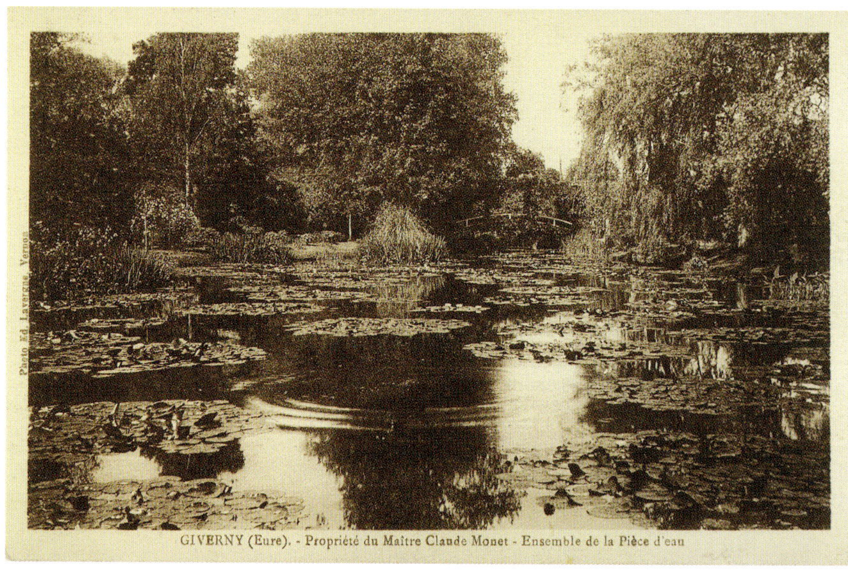

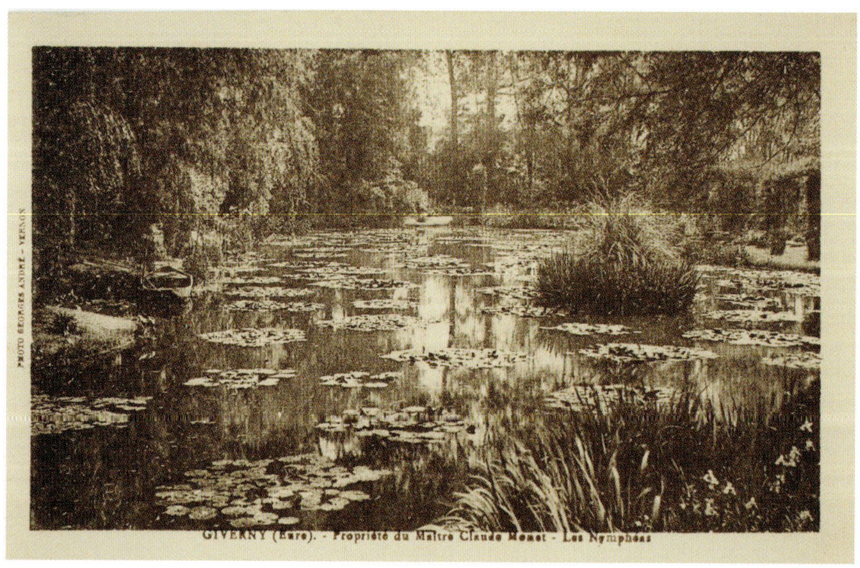

82 | Anonymous,
View of the Pond, Giverny, 1905
Annotated on the back: "The Pond is Magnificent", ca. 1905
Silver print, 5.5 × 8.30 cm (2 3/16 × 3 1/4 in.)
Philippe Piguet Collection

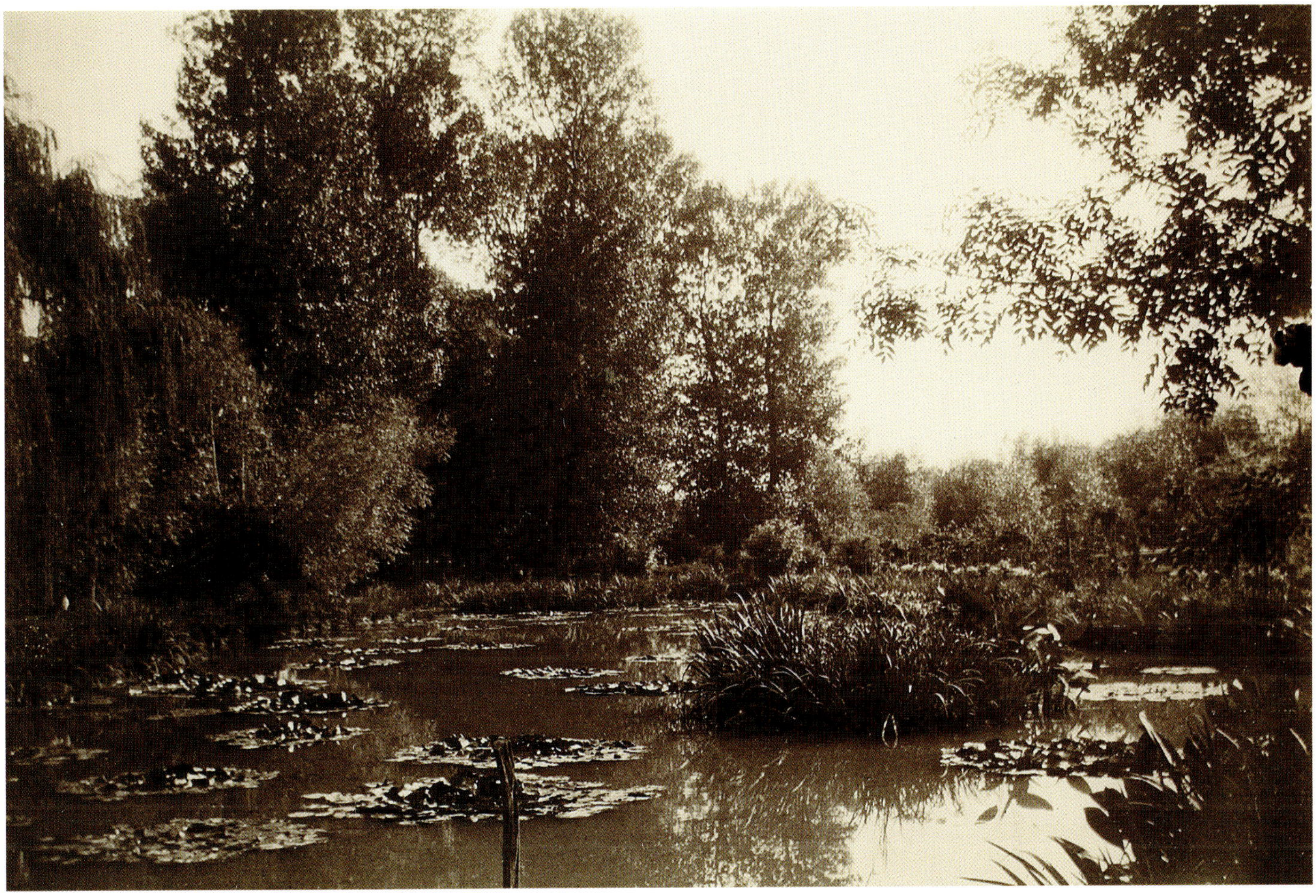

83 | *Menu for the wedding of Germaine Hoschedé and Albert Salerou with a photograph of the Japanese Bridge, Giverny*, 12 November 1902
20.8 × 12.8 cm (7 15/16 × 5 in.)
Philippe Piguet Collection

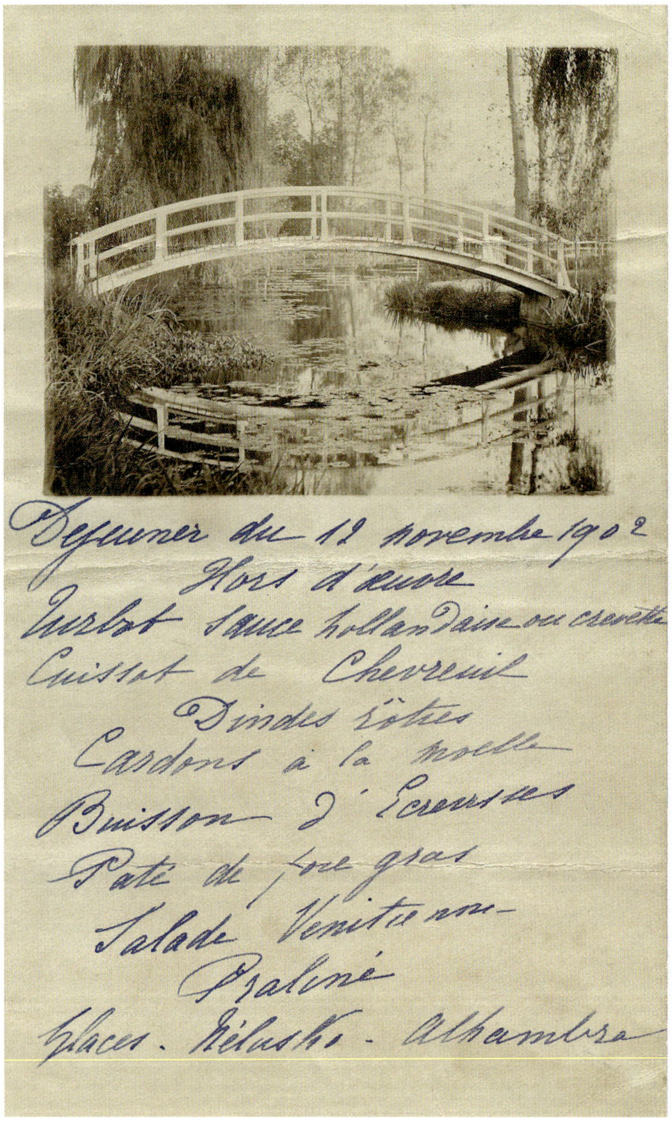

Dejeuner du 12 novembre 1902
Hors d'œuvre
Turbot sauce hollandaise ou crevettes
Cuissot de Chevreuil
Dindes rôties
Cardons à la moelle
Buisson d'Ecrevisses
Pâté de foie gras
Salade Vénitienne
Praliné
Glaces . Nélusko . Alhambra

84 | *Menu for the wedding of Simone Salerou and Robert Piguet*, 26 October 1926
23.3 × 13.9 cm (9 1/4 × 5 1/2 in.)
Philippe Piguet Collection

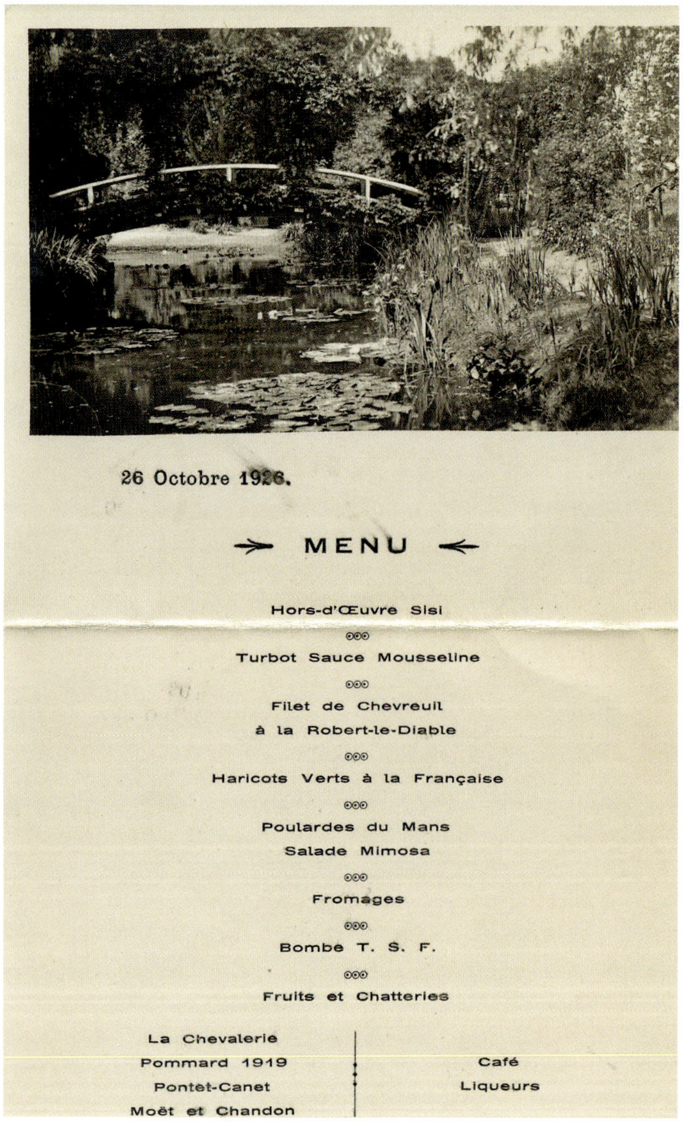

26 Octobre 1926.

MENU

Hors-d'Œuvre Sisi
Turbot Sauce Mousseline
Filet de Chevreuil
à la Robert-le-Diable
Haricots Verts à la Française
Poulardes du Mans
Salade Mimosa
Fromages
Bombe T. S. F.
Fruits et Chatteries

La Chevalerie
Pommard 1919
Pontet-Canet
Moët et Chandon

Café
Liqueurs

85 | Anonymous, *Alice Hoschedé-Monet and her granddaughter Alice Butler on one of the small bridges in the Water Lily Pond, Giverny*, July 1910
Silver print, 17.7 × 17.8 cm (7 × 7 in.)
Philippe Piguet Collection

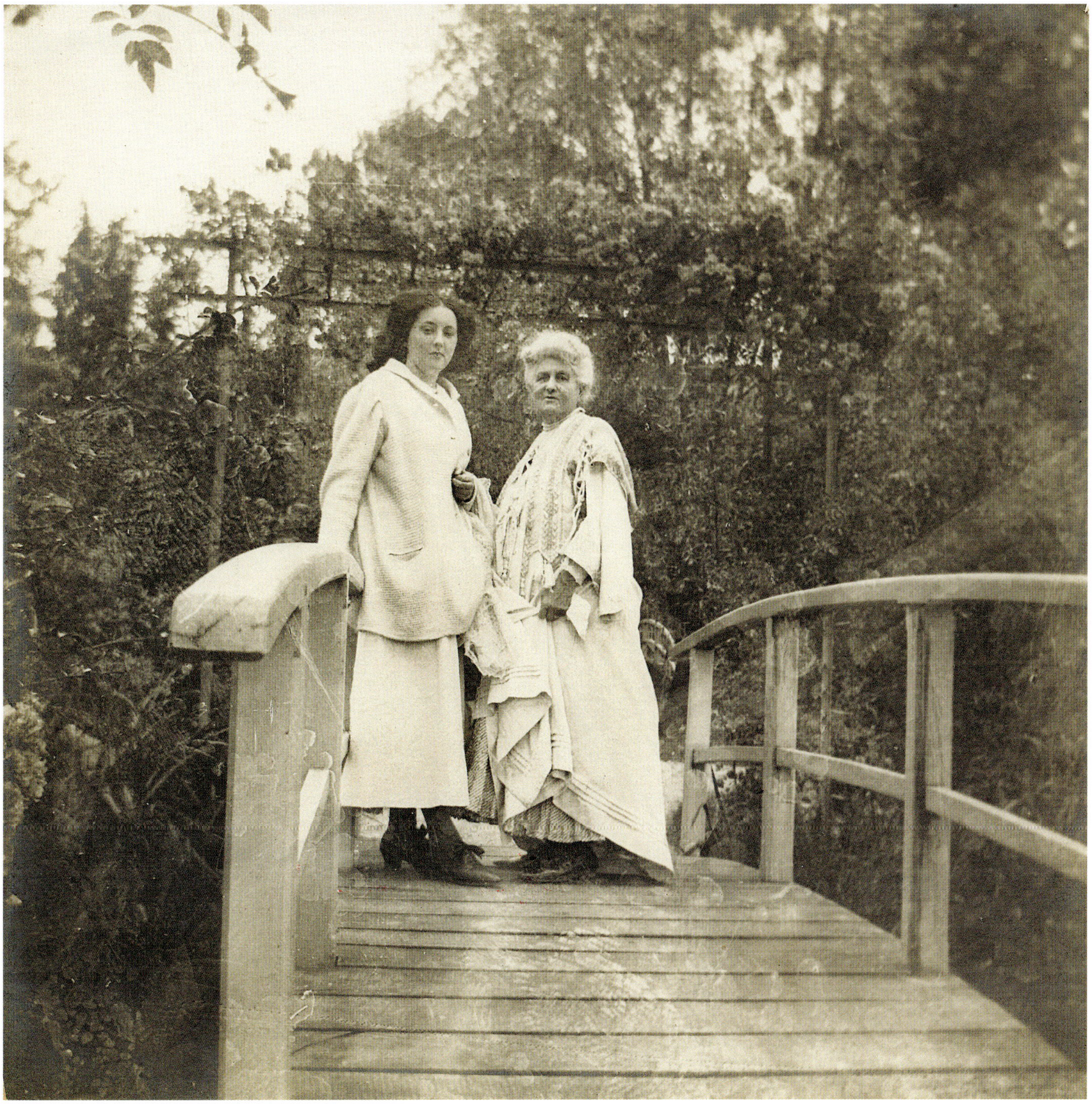

86 | Georges Truffaut,
View of the Water Lily Pond, Giverny,
ca. 1913
Silver print, 17.4 × 12.5 cm ($6\frac{7}{8}$ × $4\frac{15}{16}$ in.)
Philippe Piguet Collection

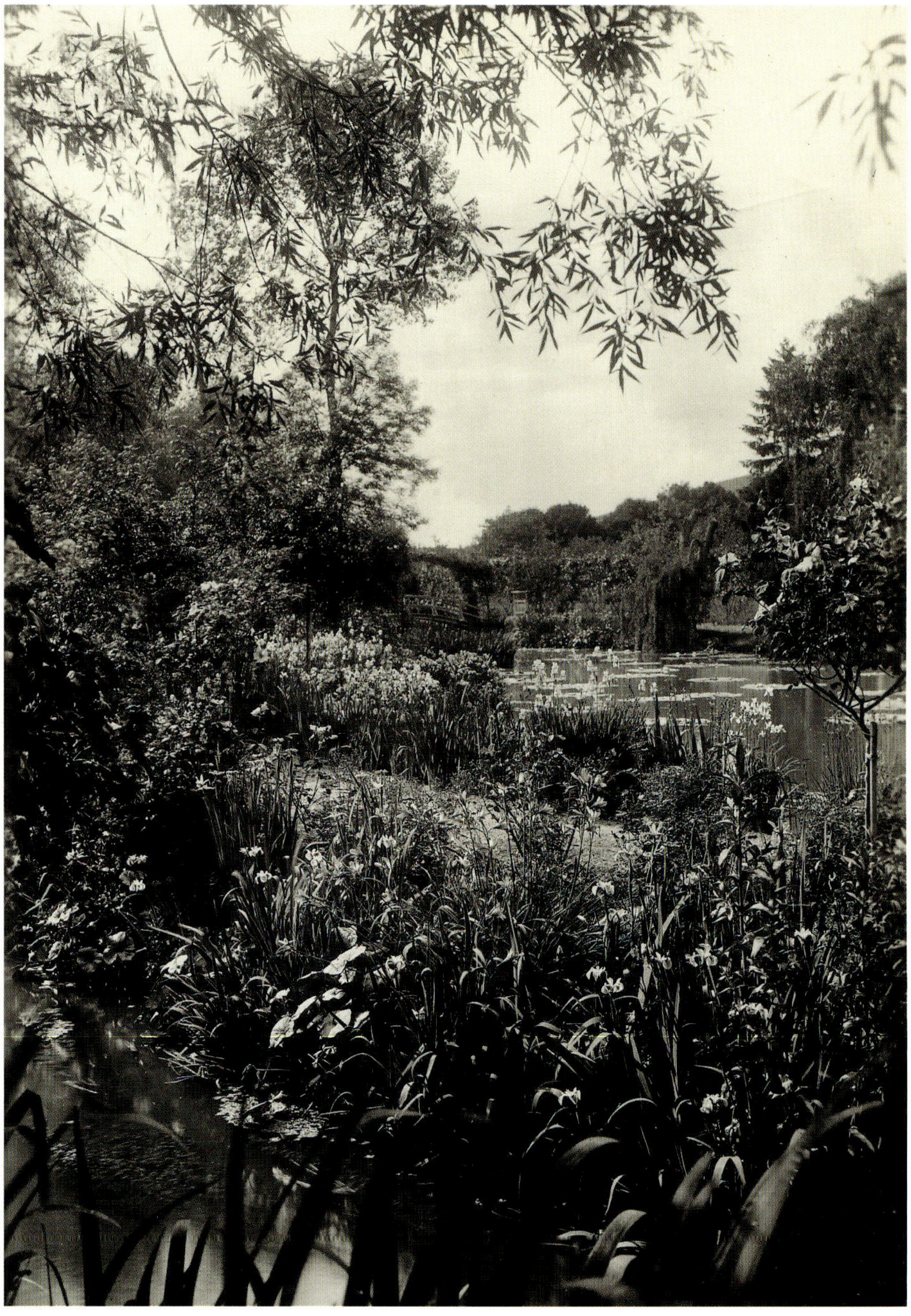

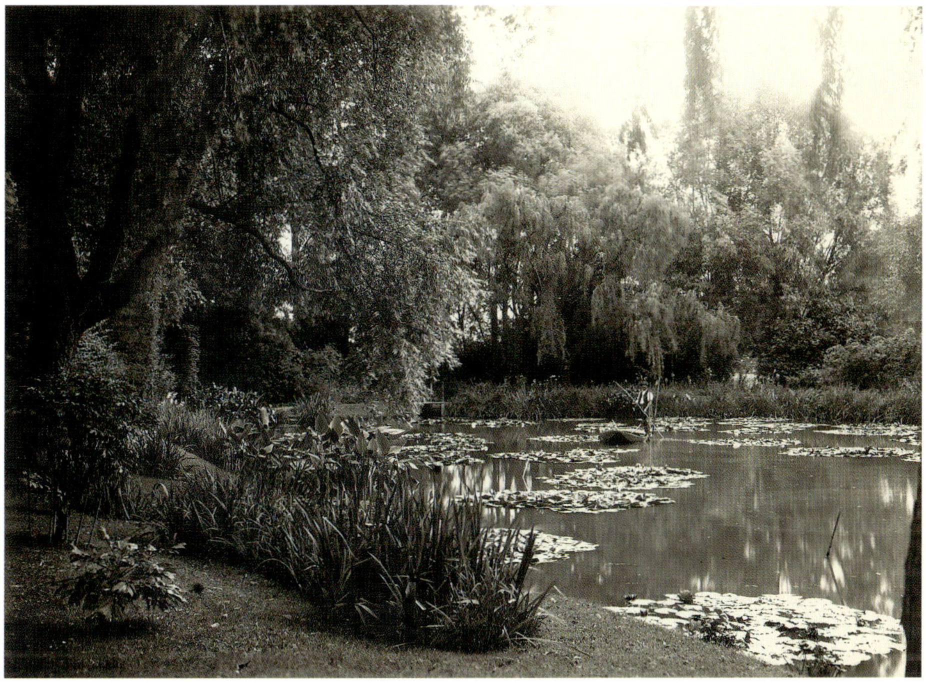

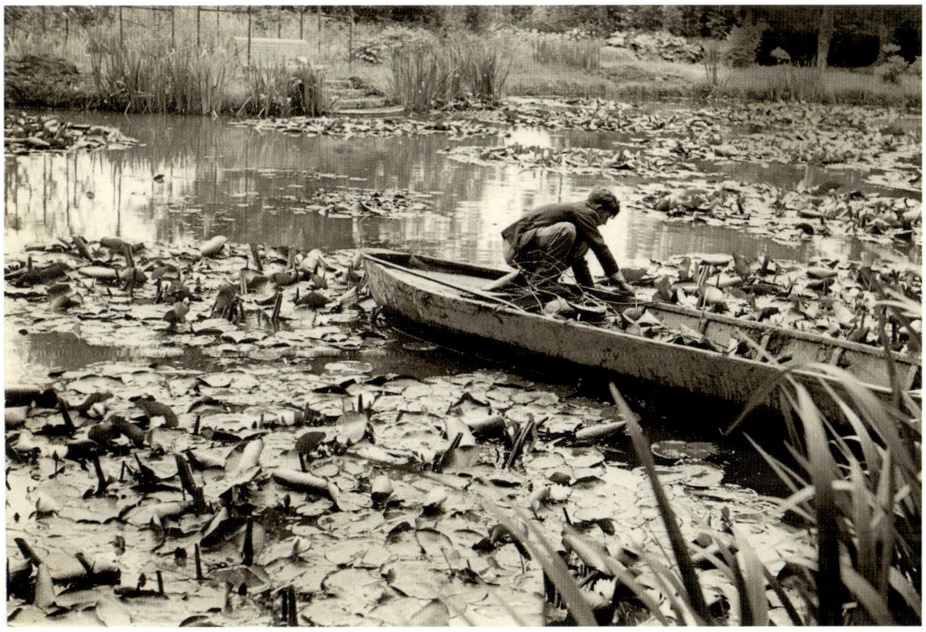

87 | Gouthière, *View of the Water Lily Pond, Giverny*, ca. 1924
Silver print, 12,5 × 17,4 cm (6⅞ × 4¹⁵⁄₁₆ in.)
Philippe Piguet Collection

88 | Anonymous, *The Gardener Félix Breuil? in the Norvégienne on the Water Lily Pond, Giverny*, n. d.
Silver print, 11.2 × 16.9 cm (4⅜ × 6⅝ in.)
Philippe Piguet Collection

89 | Anonymous, *The House seen from the Garden Path (Giverny)*, ca. 1933
Digital print
Collection of *Country Life* magazine, London

90 | Anonymous, *The Garden with the Second Studio on the Left*, ca. 1933
Digital print
Collection of *Country Life* magazine, London

91 | Anonymous, *Monet's Flower Garden*, ca. 1933
Digital print
Collection of *Country Life* magazine, London

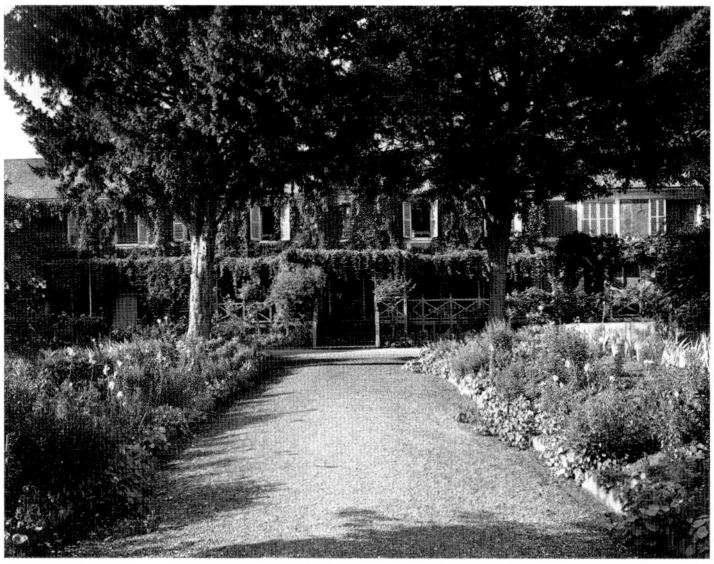

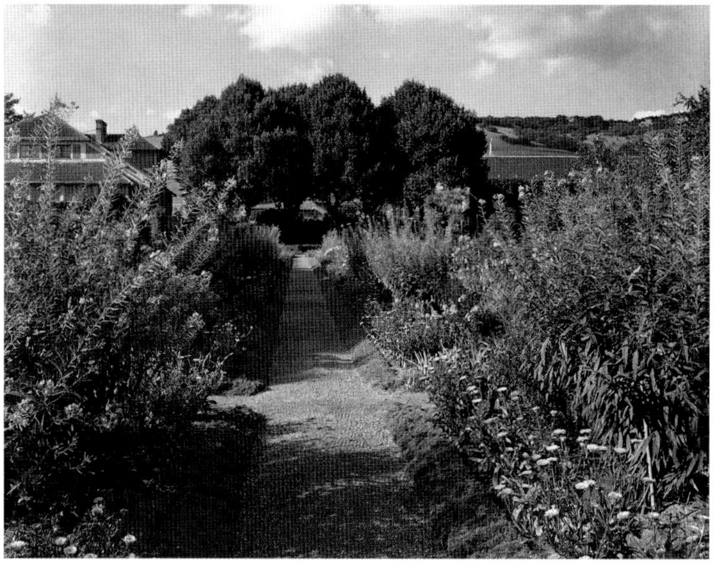

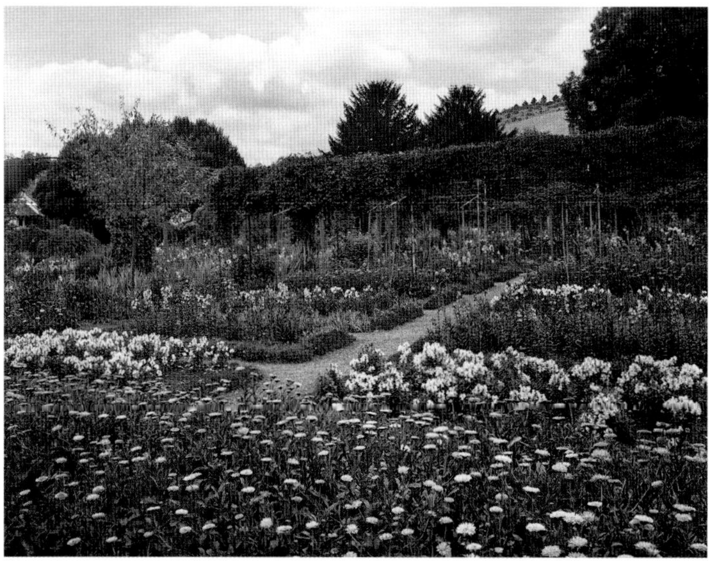

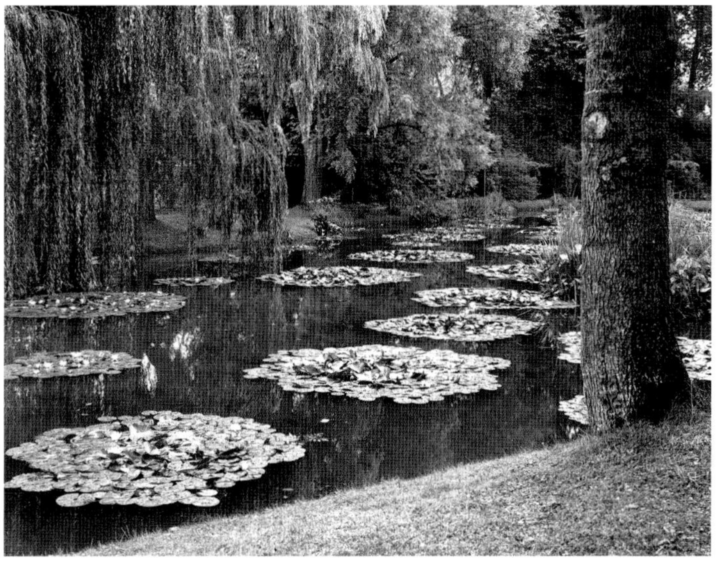

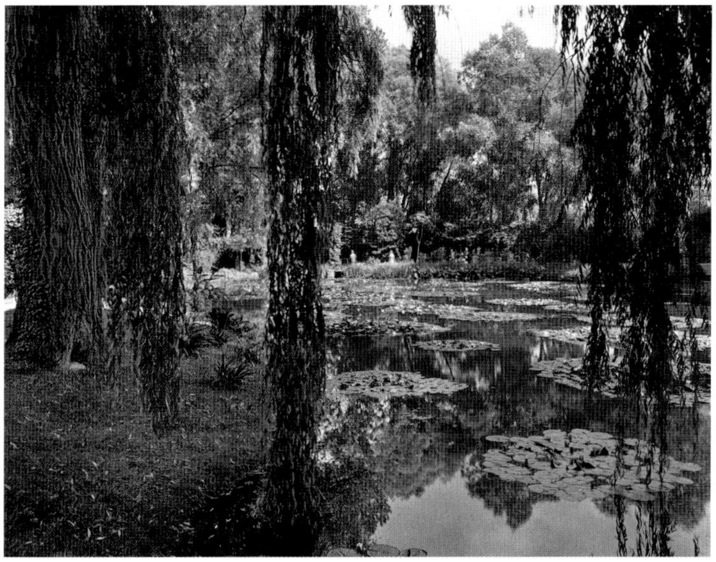

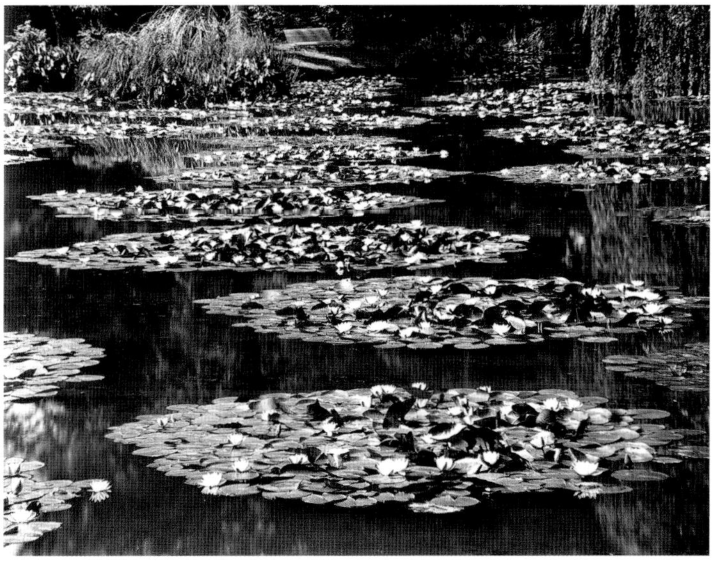

92 | Anonymous, *The Water Lily Pond*
Digital print
Collection of *Country Life* magazine, London

93 | Anonymous, *The Pond seen through Willow Branches*
Digital print
Collection of *Country Life* magazine, London

94 | Anonymous, *The Water Lily Pond*
Digital print
Collection of *Country Life* magazine, London

Letters

Letter from Claude Monet to the Prefect of the Eure, 13 August 1901
Archives Départementales de l'Eure, Évreux
(18 S 25)

Dear Sir,
I am writing you to request authorization to divert waters from a small arm of the Epte River, known as the "communal arm", within the property belonging to me, and situated within the commune of Giverny, provided that the administrative formalities and conditions that said project is likely to produce are fulfilled.

I remain, Sir, yours faithfully,
Claude Monet
This 13th day of August 1901

To the Prefect of the Eure at Évreux

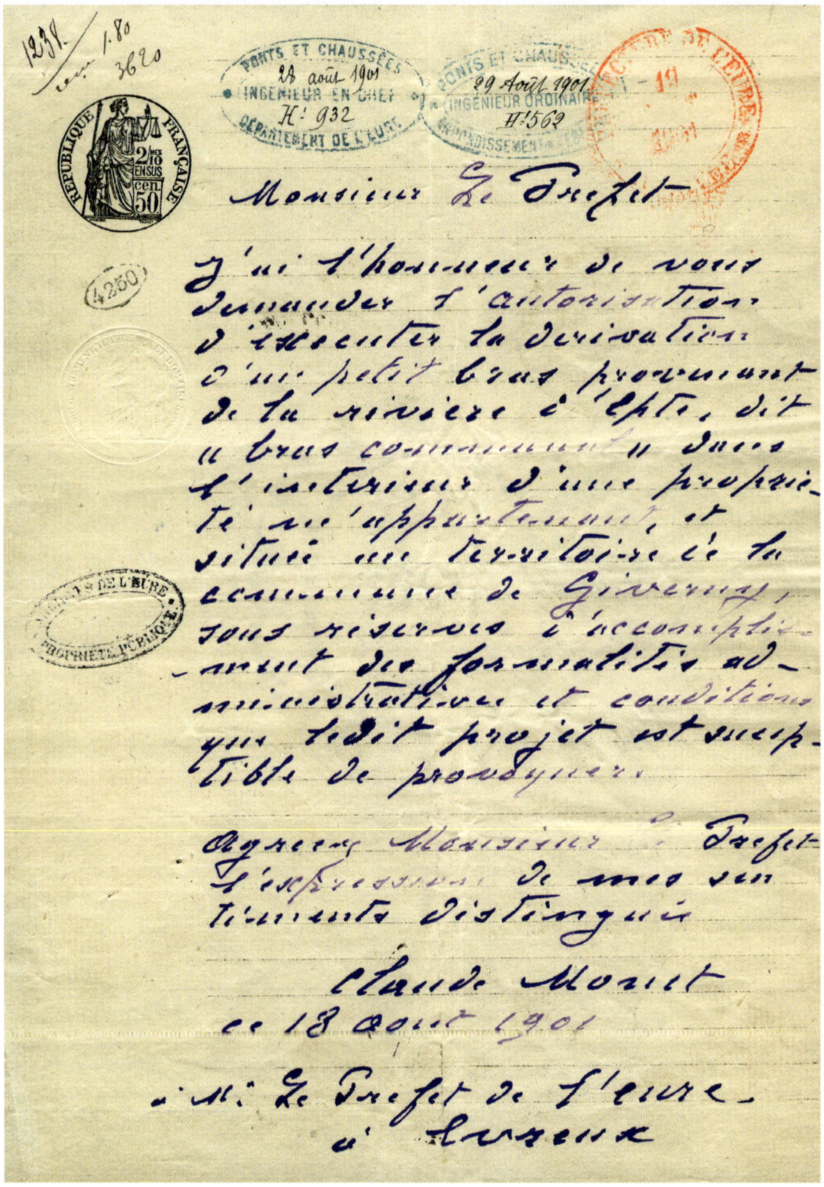

Monsieur Le Préfet

J'ai l'honneur de vous demander l'autorisation d'exécuter la dérivation d'un petit bras provenant de la rivière d'Epte, dit « bras communal » dans l'intérieur d'une propriété m'appartenant, et située au territoire de la commune de Giverny, sous réserves d'accomplissement des formalités administratives et conditions que ledit projet est susceptible de produire.

Agréez Monsieur le Préfet l'expression de mes sentiments distingués

Claude Monet
ce 13 août 1901

à M. Le Préfet de l'Eure à Evreux

Draft (for the Prefect) by Mr. Bautruche, sent by Mr. Damoy, Évreux, to Claude Monet, 11 December 1901
Archives Départementales de l'Eure, Évreux (18 S 25)

Mr. Claude Monet, artist in Giverny
(in care of the Sub-Prefect of Les Andelys)
In your request of 13 August last, you asked for authorization to divert water from the lesser arm of the Epte River, known as the "communal arm", which crosses your property, in order to enlarge a pond that you currently use for the cultivation of aquatic plants.
I am pleased to inform you that in accordance with art. 644 of the Civil Code, any landowner whose land is crossed by a water course may use it as he sees fit in the portion which crosses said land, provided that, when it leaves his property, he restores it to its ordinary course.
In these conditions, my administration cannot limit the right which is accorded to you by the code and, as a result, to rule on your request. You are therefore at liberty to carry out, rights of third parties notwithstanding, if there be any such, being expressly reserved, the works in question, as long as they in no way adversely affect the free flow of the waters of the arm of the Epte crossing your property, and this condition will be fulfilled if you give the diversion planned a minimum width of 4 meters and a uniform gradient throughout its course.

Herewith the sum of 80 francs which came with your request.
Yours faithfully,

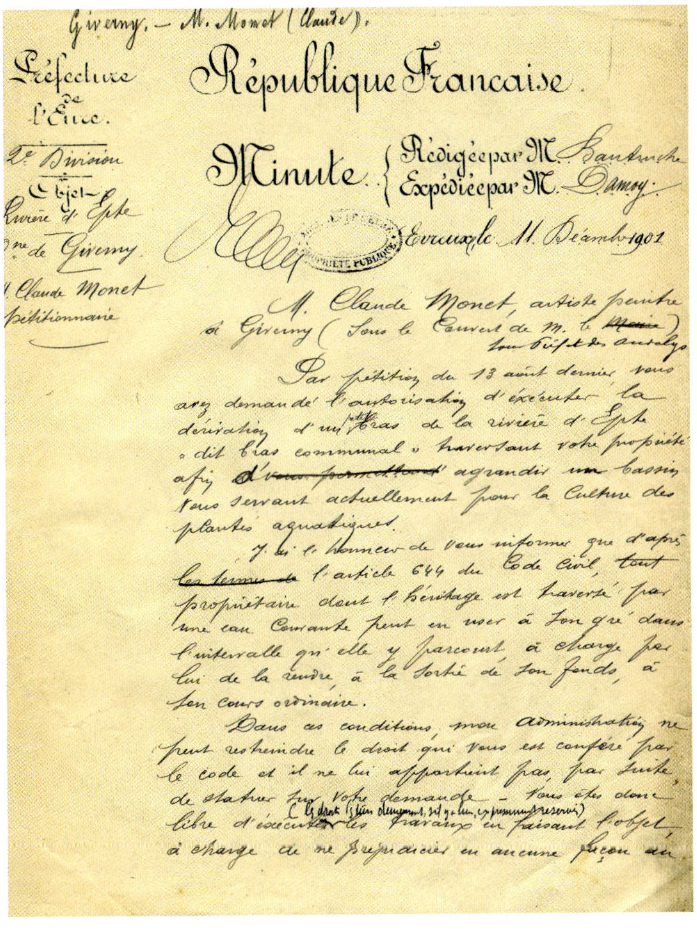
Giverny. — M. Monet (Claude).

Préfecture de l'Eure.
2e Division
Objet — Rivière d'Epte
Cne de Giverny.
M. Claude Monet pétitionnaire

République Française.

Minute. { Rédigée par M. Bautruche
Expédiée par M. Damoy.

Evreux, le 11 Décembre 1901

M. Claude Monet, artiste peintre à Giverny (Sous le couvert de M. le Sous-Préfet des Andelys)

Par pétition du 13 août dernier vous avez demandé l'autorisation d'exécuter la dérivation d'un petit bras de la rivière d'Epte « dit bras communal » traversant votre propriété afin d'agrandir un bassin vous servant actuellement pour la culture des plantes aquatiques.

J'ai l'honneur de vous informer que d'après l'article 644 du Code Civil, tout propriétaire dont l'héritage est traversé par une eau courante peut en user à son gré dans l'intervalle qu'elle y parcourt à charge par lui de la rendre, à la sortie de son fonds, à son cours ordinaire.

Dans ces conditions, mon administration ne peut restreindre le droit qui vous est conféré par le code et il ne lui appartient pas, par suite, de statuer sur votre demande — Vous êtes donc libre d'exécuter (les droits des tiers demeurant, s'il y a lieu, expressément réservés) les travaux en faisant l'objet, à charge de ne préjudicier en aucune façon au

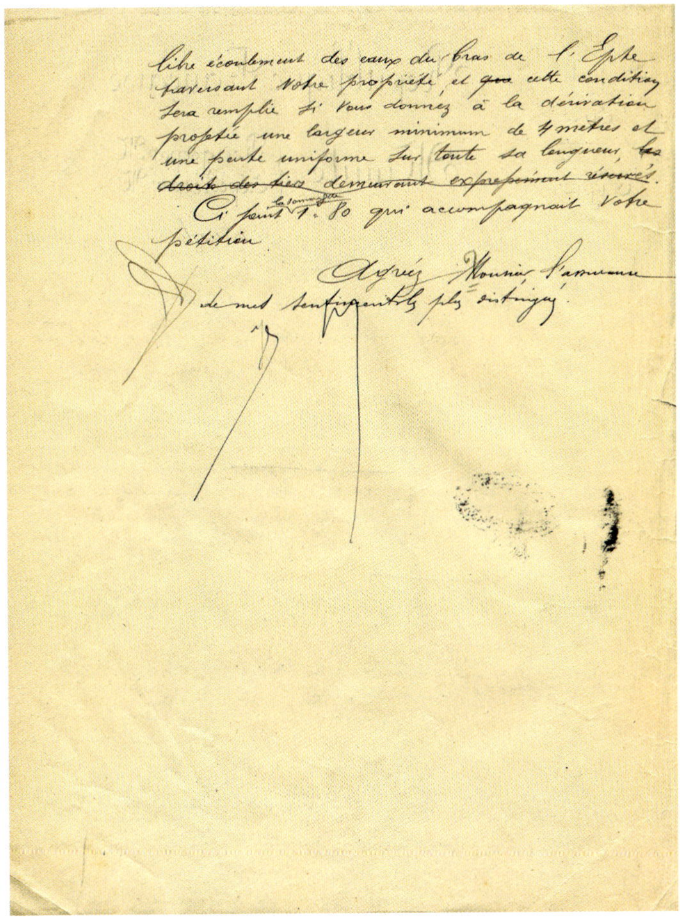
libre écoulement des eaux du bras de l'Epte traversant votre propriété, et cette condition sera remplie si vous donnez à la dérivation projetée une largeur minimum de 4 mètres et une pente uniforme sur toute sa longueur.

Ci-joint la somme de 80 qui accompagnait votre pétition.

Agréez Monsieur l'assurance de mes sentiments les plus distingués.

Letter from Claude Monet to Paul Durand-Ruel [Giverny], 5 June 1883
Archives Durand-Ruel, Paris

Dear Mr. Durand,
This is to acknowledge receipt of the 200 francs you sent. Please, I beg you, be sure to send me a large sum tomorrow. I don't know how to cope with such small sums.
I have been forced to have a shed built beside the Seine, to house my boats and keep my easels and canvases. This construction is finished. I must pay for it so I am counting on your promise. I did not mean to say that you wanted to abandon me, but I thought that, at that moment, it would be too much for you. As soon as I have something good I will send it to you. Now I shall be able to think of nothing else but painting, because I have been very disturbed by the organization of my boats. The Seine is not that close to the house, so I had to find a safe place for them; then I've had gardening to do and that has somewhat absorbed me, so that I have a few flowers to paint when the weather is bad.
Anyway, all that is over, I shall never put down my brushes again, and I will be in a position to give you things you will like.
Meanwhile, please do not forget me, for peace of mind is the first thing needed to work well.
Your most devoted
Claude Monet

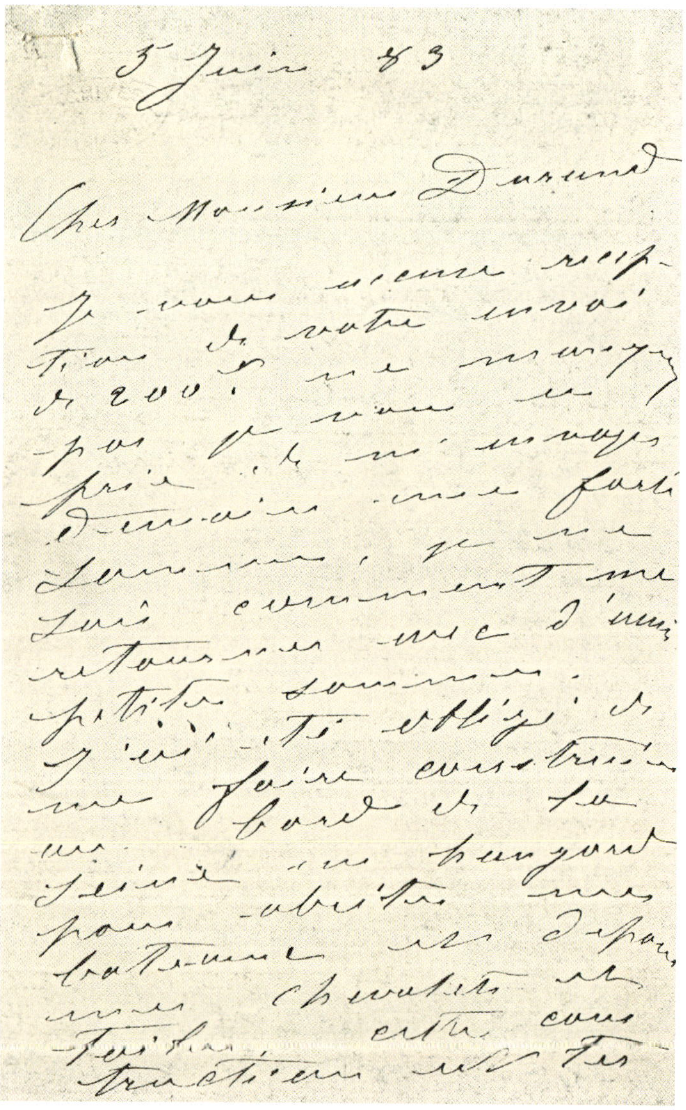

5 Juin 83

Cher Monsieur Durand

Je vous accuse récep-tion de votre envoi de 200 f. ne manquez pas je vous en prie de m'envoyer demain une forte somme; je ne sais comment me retourner avec d'aussi petites sommes. J'ai été obligé de me faire construire au bord de la Seine un hangar pour abriter mes bateaux et déposer mes chevalets et toiles; cette construction est ter-

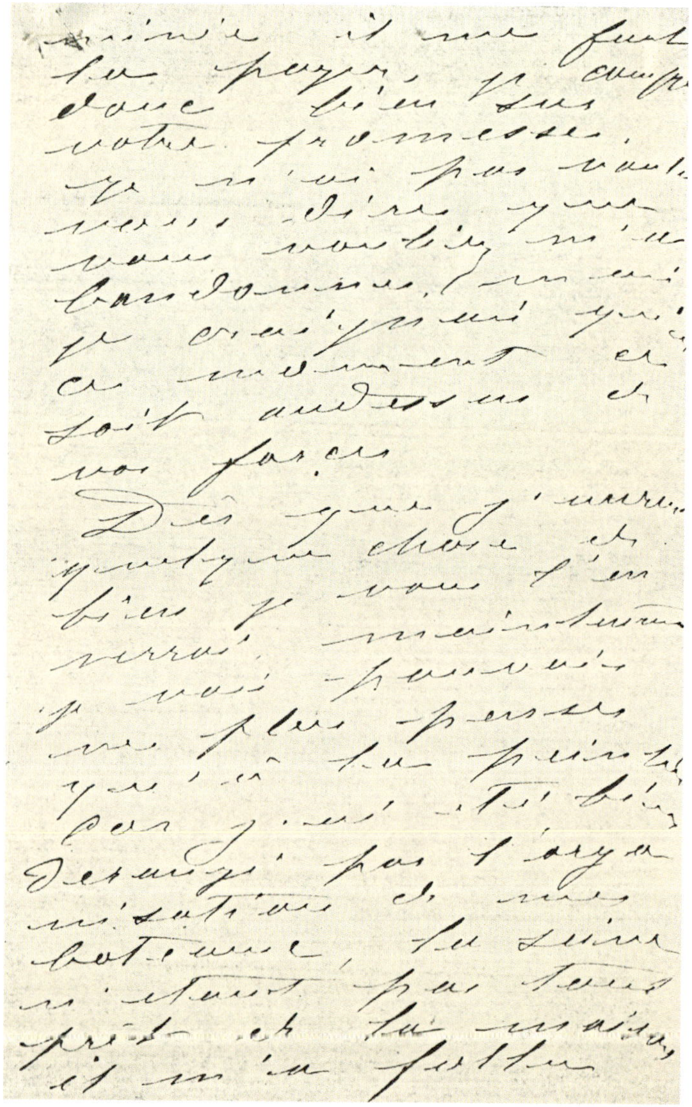

minée et il me faut la payer, je compte donc bien sur votre promesse. Je n'ai pas voulu vous dire que vous vouliez m'abandonner, mais je craignais que ce moment ce soit au dessus de vos forces.

Dès que j'aurai quelque chose de bien je vous l'enverrai; maintenant je vais pouvoir ne plus penser qu'à la peinture car j'ai été bien dérangé par l'organisation de mes bateaux, la Seine n'étant pas tout près de la maison, il m'a fallu

Letters from Claude Monet to Pierre Bonnard
Private collection

Giverny by way of Vernon, Eure
[1912]
My dear Bonnard,
As you are willing, I shall come on Tuesday with my son.
You are most kind and [I] thank you.
With my fond regards,
Claude Monet

Giverny by way of Vernon, Eure
20 February 1914
My dear Bonnard,
My thanks to you and your wife for the part you are playing in the new blow that is striking me so cruelly. I am very very touched by your kind friendship.
I don't need to tell you how much I would appreciate a visit from you on your return.
I trust that you and your wife will enjoy a pleasant stay in the south.
Yours sadly,
Claude Monet

Giverny by way of Vernon, Eure
Wednesday 26 [April 1916]
My dear Bonnard,
I am very happy to see you and if you have a spare moment today even that would suit me well, because I should like to show you where my big machines are and after tomorrow I shall have workmen here and everything will be upside down in my studio. You may come at whatever time suits you. Please remember me to your wife.
With fond regards
Claude Monet

Giverny by way of Vernon, Eure
Thursday 16 September [1920]
My dear Bonnard
Forced to stay at home on Saturday.
Would [you] be able to put off coming until Monday or Tuesday [?]. I hope that this contre-temps *[sic]* will not bother you. If it does, please tell me.
A word will do, and all my apologies.
My regards to Mrs. Bonnard.
Best wishes,
Claude Monet

Giverny by way of Vernon, Eure
[ca. 1923-1925?]
My dear Friend
This note to ask you to give me news of Mrs. Bonnard—good news, let us hope.
Our fond regards to you both.
Best wishes,
Claude Monet

Giverny by way of Vernon, Eure
18 October [ca. 1923-1925?]
My dear Bonnard,
Delighted to see you this afternoon with Vuillard.
I'm not working at the moment.
So please come by early.
Best wishes,
Claude Monet

Giverny by way of Vernon, Eure
19 January 1925
My dear Bonnard,
I am late thanking you for your good wishes and your kind letter, but I got off to a bad start this year, feeling totally dispirited, with the moment drawing near when I must deliver these panels.
I am obsessed by it and I curse the idea I had to give them to the state *[sic]* and I will be forced to give them in a lamentable state which saddens me indeed. I am doing my utmost to pull myself together a bit, but without much hope.
My very best wishes to your wife and yourself.
Blanche has asked me to thank your wife from both of us for her kind letter, until she can do so herself.
Yours,
Claude Monet

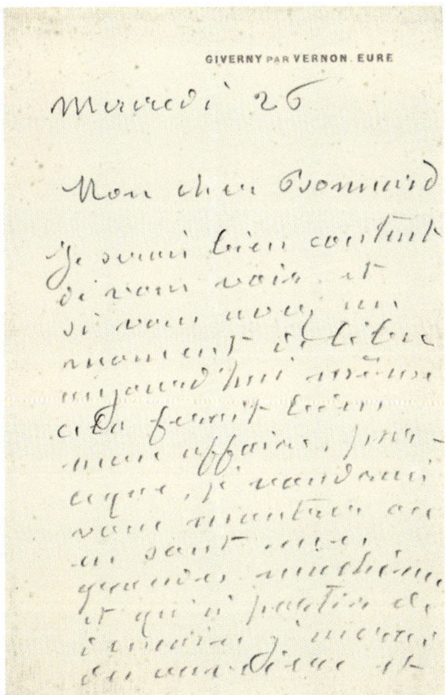
GIVERNY PAR VERNON. EURE

Mercredi 26

Mon cher Bonnard

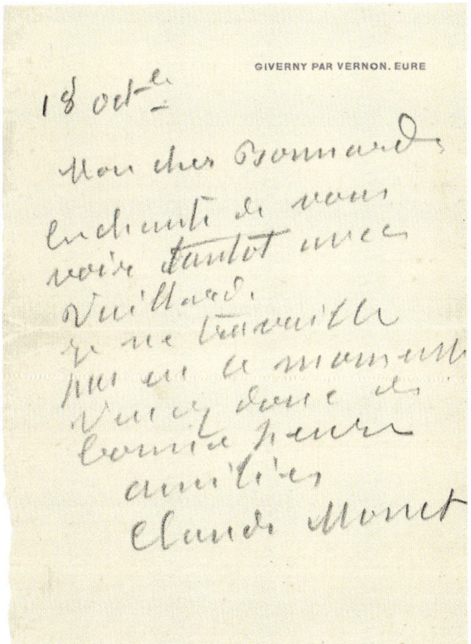
GIVERNY PAR VERNON. EURE

18 oct.

Mon cher Bonnard,
Enchanté de vous voir tantôt avec Vuillard.
Je ne travaille pas en ce moment.
Venez donc de bonne heure
amitiés
Claude Monet

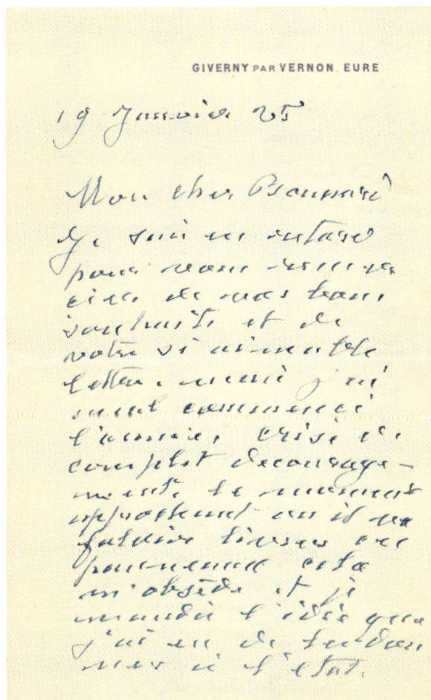
GIVERNY PAR VERNON. EURE

19 Janvier 25

Mon cher Bonnard

Checklist to the Exhibition

1. PAINTINGS: THE PAINTER AND HIS GARDEN

Claude Monet (1840–1926)

1. *Christmas Roses*, 1883
Oil on canvas, 50.5 × 37 cm ($19\frac{7}{8}$ × $14\frac{9}{16}$ in.)
Signed at bottom right, W953
Private collection (Ph 101717), cat. no. 1

2. *Pot of White Azaleas*, 1885
Oil on canvas, 50.5 × 37 cm ($19\frac{7}{8}$ × $14\frac{9}{16}$ in.)
Aigned at bottom right, W948
Private collection (Ph 17043), cat. no. 2

3. *A Palm Tree at Bordighera*, 1884
Oil on canvas, 61.3 × 74 cm ($24\frac{1}{8}$ × $29\frac{1}{8}$ in.)
Studio stamp at bottom right, W876
Private collection, cat. no. 3

4. *Under the Lemon Trees*, 1884
Oil on canvas, 73.5 × 60.5 cm ($28\frac{15}{16}$ × $23\frac{13}{16}$ in.)
Signed at bottom left, W873
Ny Carlsberg Glyptotek, Copenhagen (MIN 1968), cat. no. 4

5. *A Field of Tulip in Holland*, 1886
Oil on canvas, 65 × 81,5 cm, ($25\frac{1}{2}$ × 32 in.)
Signed at bottom left, W1067
Musée d'Orsay, Paris (RF 1944 19), cat. no. 5

6. *Peonies*, 1887
Oil on canvas, 73 × 100 cm ($28\frac{3}{4}$ × $39\frac{3}{8}$ in.)
Studio stamp at bottom right, W1141
Musées d'Art et d'Histoire, Geneva
On long term loan from the Fondation Jean-Louis Prevost (1985–29), cat. no. 9

7. *In the 'Norvégienne'* or *The Boat at Giverny*, ca. 1887
Oil on canvas, 98 × 131 cm ($38\frac{5}{8}$ × $51\frac{9}{16}$ in.)
Signed at bottom right, W1151
Musée d'Orsay, Paris. Bequest of the princess Edmond de Polignac, 1947 (RF 1944 20), cat. no. 6

8. *Poplars on the Banks of the River Epte*, 1891
Oil on canvas, 81 × 92 cm ($31\frac{7}{8}$ × $36\frac{1}{4}$ in.)
Signed at bottom left, W1311
Private collection
Courtesy Galerie Bernheim-Jeune, Paris, cat. no. 7

9. *Morning on the Seine, near Giverny*, 1896
Oil on canvas, 89.3 × 91.8 cm ($35\frac{1}{8}$ × $36\frac{1}{8}$ in.)
Signed and dated at bottom left, W1436
Private collection, United Kingdom, cat. no. 8

10. *Monet's garden at Giverny*, 1895
Oil on canvas, 81,5 × 92 cm, ($32\frac{1}{8}$ × $36\frac{1}{4}$ in.)
Signed at bottom right, W1420
E. G. Bührle Foundation, Zurich, cat. no. 10

11. *Pink Water Lilies*, 1897–99
Oil on canvas, 81 × 100 cm ($31\frac{7}{8}$ × $39\frac{3}{8}$ in.)
Signed at bottom right, W1507
Galleria Nazionale d'Arte Moderna, Rome (5163), cat. no. 11 and detail p. 60-61

12. *The Water Lily Pond, Symphony in green*, 1899
Oil on canvas, 89 × 93.5 cm (35 × $36\frac{13}{16}$ in.)
Signed and dated at bottom right, W1515
Musée d'Orsay, Paris. Bequest of the count Isaac de Camondo, 1911 (RF 2004), cat. no. 12

13. *The Artist's Garden at Giverny* or, *Irises in Monet's Garden*, 1900
Oil on canvas, 81 × 92 cm ($31\frac{7}{8}$ × $36\frac{1}{4}$ in.)
Signed and dated at bottom right, W1624
Musée d'Orsay, Paris (RF 1983 6), cat. no. 13

14. *Water Lily Pond, Symphony in Rose*, 1900
Oil on canvas, 89.5 × 100 cm ($35\frac{1}{4}$ × $39\frac{3}{8}$ in.)
Signed at bottom left, W1629
Musée d'Orsay, Paris. Bequest of the count property of Isaac de Camondo, 1911 (RF 2005), cat. no. 14

15. *Water Lilies*, 1904
Oil on canvas, 87 × 93 cm ($34\frac{1}{4}$ × $36\frac{5}{8}$ in.)
Signed and dated at bottom right, W1664
Musée Malraux, Ville du Havre (A 486), cat. no. 15

16. *Water Lilies*, 1908
Oil on canvas, diam.: 81 cm ($31\frac{7}{8}$ in.)
Signed and dated at bottom right, W1724
Musée Municipal A.-G. Poulain, Vernon (25.4.1), cat. no. 16

17. *Water Lilies*, 1914–17
Oil on canvas, 150 × 200 cm ($59\frac{1}{16}$ × $78\frac{3}{4}$ in.)
Studio stamp at bottom right, W1814
Galerie Beyeler, Basel, cat. no. 17

18. *Water Lilies*, ca. 1914–17
Oil on canvas, 135 × 145 cm ($53\frac{3}{16}$ × $57\frac{1}{8}$ in.)
Studio stamp at bottom right, W1787
Private collection, cat. no. 18

19. *Water Lilies and Agapanthus*, ca. 1914–17
Oil on canvas, 140 × 120 cm ($55\frac{1}{8}$ × $47\frac{1}{4}$ in.)
Studio stamp at bottom left, W1821
Musée Marmottan Monet, Paris (5084), cat. no. 19

20. *Hemerocallis*, ca. 1914–17
Oil on canvas, 150 × 140 cm ($59\frac{1}{16}$ × $55\frac{1}{8}$ in.)
W1818
Musée Marmottan Monet, Paris (5097), cat. n. 20

21. *Water Lilies with Weeping Willow Branches*, ca. 1916–19
Oil on canvas, 160 × 180 cm (63 × $70\frac{7}{8}$ in.)
Studio stamp at bottom right, W 1851
Paris, Lycée Claude Monet, cat. no. 21

22. *Blue Water Lilies*, ca. 1916–19
Oil on canvas, 200 × 200 cm ($78\frac{3}{4}$ × $78\frac{3}{4}$ in.)
Signed at bottom right, W1853
Musée d'Orsay, Paris (RF1981 40), cat. no. 22

23. *The Japanese Bridge*, ca. 1918–24
Oil on canvas, 89 × 115.5 cm ($35\frac{1}{16}$ × $45\frac{7}{16}$ in.)
W1921
Fondation Beyeler, Basel, cat. no. 24

24. *The Japanese Bridge*, ca. 1918–24
Oil on canvas, 89.5 × 116.3 cm ($35\frac{1}{4}$ × $45\frac{3}{4}$ in.)
W1921a
Private collection, cat. no. 25

25. *Wisteria*, 1919–20
Oil on canvas, 100 × 200 cm ($39\frac{3}{8}$ × $78\frac{3}{4}$ in.)
Studio stamp at bottom right, W1905
Musée d'Art et d'Histoire Marcel Dessal, Dreux
Gift of Michel Monet (964.1.1), cat. no. 23

26. *Weeping Willow*, 1920–22
Oil on canvas, 110 × 100 cm ($43\frac{5}{16}$ × $39\frac{3}{8}$ in.)
Studio stamp at bottom left, W1942
Musée d'Orsay, Paris. Gift of Mr. Philippe Meyer, subject to usufruct, 2000, in the collection since 2007 (RF 2000 21), cat. no. 26

27. *The House among Roses*, 1925
Oil on canvas, 92.3 × 73.3 cm ($38^{3}/_{8}$ × $28^{7}/_{8}$ in.)
Studio stamp at bottom right, W 1957
Carmen Thyssen-Bornemisza Collection, Madrid
Long term loan at the Museo Thyssen-Bornemisza (1998.52), cat. no. 28

28. *The House among Roses*, 1925
Oil on canvas, 89 × 100 cm (35 × $39^{3}/_{8}$ in.)
W1953
Private collection, cat. no. 27

29. **John Leslie Breck (1860–99)**
Garden at Giverny (In Monet's Garden), between 1887 and 1891
Oil on canvas, 46 × 55.6 cm ($18^{1}/_{8}$ × $21^{7}/_{8}$ in.)
Terra Foundation for American Art, Chicago
Collection Daniel J. Terra (1988.22), cat. no. 29

30. **Blanche Hoschedé-Monet (1865–1947)**
Garden at Giverny (The Rose Path), after 1926
Oil on canvas, 73 × 74.5 cm ($28^{3}/_{4}$ × $29^{5}/_{16}$ in.)
Musée Clemenceau, Paris. Gift of the artist, cat. no. 30

2. PHOTOGRAPHS: MONET PHOTOGRAPHED

31. **Schaarwachter (dates unknown)**
Monet, painter, ca. 1880
Modern print from a silver print glued on board, 7.4 × 4.2 cm ($2^{15}/_{16}$ × $1^{5}/_{8}$ in.)
Musée d'Orsay, Paris. Second Félix Potin collection
Gift of the Fondation Kodak-Pathé
(PHO 1983 165 548 328), cat. no. 31

32. **Theodore Robinson (1852–96)**
Portrait of Claude Monet at Giverny, ca. 1888–90
Modern print from a cyanotype, 24 × 16.8 cm ($9^{1}/_{2}$ × $6^{1}/_{2}$ in.)
Terra Foundation for American Art, Chicago
Gift of Ira Spanierman (C 1985.1.6), cat. no. 32

33. **Anonymous**
Michel and Claude Monet photographing the Pond, Giverny, ca. 1895-1900
Original silver print 5.8 × 8.4 cm ($2^{1}/_{4}$ × $3^{5}/_{16}$ in.)
Philippe Piguet Collection, cat. no. 33

34. **Jacques-Ernest Bulloz (1858–1942)**
Claude Monet beside the Water Lily Pond, summer 1905
Modern print, 29 × 20 cm ($11^{7}/_{16}$ × $7^{7}/_{8}$ in.)
Musée Municipal A.-G. Poulain, Vernon (80008), cat. no. 36

35. **Baron Adolf de Meyer (1868–1946)**
Claude Monet in Profile Looking at his Garden, Giverny, 27 October 1905
Platinum print on Japan paper, 21 × 16.5 cm ($8^{1}/_{4}$ × $6^{1}/_{2}$ in.)
Philippe Piguet Collection, cat. no. 37

36. **Baron Adolf de Meyer (1868–1946)**
Claude Monet Entering the Second Studio, Giverny, 27 October 1905
Platinum print on Japan paper, 22.8 × 11.6 cm (9 × $4^{9}/_{16}$ in.)
Philippe Piguet Collection, cat. no. 38

37. **Claude Monet (1840–1926)**
Self-Portrait on the Surface of the Water Lily Pond in Giverny, ca. 1905
Citrate print from negative, 4.3 × 5.7 cm ($1^{11}/_{16}$ × $2^{1}/_{4}$ in.)
Philippe Piguet Collection, cat. no. 34

38. **Sacha Guitry (1885–1957)**
Claude Monet in the Giverny Garden, ca. 1915
Enlarged palladium print, 38.4 × 29.5 cm ($15^{1}/_{8}$ × $11^{5}/_{8}$ in.)
Musée d'Orsay, Paris. Gift of the Galerie Texbraun, 1986 (PHO 1986 35), cat. no. 41

39. **Sacha Guitry**
Claude Monet in his Garden, Giverny, ca. 1915
Enlarged silver print, 30 × 40 cm ($11^{13}/_{16}$ × $15^{3}/_{4}$ in.)
Musée Clemenceau, Paris, cat. no. 39

40. **Pierre Choumoff (1872–1936)**
Claude Monet before the Japanese Bridge, Giverny, 1920
Silver print, 16.2 × 21.9 cm ($6^{3}/_{8}$ × $8^{5}/_{8}$ in.)
Musée Clemenceau, Paris, cat. no. 35

41. **[Sacha Guitry]**
Claude Monet and Gustave Geffroy, ca. 1920
Modern print
Whereabouts unknown, cat. no. 40

42. **Étienne Clémentel**
Claude Monet Standing before the Water Lilies, in the Giverny Garden, ca. 1920
Ektachrome by Patrice Schmidt from the stereoscopic autochrome, 4.5 × 10.5 cm ($1^{3}/_{4}$ × $4^{1}/_{8}$ in.)
Musée d'Orsay, Paris. Gift of Mme Arizzoli-Clémentel and Mme Barrelet-Clémentel, through the Société des Amis du Musée d'Orsay, 1988 (PHO 1988 2 2), cat. no. 42

43. **Étienne Clémentel (1864–1936)**
Claude Monet Standing by the Bridge in Giverny, ca. 1920
Ektachrome by Patrice Schmidt from the stereoscopic autochrome, 4.5 × 10.5 cm ($1^{3}/_{4}$ × $4^{1}/_{8}$ in.)
Musée d'Orsay, Paris. Gift of Mme Arizzoli-Clémentel and Mme Barrelet-Clémentel, through the Société des Amis du Musée d'Orsay, 1988 (PHO 1988 2 1), cat. no. 43

44. **Étienne Clémentel**
Path in the Giverny Garden, ca. 1920
Ektachrome by Patrice Schmidt from the stereoscopic autochrome, 4.5 × 10.5 cm ($1^{3}/_{4}$ × $4^{1}/_{8}$ in.)
Musée d'Orsay, Paris. Gift of Mrs.Arizzoli-Clémentel and Mme Barrelet-Clémentel, through the Société des Amis du Musée d'Orsay, 1988 (PHO 1988 2 3)

45. **Étienne Clémentel**
Path in the Garden and the House in Giverny, ca. 1920
Ektachrome by Patrice Schmidt from the stereoscopic autochrome , 4.5 × 10.5 cm ($1^{3}/_{4}$ × $4^{1}/_{8}$ in.)
Musée d'Orsay, Paris. Gift of Mme Arizzoli-Clémentel and Mme Barrelet-Clémentel, through the Société des amis du musée d'Orsay, 1988 (PHO 1988 2 4)

46. **Étienne Clémentel**
Path and Water Lilies in the Giverny Garden, ca. 1920
Ektachrome by Patrice Schmidt from the stereoscopic autochrome, 4.5 × 10.5 cm ($1^{3}/_{4}$ × $4^{1}/_{8}$ in.)
Musée d'Orsay, Paris. Gift of Mme Arizzoli-Clémentel and Mme Barrelet-Clémentel, through the Société des Amis du Musée d'Orsay, 1988 (PHO 1988 2 8)

47. **Anonymous for *L'Illustration***
Claude Monet before his House in Giverny, spring 1921
Ektachrome by Patrice Schmidt from the stereoscopic autochrome made for *L'Illustration*, 18 × 24 cm ($7^{1}/_{8}$ × $9^{7}/_{16}$ in.)
Musée d'Orsay, Paris (PHO 2006 9 1), cat. no. 45 and back cover

48. **Anonymous for *L'Illustration***
The Water Lily Pond in Giverny, spring 1921
Ektachrome by Patrice Schmidt from the autochrome made for *L'Illustration*, 18 × 24 cm ($7^{1}/_{8}$ × $9^{7}/_{16}$ in.)
Musée d'Orsay, Paris (PHO 2006 9 2), cat. no. 44

49. **Anonymous for *L'Illustration***
The Rose Garden in Giverny, spring 1921
Ektachrome by Patrice Schmidt from the autochrome made for *L'Illustration*, 18 × 24 cm ($7^{1}/_{8}$ × $9^{7}/_{16}$ in.)
Musée d'Orsay, Paris (PHO 2006 9 3), cat. no. 46

50. **Anonymous**
Claude Monet and Georges Clemenceau on a Path in the Giverny Garden (facing), 1921
Silver print, 17.8 × 12.7 cm (7 × 5 in.)
Musée Clemenceau, Paris, cat. no. 50

51. **Henri Martinie (1881–1940)**
Claude Monet and Georges Clemenceau in a Path in the Giverny Garden (from behind), 1921
Silver print, 12.7 × 17.8 cm (5 × 7 in.)
Musée Clemenceau, Paris
Gift of Blanche Hoschedé-Monet, 1937, cat. no. 51

52. **Henri Martinie**
Mme Kuroki, Claude Monet, Lili Butler, Blanche Hoschedé-Monet and Georges Clemenceau in the Giverny Garden, June 1921
Silver print, 17.5 × 23.6 cm ($6^{7}/_{8}$ × $9^{1}/_{4}$ in.)
Musée Clemenceau, Paris. Gift of Mme Langlois Berthelot, 1973, cat. no. 47

53. **Henri Martinie**
Georges Clemenceau, Claude Monet and Alice Butler on the Japanese Bridge, Giverny, June 1921
Sepia silver print, 19.8 × 24.5 cm ($7^{13}/_{16}$ × $9^{5}/_{8}$ in.)
Musée Clemenceau, Paris, cat. no. 48

54. **Sacha Guitry**
Claude Monet and the American Singer Marguerite Namara at the Pond, Giverny, 1922
Modern silver print,12.5 × 9.7 cm ($4^{15}/_{16}$ × $3^{13}/_{16}$ in.)
Philippe Piguet Collection, cat. no. 49

55. **[Michel Monet]**
Claude Monet during his Cataract Operation at the Neuilly Clinic, 1923
Modern silver print, 12.1 × 17.8 cm (5 × 7 in.)
Philippe Piguet Collection, cat. no. 53

56. **Anonymous**
Claude Monet in the Great Rose Path, Giverny, ca. 1923
Silver print, 29 × 39.1 cm ($11^{7}/_{16}$ × $15^{3}/_{8}$ in.)
Philippe Piguet Collection, cat. no. 52

57. **Thérèse Bonney (1894–1976)**
Claude Monet near the Water Garden, 1925
Original silver print, 17.4 × 22.8 cm ($6^{7}/_{8}$ × 9 in.)
Musée Clemenceau, Paris, cat. no. 54

58. **Thérèse Bonney (1894–1976)**
Claude Monet on the Japanese Bridge in his Giverny Garden, 1925
Original silver print, 22.5 × 17.4 cm ($8^{7}/_{8}$ × $6^{7}/_{8}$ in.)
Musée Clemenceau, Paris, cat. no. 55

59. **Jacques Salomon**
Édouard Vuillard, Ker Xavier Roussel, Claude Monet, Blanche Hoschedé-Monet and Mme Salomon in Giverny, 1926
Enlarged and tinted silver print, 16 × 18.4 cm ($6^{5}/_{16}$ × $7^{1}/_{4}$ in.)
Private collection, cat. no. 57

60. **Reine Natanson (1886–1953)**
Pierre Bonnard with Claude Monet in Giverny, 1926
Enlarged silver print, 11.2 × 16 cm (4 3/8 × 6 5/16 in.)
Private collection, cat. no. 56

61. **Nickolas Muray (1892–1965)**
Claude Monet Seated in his Garden in Giverny, 1926
Original silver print, signed and dated, 19 × 23.5 cm
(7 1/2 × 9 1/4 in.)
Musée Clemenceau, Paris, cat. no. 58

3. PHOTOGRAPHS: THE GARDEN AT GIVERNY

62. **Anonymous**
The Hoschedé-Monet Family by the House, Giverny,
ca. 1886
Silver print, 16.6 × 23 cm (6 1/2 × 9 1/16 in.)
Philippe Piguet Collection, cat. no. 60

63. **Anonymous**
The Hoschedé-Monet Family, n. d.
Silver print, 9 × 9.5 cm, (3 9/16 × 3 3/4 in.)
Musée Municipal A.-G. Poulain, Vernon, cat. nos. 61-63

64. **Anonymous**
Alice Hoschedé-Monet and her Daughters Having Tea on the Terrace, n. d.
Silver print, 9 × 9.5 cm (3 9/16 × 3 3/4 in.)
Véronique and Philippe Perdrix Collection, cat. no. 64

65. **Anonymous**
Michel Monet on his Bicycle in front of the Family Home, n. d.
Silver print, 9 × 9.5 cm (7 1/8 × 9 7/16 in.)
Véronique and Philippe Perdrix Collection, cat. no. 65

66. **Anonymous**
View of the Orchard with the House in the Background, Giverny, 1890s
Silver print, 15.6 × 22.4 cm (6 1/8 × 8 13/16 in.)
Philippe Piguet Collection, cat. no. 69

67. **Joseph Durand-Ruel (1862–1928)**
Claude Monet, his Family and Paul Durand-Ruel in the Garden, Giverny, June 1893
Silver print, 9.8 × 11.7 cm (3 3/4 × 4 1/2 in.)
Philippe Piguet Collection, cat. no. 67

68. **Joseph Durand-Ruel**
The Durand-Ruel Family Visiting Giverny, the Hoschedé-Monet Family, Butler, Durand-Ruel with Paul in a Bowler Hat, June 1893
Digital print, 12 × 15 cm (4 3/4 × 6 in.)
Archives Durand-Ruel, Paris (Ph 17385),
cat. no. 68

69. **Anonymous**
Monet's Garden in Giverny, View of the Greenhouse, 1897
Silver print, 3.8 × 5.5 cm (1 1/2 × 2 3/16 in.)
Philippe Piguet Collection, cat. no. 70

70. **Paul Nadar (1856–1939)**
Portrait of Alice Monet, 1899
Signed original silver print, 24.2 × 15.5 cm
(9 1/2 × 6 1/8 in.)
Philippe Piguet Collection, cat. no. 59

71. **Joseph Durand-Ruel**
Germaine Hoschedé, Lili Butler, Mme Joseph Durand-Ruel, Georges Durand-Ruel and Claude Monet, September 1900
Digital print, 12 × 15 cm (4 3/4 × 6 in.)
Archives Durand-Ruel, Paris (Ph 16424), cat. no. 66

72. **Anonymous**
View of Paul Durand-Ruel's Living Room, Rue de Rome, n. d.
Digital print, 12 × 15 cm (4 3/4 × 6 in.)
Archives Durand-Ruel, Paris (Ph 16508), fig. 1 p. 149

73. **Anonymous**
View of the Pond, Giverny, ca. 1905
Annotated on the back:
"Le bassin est magnifique" [the pond is magnificent]
Silver print, 5.5 × 8.3 cm (2 3/16 × 3 1/4 in.)
Philippe Piguet Collection, cat. no. 82

74. **Anonymous**
Monet's House in Giverny with a Flowerbed in the Foreground, 1910
Silver print, 7.8 × 10.8 cm (3 1/16 × 4 1/4 in.)
Philippe Piguet Collection, cat. no. 71

75. **Anonymous**
Alice Hoschedé-Monet and her granddaughter Alice Butler on one of the small bridges in the Water Lily Pond, Giverny, July 1910
Silver print, 17.7 × 17.8 cm (7 × 7 in.)
Philippe Piguet Collection, cat. no. 85

76. **Anonymous**
Monet's Garden in Giverny, Flowerbeds and View of the Second Studio, ca. 1910
Silver print, 5.5 × 8.2 cm (2 3/16 × 3 1/4 in.)
Philippe Piguet Collection, cat. no. 72

77. **Georges Truffaut**
View of the Water Lily Pond, Giverny, ca. 1913
Silver print, 17.4 × 12.5 cm (6 7/8 × 4 15/16 in.)
Philippe Piguet Collection, cat. no. 86

78. **Pogany**
Félix Breuil, the Head Gardener at Work, Giverny, ca. 1913
Modern silver print, 12.6 × 17.7 cm (5 × 7 in.)
Philippe Piguet Collection, cat. no. 73

79. **Anonymous**
The Gardener Félix Breuil? in the "Norvégienne" on the Water Lily Pond, Giverny, no date
Silver print, 11.2 × 16.9 cm (4 3/8 × 6 5/8 in.)
Stamp Foto-Dräyer, Zurich
Philippe Piguet Collection, cat. no. 88

80. **Gouthière**
View of the Water Lily Pond, Giverny, ca. 1924
Silver print, 12.5 × 17.4 cm (4 15/16 × 6 7/8 in.)
Philippe Piguet Collection, cat. no. 87

81. **Anonymous**
The House seen from the Central Path (Giverny),
ca. 1933
Digital print
Country Life magazine Collection, London, cat. no. 89

82. **Anonymous**
The Garden with the Second Studio on the Left, ca. 1933
Digital print
Country Life magazine Collection, London, cat. no. 90

83. **Anonymous**
Monet's Flower Garden, ca. 1933
Digital print
Country Life magazine Collection, London, cat. no. 91

84. **Anonymous**
The Water Lily Pond, ca. 1933
Digital print
Country Life magazine Collection, London, cat. no. 92

85. **Anonymous**
The Pond seen through Willow Branches, ca. 1933
Digital print
Country Life magazine Collection, London, cat. no. 93

86. **Anonymous**
The Water Lily Pond, ca. 1933
Digital print
Country Life magazine Collection, London, cat. no. 94

4. DOCUMENTS

87. *Handwritten letter signed by Claude Monet to Paul Durand-Ruel*, 5 June 1883
Archives Durand-Ruel, Paris, p. 134

88. *Plan of the first pond project by the engineer of the Ponts et Chaussées [Department of Civil Engineering] of the département of the Eure*,
22 June 1893
Archives Départementales de l'Eure, Évreux (18 S 25),
fig. 4 p. 51

89. *Receipt of authorization to take water from the arm of the Epte known as the "communal arm", signed by Claude Monet*, 28 July 1893
Archives Départementales de l'Eure, Évreux (18 S 25),
fig. 2 p. 50

90. *Receipt of authorization to build two footbridges signed by Claude Monet*, 28 July 1893
Archives Départementales de l'Eure, Évreux (18 S 25),
fig. 3 p. 50

91. *Delivery slip from the Latour-Marliac Nursery to Claude Monet (no. 261 and 262)*, 15 May [1894]
Latour-Marliac Sarl, Le Temple-sur-Lot,
fig. 5 and 6 p. 52

92. *Plan of the pond with the project to divert water from the arm of the Epte known as the "communal arm", report of the subdivisional foreman*,
8 October 1901
Archives Départementales de l'Eure, Évreux (18 S 25),
fig. 9 p. 54

93. *Handwritten letter signed by Claude Monet to the Prefect of the Eure*, 13 August 1901
Archives Départementales de l'Eure, Évreux (18 S 25),
p. 132

94. *Draft (for the Prefect) by Mr. Bautruche, sent by M. Damoy, Évreux, to Mr. Claude Monet*,
11 December 1901
Archives Départementales de l'Eure, Évreux (18 S 25),
p. 133

95. *Menu for the wedding of Germaine Hoschedé and Albert Salerou with a photograph of the Japanese Bridge, Giverny*, 12 November 1902
20.8 × 12.8 cm (7 15/16 × 5 in.)
Philippe Piguet Collection, cat. no. 83

96. *Catalogue of the Latour-Marliac Nursery*, 1904
Latour-Marliac Sarl, Le Temple-sur-Lot

97. **Jean-Claude-Nicolas Forestier**
"Le Jardin de M. Claude Monet," in *Fermes et Châteaux*, no. 39, 1st September 1908, p. 13
Musée des Impressionnismes, Giverny, fig. 4 p. 42

98. *Catalogue of the Latour-Marliac Nursery*, 1912
Latour-Marliac Sarl, Le Temple-sur-Lot

99. **Anonymous**
Giverny - Claude Monet's Garden – Central Path, n. d.
Vintage postcard, 9 × 14 cm (3⁹⁄₁₆ × 5½ in.)
Terra Foundation for American Art, Chicago, cat. no. 74

100. **[Ed. Lavergne, Vernon]**
Giverny (Eure) – Property of the Painter Claude Monnet (sic), n. d.
Vintage postcard, 9 × 14 cm (3⁹⁄₁₆ × 5½ in.)
Terra Foundation for American Art, Chicago, cat. no. 75

101. **Anonymous**
Giverny (Eure) – Property of Master Claude Monet – Central Path, n. d.
Vintage postcard, 9 × 14 cm (3⁹⁄₁₆ × 5½ in.)
Terra Foundation for American Art, Chicago, cat. no. 76

102. **Anonymous**
Giverny – Artist's Studio, n. d.
Vintage postcard, 9 × 14 cm (3⁹⁄₁₆ × 5½ in.)
Terra Foundation for American Art, Chicago, cat. no. 77

103. **Anonymous**
Giverny (Eure) – Property of Master Claude Monet – Irises, n. d.
Vintage postcard, 9 × 14 cm (3⁹⁄₁₆ × 5½ in.)
Terra Foundation for American Art, Chicago, cat. no. 78

104. **Anonymous**
Giverny – Claude Monet's Garden – Water Lilies, n. d.
Vintage postcard, 9 × 14 cm (3⁹⁄₁₆ × 5½ in.)
Terra Foundation for American Art, Chicago, cat. no. 79

105. **[Ed. Lavergne, Vernon]**
Giverny (Eure) – Property of Master Claude Monet – Irises and Water Lilies, n. d.
Vintage postcard, 9 × 14 cm (3⁹⁄₁₆ × 5½ in.)
Terra Foundation for American Art, Chicago

106. **Anonymous**
Giverny (Eure) – Property of Master Claude Monet – The Water Garden, n. d.
Vintage postcard, 9 × 14 cm (3⁹⁄₁₆ × 5½ in.)
Terra Foundation for American Art, Chicago, cat. no. 80

107. **[Georges André, Vernon]**
Giverny (Eure) – Property of Master Claude Monet – Water Lilies, n. d.
Vintage postcard, 9 × 14 cm (3⁹⁄₁₆ × 5½ in.)
Terra Foundation for American Art, Chicago, cat. no. 81

108. **[Ed. Lavergne, Vernon]**
Giverny (Eure) – Property of Master Claude Monet – Irises and Water Lilies, n. d.
Vintage postcard, 9 × 14 cm (3⁹⁄₁₆ × 5½ in.)
Terra Foundation for American Art, Chicago

109. *Handwritten letter signed by Claude Monet to Pierre Bonnard*, [1912]
Private collection

110. *Handwritten letter signed by Claude Monet to Pierre Bonnard*, 20 February 1914
Private collection

111. *Handwritten letter signed by Claude Monet to Pierre Bonnard*, 26 [April 1916]
Private collection, p. 135

112. *Handwritten letter signed by Claude Monet to Pierre Bonnard*, 16 September [1920]
Private collection

113. *Handwritten letter signed by Claude Monet to Pierre Bonnard*, [ca. 1923–25?]
Private collection

114. *Handwritten letter signed by Claude Monet to Pierre Bonnard*, 18 October [ca. 1923–25?]
Private collection, p. 135

115. *Handwritten letter signed by Claude Monet to Pierre Bonnard*, 19 January 1925
Private collection, p. 135

116. **Félix Breuil**
"Les iris pour bords de rivières, étangs et territoires humides"
Jardinage magazine, no. 21, October 1913, pp. 2–9
Truffaut, Évry, cat. nos. 73 and 86

117. **M. Lagrange**
"Les nymphéas rustiques dans les jardins"
Jardinage magazine, no. 28, May 1914, pp. 309–19
Truffaut, Évry, fig. 14 p. 57

118. **Georges Truffaut**
"Le Jardin de Claude Monet," *Jardinage* magazine, no. 87, November 1924, pp. 54–59
Truffaut, Évry, fig. 15 p. 58, fig. 3 p. 42, fig. 6 p. 45 and cat. no. 87

119. *Menu for the wedding of Simone Salerou and Robert Piguet*, 26 October 1926
23.3 × 13.9 cm
Philippe Piguet Collection, cat. no. 84

120. **Georges Clemenceau**
Claude Monet, Les Nymphéas, 1928
Paris, Librairie Plon, Collection Nobles Vies
Musée Clemenceau, Paris

121. **Georges Truffaut**
"Les pivoines et plantes vivaces"
Jardinage magazine, no. 138, December 1929, pp. 76–79, Truffaut, Évry

122. *La Petite Illustration* magazine, 21 December 1929
Musée Clemenceau, Paris

Selected Bibliography

ARTICLES AND CONTRIBUTIONS

Alexandre, Arsène. "La vie artistique: exposition Claude Monet." *Le Figaro*, no. 327, 23 November 1900, p. 5.

—. "Le jardin de Monet." *Le Figaro*, no. 221, 9 August 1901, p. 1.

—. "Un jardinier." *Le Courrier de l'Aisne*, no. 193, 9 June 1904, p. 1.

—. "La vie artistique: les Nymphéas de Claude Monet." *Le Figaro*, no. 127, 7 May 1909, p. 5.

—. "La semaine artistique: un paysagiste d'aujourd'hui et un portraitiste de jadis." *Comœdia*, no. 386, 8 May 1909, p. 3.

—. "L'Epopée des *Nymphéas*." *Le Figaro*, no. 294, 21 October 1920, p. 1.

Anonymous. "Chez les peintres: Claude Monet - Albert Besnard." *Le Temps*, no. 11242, 1 March 1892, p. 2.

—. "L'impressionnisme: exposition d'œuvres nouvelles de Claude Monet." *La Justice*, no. 7570, 5 December 1900, p. 1.

—. "Nouvelles: musées." *Chronique des Arts et de la Curiosité*, no. 16, 15 October 1920, p. 134.

Arnyvelde, André. "Chez le peintre de la lumière: Je sais tout interviewe Claude Monet." *Je sais tout*, 15 January 1914, pp. 29–38.

Bachelard, Gaston. "Les *Nymphéas* ou les surprises d'une aube d'été." *Verve*, 7, nos. 27 and 28, December 1952, pp. 59–64.

Blanche, Jacques-Émile. "Claude Monet." *La Revue de Paris*, no. 3, 1 February 1927, pp. 557–75.

Blume, Mary. "The Gardener of Giverny." *Art News*, 77, no. 4, April 1978, pp. 50–54.

Bonnef, François. "Aux rives de l'Huisne, le jardinier des *Nymphéas* – cultive – des Roses." *Paris-Normandie* (Évreux Edition), no. 1611, 28 November 1949, p. 1 and 8.

Breuil, Félix. "Les iris pour bords de rivières, étangs et territoires humides." *Jardinage*, no. 21, October 1913, pp. 2–9.

Ciolkowska, Muriel. "Monet-His Garden, His World." *International Studio*, 76, no. 309, February 1923, pp. 371–78.

Delange, René. "Claude Monet." *L'Illustration*, no. 4376, 15 January 1927, pp. 54–60.

Descaves, Lucien. "Ceux dont on parlera longtemps: chez Claude Monet." *Paris-Magazine*, 25 August 1920, p. 354.

Elder, Marc. "Le peintre à la campagne : une visite à Giverny chez M. Claude Monet." *Excelsior*, no. 3404, 6 April 1920.

—. "Une visite à Giverny chez Claude Monet." *Excelsior*, January 1921.

— [pseud. Marcel Tendron]. "Une visite à Claude Monet." *Le Bulletin de la Vie Artistique*, no. 11, 1 May 1920, p. 305

FitzGerald, Desmond. "Claude Monet. The Master of Impressionism." *Outlook* (1893-1924), 80, no. 12, 22 July 1905, pp. 766–75.

Forestier, Jean-Claude-Nicolas. "Le jardin de M. Claude Monet." *Fermes et Châteaux*, no. 39, 1 September 1908, p. 13-16.

Fourcaud, Louis de. "M. Claude Monet et le lac du jardin des fées." *Le Gaulois*, 22 May 1909, p. 1.

—. "Exposition internationale, à la Galerie Georges Petit." *Le Gaulois*, 19 June 1886, p. 2.

Geffroy, Gustave. "Claude Monet." *Le Journal*, 7 June 1898, p. 1.

—. "Causeries : les paysages d'eau de Claude Monet." *La Dépêche de Toulouse*, no. 14920, 15 May 1909, p. 1.

—. "Claude Monet." *L'Art et les Artistes*, no. 11, November 1920, pp. 51–81.

—. "Hommes et choses: Hommage de Claude Monet au Japon." *La Dépêche de Toulouse*, 12 January 1924, p. 1.

Gillet, Louis. "L'épilogue de l'impressionnisme: les Nymphéas de M. Claude Monet." *La Revue hebdomadaire*, 8, 21 August 1909, pp. 397–415.

—. "Après l'exposition Claude Monet - le testament de l'impressionnisme." *Revue des Deux Mondes*, 1 February 1924, pp. 661–73.

Gimpel, René. "At Giverny with Claude Monet." *Art in America*, 15, no. 4, June 1927, pp. 168–74.

Godefroy, Louis de. "Claude Monet, peintre de nymphéas." *La Flamme*, 20 September 1909, pp. 468–72.

Grappe, Georges. "Visites et promenades: chez Claude Monet." *L'Opinion*, 16 October 1920, pp. 442–43.

Grignan, G.-T. "Les floraisons de juin." *Jardinage*, no. 34, June 1919, pp. 92–94.

Guillemot, Maurice. "Claude Monet." *La Revue Illustrée*, no. 7, 15 March 1898, n. p.

Gwynn, Stephen. "In Monet's Country II-Claude Monet's Garden." *Country Life*, 31 December 1932, p. 740-741.

—. "Claude Monet's Lily Garden." *Country Life*, 7 October 1933, p. 355–58.

H. G. [Henri Ghéon]. "Notes : les 'paysages d'eau' de Claude Monet." *La Nouvelle Revue Française*, no. 6, 1 July 1909, pp. 533–35.

Herbert, Robert. "Method and Meaning in Monet," *Art in America*, September 1979, pp. 90–108.

Howard-Johnston, Paulette. "Une visite à Giverny en 1924." *L'Œil*, no. 171, March 1969, pp. 28–33, 76.

HSC [Henri Saulnier-Ciolkowski]. "Monet, at 84, still a Master Painter." *Art News*, 23, no. 5, 8 November 1924, pp. 1, 7.

G. J. [Jeanniot, Georges]]. "Notes sur l'Art, Claude Monet." *La Cravache Parisienne*, no. 388, 23 June 1888, pp. 1–2.

Kahn, Maurice. "Au jour le jour-le jardin de Claude Monet." *Le Temps*, no. 15606, 7 June 1904, pp. 2–3.

Kuhn, Alice. "Claude Monet à Giverny." *Femme d'aujourd'hui*, 10 August 1904, pp. 454–56.

Lagrange, M. "Les nymphéas rustiques dans les jardins." *Jardinage*, no. 28, May 1914, pp. 309–19.

Leclercq, Julien. "Petites expositions: Le Bassin aux nymphéas de Claude Monet." *Chronique des Arts et de la curiosité*, no. 37, 1 December 1900, pp. 363–64.

Marx, Roger. "Les Nymphéas de M. Claude Monet." *Gazette des Beaux-Arts*, June 1909, pp. 523–31.

Masson, André. "Monet le fondateur," *Verve*, 7, nos. 27-28, December 1952, pp. 68-70.

Maupassant, Guy de. "La vie d'un paysagiste." *Gil Blas*, no. 2506, 28 September 1886, p. 1.

Mille, Pierre. "En passant - Écrits sur l'eau." *Le Temps*, no. 17487, 13 May 1909, p. 3.

Mirbeau, Octave. "Claude Monet." *L'Art dans les Deux Mondes*, no. 16, 7 March 1891, pp. 183–85.

—. "Lettres à Claude Monet.' *Les Cahiers d'Aujourd'hui*, 5, no. 7, 29 November 1922, pp. 161–76.

Morgan, Jean. "Causeries chez quelques maîtres : M. Claude Monet." *Le Gaulois*, 5 May 1909, pp. 1–2.

Natanson, Thadée. "Monet le taciturne," in *Peints à leur tour*, Paris: Albin Michel, 1948, pp. 33–41.

Pays, Marcel. "Un grand maître de l'impressionnisme: une visite à M. Claude Monet dans son ermitage à Giverny." *Excelsior*, no. 3698, 26 January 1921, pp. 2–3.

Perry, Lilla Cabot. "Reminiscences of Claude Monet from 1889 to 1909." *The American Magazine of Art*, 18, no. 3, March 1927, pp. 119–25.

Proust, Marcel. "Les *Éblouissements*, par la comtesse de Noailles." *Le Figaro*, literary supplement, no. 166, 15 June 1907.

Raitif de la Bretonne [Jean Lorrain], "Poussières de Paris. Féeries peintes." *Le Journal*, 10 December 1900.

Robinson, Theodore. "Claude Monet." *Century Illustrated Magazine*, 44, no. 5, September 1892, pp. 696–701.

Salomon, Jacques. "Giverny, 14 juin 1926. Aujourd'hui, déjeuner chez Claude Monet." *Les Arts*, p. 10.

—. "Chez Monet, avec Vuillard et Roussel." *L'Œil*, no. 197, May 1971, pp. 20–25.

Sauvage, Marcel. "Après la mort de Claude Monet. Dans le paradis fleuri du maître à Giverny." *Comœdia*, 7 December 1926, p. 1.

Sée, Edmond. "Devant les 'paysages d'eau.'" *Gil Blas*, no. 10791, 20 May 1909, p. 1.

Thiébault-Sisson, François. "Claude Monet: les années d'épreuves." *Le Temps*, no. 14414, 26 November 1900, p. 3.

—. "Au jour le jour: Choses d'art - Les derniers travaux de Claude Monet." *Le Temps*, no. 17482, 8 May 1909, p. 3.

—. "Feuilleton du temps: La vie artistique - Claude Monet." *Le Temps*, no. 21435, 6 April 1920, p. 3.

—. "Claude Monet." *Le Temps*, no. 23855, 7 December 1926, p. 3.

—. "Autour de Claude Monet: Anecdotes et souvenirs." *Le Temps*, no. 23877, 29 December 1926, p. 3.

—. "Autour de Claude Monet: anecdotes et souvenirs, II." *Le Temps*, no. 23886, 8 January 1927, p. 3.

—. "Un nouveau musée parisien, les Nymphéas de Claude Monet à l'Orangerie des Tuileries." *La Revue de l'Art Ancien et Moderne*, no. 52, June 1927, pp. 40–52.

Trévise, Duc de. "Les quatre-vingts ans du peintre Claude Monet." *La Vie aux Champs*, 25 janvier 1921, p. 18.

—. "Le pèlerinage de Giverny". *La Revue de l'Art ancien et moderne*, 31st year, vol. LI, no. 282, January 1927, pp. 42–50.

—. "Le pèlerinage de Giverny." *La Revue de l'Art Ancien et Moderne*, 31st year, vol. LI, no. 283, February 1927, pp. 121–34.

Truffaut, Georges. "Le jardin de Claude Monet." *Jardinage*, no. 87, November 1924, pp. 55–59.

Vaudoyer, Jean-Louis. "Petites expositions: Claude Monet, galerie Durand-Ruel." *Chronique des Arts et de la Curiosité*, no. 20, 15 May 1909, p. 159.

Vauxcelles, Louis [Louis Meyer]. "La mort de Claude Monet." *Excelsior*, no. 5838, Monday 6 December 1926, p. 3.

—. "Chez les peintres: une après-midi chez Claude Monet." *L'Art et les Artistes*, 2, December 1905, pp. 85–90.

Villemer, Jean. "Les *Nymphéas* de M. Claude Monet." *Le Gaulois*, 16 October 1920, p. 1.

Whitsey, Fred. "The Puzzle at Giverny: Claude Monet's Garden Restored." *Country Life*, 170, no. 4378, 16 July 1981.

GENERAL WORKS AND EXHIBITION CATALOGUES

Claude Monet, exhib. cat., Paris, Galerie Durand-Ruel, 1900.

Hommage à Claude Monet, exhib. cat., Paris, Galeries Nationales du Grand Palais / Réunion des Musées Nationaux, 1980.

Blanche Hoschedé-Monet, 1865–1947, une artiste de Giverny, exhib. cat., Vernon, Musée Municipal A.-G. Poulain, 1991.

Monet's Years at Giverny: Beyond Impressionism. New York: The Metropolitan Museum of Art / Harry N. Abrams, [1978] 1995.

Voyage à Giverny. De Monet à Joan Mitchell, exhib. cat., Paris, Musée Marmottan Monet / Scala, 2007.

Monet, l'œil impressionniste. Paris: Musée Marmottan Monet, 2008.

Aitken, Geneviève, and Marianne Delafond. *La Collection d'estampes japonaises de Claude Monet.* Giverny: Fondation Claude Monet / Lausanne; and Paris: Bibliothèque des Arts, 2003.

Alexandre, Arsène. *Claude Monet.* Paris: Bernheim-Jeune, 1921.

Alphant, Marianne. *Claude Monet: une vie dans le paysage.* Paris: Hazan, 1993.

Aragon, Louis. *Aurélien.* Paris: Gallimard, 1944, chap. LXIII.

Bayle, Françoise. *Une visite à Giverny.* Versailles: Artlys, 1991.

Becker, Christoph. *Monet's Garden.* Zurich: Kunsthaus, 2004.

Bourguignon, Katherine M. *Impressionist Giverny. A colony of Artists, 1885–1915.* Giverny: Musée d'Art Américain / Terra Foundation for American Art, The University of Chicago Press, 2007.

Clemenceau, Georges. *Claude Monet: Les Nymphéas.* Paris: Plon, 1928.

—. *Georges Clemenceau à son ami Claude Monet: correspondance.* Paris: Réunion des Musées Nationaux, [1993] 2008.

Dauberville, Henry. *Le Bataille de l'impressionnisme.* Paris: Éditions Bernheim-Jeune, 1967.

Elder, Marc, [Marcel Tendron]. *À Giverny, chez Claude Monet.* Paris: Bernheim-Jeune, 1924.

Fels, Florent. *Claude Monet, La Nouvelle Revue Française*, 1925.

Fels, Marthe de. *La Vie de Claude Monet.* Paris: Gallimard, 1929.

Geffroy, Gustave. *Claude Monet: sa vie, son temps, son œuvre*, vol. II. Paris: G. Grès, [1922] 1924.

Georgel, Pierre. *Monet : le cycle des Nymphéas.* Paris: Musée de l'Orangerie, 1999.

Gimpel, René. *Journal d'un collectionneur, marchand de tableaux.* Paris: Calmann-Lévy, 1963.

Gordon, Robert, and Sydney Eddison. *Monet the Gardener.* New York: Universe, 2002.

Gordon, Robert, and Andrew Forge. *Monet.* New York: Harry N. Abrams, 1983.

Guillaud, Jacqueline and Maurice Guillaud, (eds.). *Claude Monet au temps de Giverny*, exhib. cat. Paris: Centre Culturel du Marais, 1983.

Gwynn, Stephen. *Claude Monet and his Garden. The Story of an Artist's Paradise.* London: Country Life Limited, 1934.

Holmes, Caroline. *Le Jardinier impressionniste,* Paris, Gründ, 2002, trans. from *Monet at Giverny,* London, Cassel, 2001.

Hoog, Michel. *The Nymphéas of Claude Monet at the Musée de l'Orangerie.* Paris: Éditions de la Réunion des Musées Nationaux, 1990.

Hoschedé, Jean-Pierre. *Claude Monet ce mal connu: intimité familiale d'un demi-siècle à Giverny de 1883 à 1926,* 2 vols. Geneva: Pierre Cailler, 1960.

House, John. *Monet. Nature into Art.* New Haven and London: Yale University Press, 1986.

Isaacson, Joel. *Claude Monet: Observation and Reflection.* Oxford: Phaidon, 1978.

Joyes, Claire. *Claude Monet: Life at Giverny.* New York: Vendome Press, 1985.

—. *Giverny: un village impressionniste au temps de Monet.* Paris: Flammarion, 2000.

Keller, Horst. *Monet's Years in Giverny: A Garden Becomes Painting.* Koln: DuMont Verlag, 2001.

Kendall, Richard. (ed.). *Monet by himself: Paintings, Drawings, Pastels, Letters.* London: MacDonald & Co, 1989.

Levine, Steven Z. *Monet, Narcissus, and Self-Reflection. The Modernist Myth of the Self.* Chicago: The University of Chicago, 1994.

Lobstein, Dominique. *Les Impressionnistes.* Paris: Le Cavalier Bleu, 2007.

Mancoff, Debra N. *Monet's Garden in Art.* London: Frances Lincoln, 2001.

Mirbeau, Octave. *Correspondance avec Claude Monet.* Tusson: Du Lérot Éditeur, 1990.

—. *Claude Monet et Giverny.* Paris: Séguier, 1995.

Patin, Sylvie. *Monet "un œil... mais, bon Dieu, quel œil!".* Paris: Gallimard, 1991.

—. *Regards sur les Nymphéas, de Paul Claudel à André Masson.* Paris: Réunion des Musées Nationaux, 2006.

Piguet, Philippe. *Monet et Venise.* Paris: Herscher, [1986] 2008.

Pissarro, Joachim. *Monet and the Mediterranean.* Fort Worth: Kimbell Art Museum, and New York: Brooklyn Museum of Art, 1997.

Proust, Marcel. *À la recherche du temps perdu,* vol. I: Du côté de chez Swann. Paris: La Pléiade, 1973.

Rouart, Denis, Rey Dominique et Maillard Robert. *Monet. Nymphéas ou les miroirs du temps. Suivi d'un catalogue raisonné.* Paris: Hazan, 1972.

Stuckey, Charles F. *Monet: Water Lilies.* New York: Hugh Lauter Levin Associates, 1988.

—. (ed.). *Claude Monet 1840–1926,* exhib. cat. Chicago: The Art Institute of Chicago, 1995.

—. *Monet. A Retrospective.* New York: Hugh Lauter Levin Associates, Inc., 1985.

Tucker, Paul Hayes. *Claude Monet Life and Art.* New Haven and London: Yale University Press, 1995.

Venturi, Lionello. *Les Archives de l'impressionnisme.* New York and Paris: Durand-Ruel, 1939.

Wildenstein, Daniel. *Claude Monet, biographie et catalogue raisonné* (5 vols.). Lausanne and Paris: Bibliothèque des Arts, 1974–1991.

INDEX OF NAMES OF PERSONS

This index covers the whole catalogue, apart from the acknowledgements, prefaces, endnotes, the list of works on view, and the selective bibliography. Page numbers in *italics* refer to illustrations.

PHOTO CREDITS

Every effort has been made to locate the beneficiaries; our sincere apologies to those whose names we may have omitted to mention.

Basle
Fondation Beyeler, Riehen / Galerie Beyeler: p. 78 (cat. no. 17) and 85 (cat. no. 24)
Kunstmuseum Basel, Martin Bühler: p. 21 (fig. 4)

Chicago
The Art Institute / Photo: Bob Hashimoto: p. 41 (fig. 2)
Terra Foundation of American Art: p. 90 (cat. no. 29), 93 (cat. no. 32), 122-24 (cat. no. 74-81)

Copenhagen
Ny Carlsberg Glyptotek / Photo: Ole Haupt: p. 65 (cat. no. 4)

Dreux
Musée d'Art et d'Histoire Marcel Dessal / Photo: Jean-Louis Losi: p. 84 (cat. no. 23)

Évreux
Archives Départementales de l'Eure: p. 50-51 (fig. 2, 3 and 4), 54 (fig. 9), 132-33

Évry
Truffaut: p. 42 (fig. 3), 45 (fig. 6), 57 (fig. 14), 58 (fig. 15)

Geneva
Musées d'Art et d'Histoire / Photo: Yves Siza: p. 70 (cat. no. 9)

Giverny
With the kind permission of Fondation Claude Monet: p. 43 (fig. 5)
Musée des impressionnismes / Photo: Patrice Schmidt: p. 42 (fig. 4)

Houston
Museum of Fine Arts / Photo: Bridgeman-Giraudon: p. 23 (fig. 5)

Le Havre
Musée Malraux / Photo: Florian Kleinefenn: p. 76 (cat. no. 15) and cover

Le Temple-sur-Lot
Latour-Marliac Sarl: p. 52 (fig. 5 and 6), 55 (fig. 10), 56 (fig. 11 et 12)

London
Pyms Gallery: p. 69 (cat. no. 8)
Country Life : p. 130-31 (cat. nos. 89 to 94)

Madrid
Carmen Thyssen-Bornemisza Collection, on loan at Museo Thyssen-Bornemisza: p. 89 (cat. no. 28)

New York
Metropolitan Museum of Art, Dist. RMN / Photo: Malcom Varon: p. 40 (fig. 1)

Paris
Archives Artcurial: p. 24 (fig. 6)
Archives Durand-Ruel: p. 49 (fig. 1), 62 (cat no. 1), 63 (cat no. 2), 118-19 (cat. nos. 66 and 68), 134
Galerie Berhneim-Jeune: p. 68 (cat. no. 7)
Lycée Claude Monet: p. 82 (cat. no. 21)
Musée Clemenceau: p. 30 (detail), 47 (fig. 7), 91 (cat. no. 30), 96 (cat. no. 35), 100 (cat. no. 39), 104-05 (cat nos. 47 and 48), 106-07 (cat. nos. 50 and 51), 110-11 (cat. nos. 54 and 55), 113 (cat. no. 58)
Musée Marmottan Monet / Bridgeman-Giraudon: p. 10 (detail), 32-33 (fig. 1, 2 and 3), 80-81 (cat. nos. 19 and 20)
Musée d'Orsay, Dist. RMN / Photo: Patrice Schmidt: p. 102-03 (cat. no. 43 to 46 and back cover)
RMN (musée de l'Orangerie) / Photo: Hervé Lewandowski: p. 27 (fig. 7)
RMN (musée d'Orsay) / Photo: Michèle Bellot: p. 87 (cat. no. 26) / Photo: Hervé Lewandowski: p. 14 (fig. 1), 66 (cat. no. 5), 67 (cat. no. 6), 73 (cat. no. 12), 74 (cat. no. 13), 75 (cat. no. 14), 83 (cat. no. 22), 92 (cat. no 31) / Photo: Jean Schormans: p. 101 (cat. no. 41) / All rights reserved: p. 102 (cat. no. 42)
RMN / All rights reserved: p. 100 (cat. no. 40)
Roger-Viollet: p. 35 (fig. 4)

Rome
Galleria Nazionale d'Arte Moderna. Su concessione del Ministero per i beni e le Attività Culturali / Photo: Alessandro Vasari: p. 60-61 (detail), 72 (cat. no. 11)

Saint Petersburg
Musée de l'Ermitage / Bridgeman-Giraudon: p. 17 (fig. 2)

Vernon
Musée municipal A.-G. Poulain / Musées de Vernon: p. 97 (cat. no. 36), 116 (cat. nos. 61 to 63) / Photo: Laurent Lecat: p. 77 (cat. no. 16)

Washington
Archives of American Art, Smithsonian Institution. Courtesy of the Lilla Cabot Perry photographs, ca. 1889-1909: p. 53 (fig. 7 and 8)
National Gallery of Art, Image courtesy of the Board of Trustees: p. 18 (fig. 3)

Zurich
Fondation E. G. Bührle: p. 71 (cat. no. 10)

Private collection: p. 64 (cat. no. 3) and p. 86 (cat. no. 25)
Private collection: p. 79 (cat. no. 18)
Private collection: p. 88 (cat. no. 27)
Private collection / Photo: Patrice Schmidt: p.59 (fig. 16), 112 (cat. nos. 56 and 57), 135
Véronique and Philippe Perdrix Collection: p. 117 (cat. nos. 64 and 65)
Philippe Piguet Collection: p. 38 (detail), 94 (cat. no. 33), 95 (cat. no. 34), 98-99 (cat. nos. 37 and 38), 106 (cat. nos. 49), 108-09 (cat. nos. 52 and 53), 114-15 (cat. nos. 59 and 60), 119 (cat. nos. 67), 120-21 (cat. nos. 69-73), 125-29 (cat. nos. 82-88)

Colour Separation
Pixel Studio, Milan

Printed in April 2009
by Grafiche Flaminia s.r.l., Foligno (Italy)

Printed in Italy